Visibly Muslim

Visibly Muslim

Fashion, Politics, Faith

Emma Tarlo

Oxford • New York

English edition
First published in 2010 by
Berg
Editorial offices:
First Floor, Angel Court, 81 St Clements Street, Oxford OX4 1AW, UK
175 Fifth Avenue, New York, NY 10010, USA

Berg is the imprint of Oxford International Publishers Ltd.

Library of Congress Cataloging-in-Publication Data

Tarlo, Emma.
Visibly Muslim : fashion, politics, faith / Emma Tarlo.
p. cm.
Includes bibliographical references and index.
ISBN 978-1-84520-432-7 (cloth) — ISBN 978-1-84520-433-4 (pbk.)
1. Muslim women—Clothing—Great Britain.   2. Muslim women—Great
Britain—Social conditions.   3. Hijab (Islamic clothing)—Great Britain.
4. Burqas (Islamic clothing)—Great Britain.   5. Clothing and dress—
Religious aspects—Islam.   6. Veils—Religious aspects—Islam.   7. Islam
in mass media.   8. Muslims in popular culture.   I. Title.
GT733.T37 2010
391.2088'297—dc22
2009043584

British Library Cataloguing-in-Publication Data

A catalogue record for this book is available from the British Library.

ISBN 978 1 84520 432 7 (Cloth)
978 1 84520 433 4 (Paper)

Typeset by Apex CoVantage, LLC, Madison, WI, USA
Printed in Great Britain by the MPG Books Group, Bodmin and King's Lynn

www.bergpublishers.com

CONTENTS

ILLUSTRATIONS

COLOR IMAGE SEQUENCE 1: TYING HIJAB

Zarina Saley at her home in central London. All images are courtesy of Elizabeth Scheder-Bieschin, 2009.

COLOR IMAGE SEQUENCE 2: SHOPPING

All images are courtesy of Emma Tarlo unless otherwise noted.

1. Green Street, London, 2007.
2. Global Peace and Unity Event (GPU), London, 2008.
3. Green Street, London, 2007.
4. Oxford Street, London, 2008.
5. Oxford Street, London, 2008.
6. Queens Market, Upton Park, London, 2009. Courtesy of Elizabeth Scheder-Bieschin.
7. Green Street, London, 2007.
8. Global Peace and Unity Event (GPU), London, 2008.
9. Islamic Impressions, Green Street, London, 2009. Courtesy of Elizabeth Scheder-Bieschin.
10. Pinz Pinz Pinz, GPU, London, 2008.
11. Islamic Impressions, London, 2009. Courtesy of Elizabeth Scheder-Bieschin.
12. Arabiannites, Whitechapel, East London, 2007.
13. Arabiannites, Whitechapel, East London, 2007.
14. Arabiannites, Whitechapel, East London, 2007.
15. Green Street, East London, 2008.
16. Outside Primark, Oxford Street, 2009. Courtesy of Elizabeth Scheder-Bieschin.

ACKNOWLEDGEMENTS

There are many people without whom this book could not have been written. I would like to begin by thanking the women who opened up their wardrobes and clothing biographies to me and trusted me to represent their stories. Some have chosen to remain anonymous; others preferred to be named. Amongst the latter, I would especially like to thank Rezia Wahid, Humera Khan, Shazia Mirza, Zarina Saley, Shirin D'Oyen, Sumaiyah Forbes, Laura Blizzard, Sukina Abdul Noor and Muneera Rashida for their willingness to share personal details of their clothing experiences and preferences with a wider public. I have learned much from your insights and I am sure that readers will too. To the many others who remain anonymous or appear with pseudonyms, I am no less grateful for your contributions. Your experiences have enriched my understandings of Muslim dress practices in numerous ways. I hope you will recognize your contributions when you come across them and find them accurately represented.

To Wahid Rahman, Anas Sillwood, Yasmin Arif, Sheeba Kichloo, Sadia Nosheen, Cindy van den Bremen, Sophia Kara, Zeena Altalib, Junayd Miah, Abdul R. Hummaida, Sarah Elenany and Faisel Ibn Dawood Atcha, a special thank you for answering all my many questions about the design and marketing of Islamic fashions and for generously offering images for reproduction in this book. I wish you all the best with your enterprises.

For their involvement in the research process, I would like to thank Shelina Begum and Hilal Ahmed. Shelina acted as interpreter for my interviews with Bengali women in Somerstown in the summer of 2005 whilst Hilal worked as part-time research assistant in 2006. His intellectual insights, personal experience and local knowledge were an inspiration. My thanks also to staff at the Hopskotch Community Centre in Somerstown, Faith in the Future and the North London Muslim Community Centre in Stamford Hill for opening up their doors for me to conduct group discussions with members. For all those who participated in those discussions, further thanks.

Many have also contributed images for this book. A special thanks to Elizabeth Scheder-Bieschin, Kuranya Paramaguru and Arzu Unal. I am especially grateful to Elisabeth for providing the colour sequence of images showing different techniques of tying hijab and to Zarina Saley for sharing her hijab-tying skills with us with such patience and generosity. My thanks also to all those who have contributed photographs from their own personal collections and albums as well as those who agreed to be photographed for the book. My apologies to those whose images were not included in the final selection. Credits for the black and white photos are given with each image. This is not the case with the colour sequences where the emphasis is on providing an uninterrupted visual narrative. Credits for these images can be found at the end of the list of illustrations. A special thanks to Arranbainnites, Pinz Pinz Pinz and Islamic Impressions which feature in the sequence on shopping. In addition I would like to thank Berg for agreeing to include so many images and Norface for contributing towards the cost of coloured reproductions. Finally I would like to thank Julia Rosen, Anna Wright, Emily Metcalf and Ken Bruce for their contributions at different stages of the production process. Our relations may have remained virtual throughout but our exchanges have been frequent and steeped in detail signalling genuine and prolonged engagement.

There are many colleagues whose insights, conversations, enthusiasm, criticisms and support I have valued. First I would like to thank Stephanie Jones, Kaushik Bhaumik, Suman Gupta, Sandip Hazareesingh, Bob Wilkinson, Heather Scott, Lotte Hughes and David Richards—all fellow members of the Ferguson Centre for African and Asian Studies at the Open University where I was employed when I began this study. Our conversations which took us from the OU canteen in Milton Keynes to conferences and banquets in Marakesh and Beijing have undoubtedly enriched this study. To the many scholars we met on the way, especially Taieb Belghazi and Khalid Bekkaoui, an additional thanks. Thanks also to students and colleagues in the Department of Anthropology at Goldsmiths where I am currently employed, especially Sophie Day and Frances Pine, for their comments, suggestions and support.

Halfway through the research for this book I was invited by Annelies Moors to join a Norface-funded comparative research project on the emergence of Islamic fashion in Europe. Participating in this collective project has undoubtedly shaped my reflections and observations in numerous ways, and I am especially grateful to Annelies for her passion, intellect and powers of observation as well as for being a wonderful person with whom to work. My thanks also to all my fellow researchers on this project: Connie Christiansen, Annika Rabo, Sigrid Noekel, Dijla Salim, Leila Osterlind, Arzu Unal and Irene Bregenzer. Our research workshops and field trips in Leiden, London and Stockholm were always stimulating.

Other scholars with whom I have had valuable conversations at different stages of the research include Claire Dwyer, Danny Miller, Reina Lewis, Amina Yaqin, Peter Morey, Fauzia Ahmed, Pnina Werbner, Mukulika Bannerjee, Inderpal Grewal, Carla Jones, Ozlem Sandikci, Caroline Osella, Dorathea Schulz, Mona Abaza and Alexandru Balasescu. A conversation with Fauzia in 2004 was particularly influential at the early stages.

The research would not have been possible without institutional support from Goldsmiths, University of London and the Ferguson Centre of African and Asian Studies at the Open University. To the Ferguson Centre for generously supporting the earlier phases of research and to the British Academy, ArtMap and Norface for supporting the latter phases, I would like to express my gratitude. Without the funding and the time that this allows for concentration on research, the writing of this book would not have been possible.

Throughout the research process I have benefited from participation in various collective research networks and projects: 'Constructions identitaires et mondialisation' (project of IRD, Paris); 'Globalisation, Identity Politics and Social Conflict' (Ferguson Centre, Open University); 'ArtMap' (CNRS/IRD); 'Framing Muslims: Representations of Muslims post 9/11' (SOAS and University of East London) and 'The Emergence of Islamic Fashion in Europe' which was part of the Norface research programme 'The Re-emergence of Religion as a Social Force in Europe'. I have also benefited from the feedback I have received through presenting my research in conferences, workshops and public lectures at University College London, Oxford University, Goldsmiths, the London School of Economics and Political Science, the School of Oriental and African Studies, University of East London, the Victoria and Albert Museum, University of Princeton, University of California Irvine, Stockholm University, Beijing University, Mohammed V University Rabat, IRD Paris, University of Leiden and the University of Amsterdam. Earlier versions of some of the material discussed in chapters 2, 3 and 5 have been published in the journals *Moving Worlds, Fashion Theory, Anthropology Today* and *The Journal of Material Culture*. I am grateful to these journals for permission to reproduce some of this material.

Finally it remains for me to thank friends and family. In particular I thank Denis Vidal for his stimulating companionship, support and incisive comments, Julius for his patience and capacity to distract me and Iris for popping up at the right time to offer a helping hand.

Emma Tarlo

1   INTRODUCTION

The past decade has seen a rapid increase in visible expressions of faith amongst Muslims living in the cosmopolitan cities of Britain, Europe and America. Whether by wearing coloured or decorative headscarves or plainer, more encompassing forms of covering, women are often at the forefront of this increased Muslim visibility. But what is such visibility about? And why has it generated so much public attention and controversy in politics, media and the law? Do distinctive forms of dress make Muslims the unwilling targets of attention or is visibly Muslim dress better understood as a self-chosen visible declaration of identity and faith? Is it a quest for religiously based recognition? Furthermore, if Islam is providing an increasingly important frame and reference for Muslim dress practices in the West, how does this explain the diversity of interpretations of Muslim dress visible in the streets? In short, how can we better understand what it means to look Muslim in the first decade of the new millennium?

Popular media representations of Muslim women swathed in black often give the impression that Islamic dress is about sombre uniformity and conformity to type. A stroll down any multicultural British high street does, however, create a very different impression. Here fashionable Muslim girls, like other young women of their generation, can be seen wearing the latest jeans, jackets, dresses, skirts and tops which signal their easy familiarity with high street fashion trends. Often the only feature of their clothing which clearly identifies them as Muslim is the headscarf, but here too, one finds much diversity. In fact, far from promoting an image of dull uniformity, the headscarf is often the most self-consciously elaborated element of an outfit, carefully co-ordinated to match or complement other details of a woman's appearance. Worn in a diverse range of colours and textures, built using different techniques of wrapping, twisting and layering and held together with an increasing variety of decorative hijab pins designed for the purpose, the headscarf has in recent years become a new form of Muslim personal art. In many cases, it provides the aesthetic focal point of a young woman's appearance. Such scarf-led outfits, known by many as hijabi[1] fashions, often lend a splash of colour and light to the grey uniformity of British high streets and university corridors. They also contrast strongly with some of the more austere full-length all-black covered outfits favoured by some Muslim women.

This book invites reflection about the huge diversity of visibly Muslim dress practices which co-exist in the streets of multicultural British cities from strict forms of total body and face covering to the latest hijabi trends and the new range of garments designed and marketed as 'Islamic fashion'. It questions how and why all forms of dress which identify their wearers as Muslim tend to be lumped together and perceived by outsiders as monotone, retrograde and repressive. Readers are invited to suspend whatever judgements or assumptions they might have about particular garments in favour of trying to comprehend what clothes mean to the people who wear them. At the same they might reflect on the possible social, political, ethical and aesthetic effects of particular clothing choices. This involves consideration of not only the impact different clothes have on their wearers but also what sort of public intervention they make in a multicultural urban environment.

What is presented here is not an argument for or against particular types of dress. Readers who are interested only in confirming their approval or disapproval of headscarves (hijabs), face veils (niqabs) and full-length gowns (jilbabs) should turn instead to the vast bodies of literature which promote or condemn covering for women on religious, moral or political grounds. Nor does this book seek to provide a definitive guide to decoding what particular garments mean, since meaning is above all about interpretation, is often highly contested and is always contingent on particular circumstances. Rather, what is presented is insight into the changing landscape of visibly Muslim dress practices in Britain, practices which are undergoing major transformations, shaped both by local and global social, religious and political forces and by issues of personal aesthetics, ethics, fashion, identity and faith. It is suggested that this changing visual and material landscape is best understood, not in terms of some mythical opposition between Islam and the West, religion and secularism or tradition and modernity but rather in terms of complex debates about identity, faith, politics, ethics, aesthetics and belonging. What is highlighted is the diversity of modern Muslim perspectives on these issues and the different sartorial possibilities they are generating.

If readers, whatever their religious, political or cultural persuasion, come away from this book with more questions than answers, with heightened curiosity rather than a feeling of knowing it all, with more nuanced interest rather than a sense of closure, then the book will have performed its function.

BEYOND THE VEIL

The topic of Muslim women's appearances is by no means a blank canvas. Rather, it has the quality of a familiar painting, so often reproduced that representation gets confused for reality and we fail to see what might have been left out of the picture or how things could have been painted differently. Representations of Muslim women are dominated by one single all-consuming image, word and concept—*the veil*. This word which does not correspond directly to any clear-cut Arabic or Islamic category,[2] has come to stand for anything from shawls and headscarves to face veils and full head-to-toe coverings and has long been the key trope through which Muslim women's identity has been defined and imagined by non-Muslims in the West. Library shelves literally groan under the weight of volumes with 'veil' in their titles which offer a plethora of interpretations of life within, beyond and behind the veil. There are feminists critiquing it, anthropologists interpreting it, religious authorities prescribing it, hijab wearers defending it, politicians and activists promoting or opposing it, legal professionals judging it, governments prohibiting or imposing it and artists and novelists exploiting its multivalent semiotic potential for expressing a whole range of ideas about beauty, eroticism, secrecy, mystery, piety, holiness, freedom, protection and oppression.

Such contemporary readings of the veil are in turn informed by a long legacy of Orientalist images and texts, integrated within the cannons of Western art history, literature and colonial writings.[3] In these historic male-dominated Western traditions veiled and semi-veiled women from various Eastern and North African countries were represented as passive, exotic, oppressed and sensually alluring figures in need of protection and liberation—discourses which justified imperialist interventions and contributed to the building of long-lasting stereotypes. In the sea of images of veiled women that have gained currency in the Western media since the terrorist attacks of 9/11, Muslim women continue to be portrayed within a highly restricted repertoire of roles. More often than not they are represented either as victims in foreign lands in need of rescue through the supposed civilizing influence of the West or as migrants from foreign lands, who, by stubbornly retaining their alien and backward ways, seem to threaten the very notions of individuality and freedom on which contemporary democratic Western societies are founded. Hence images of Afghan women enveloped in billowing burqas were used in the British and American press to justify military intervention in Afghanistan in 2001 just as images of British Muslim women in face veils have become a convenient shorthand for expressing anxieties about multiculturalism and the threat of religiously sanctioned terrorism. The assumption that Muslim women remain forever incapable of defending themselves, whether against patriarchal family structures, religious ideologies or fundamentalist discourses has in turn been used to support recent attempts in a number of European countries to control and restrict clothing practices in the public sphere. What seems to unite these images, old and new, is the equation of covering with oppression and the implicit or explicit quest to uncover Muslim women in their own best interests as defined by others.

All too often, then, anxieties and concerns about 'the veil' translate into actions and legislation against it. In the first half of the twentith century, for example, the unveiling of women was promoted and enforced in many parts of the world, both by Western imperialists and by local elites who internalized the notion that veiling was above all a sign of backwardness and an impediment to modernity. Hence both the Turkish leader, Kemal Ataturk, and the Iranian ruler, Reza Shah Pahlavi, were vociferous in their condemnation of covering practices and made great efforts to force women out of headscarves and long outer garments in the name of secularism and progress. Whilst men's dress underwent some modification at the time, as the banning of the fez in Turkey clearly demonstrates, it was women's bodies that became the central symbol of national identity and concern and the ground on which debates about modernity and tradition were waged most forcefully.

The attack and defence of 'the veil' does not, however, split neatly along gender or class lines. Early Egyptian and Iranian feminists, mostly from elite educated backgrounds, sided with the modernist portrayal of the veil as a form female imprisonment.[4] This view continues to find expression in the discourses of some contemporary feminists who consider the act of unveiling a necessary step towards female emancipation. Hence French feminists were particularly active in supporting the legislation, introduced in 2005, banning the wearing of conspicuous symbols of religious identity in French state schools—a ruling largely designed to eliminate the presence of the headscarf in the classroom.[5]

One consequence of early-twentieth-century attempts to suppress 'the veil' was its later emergence as a powerful symbol of authenticity and resistance in many parts of the world from Egypt, Algeria, Turkey and Iran to Indonesia and Pakistan.[6] Similarly the recent wave of clothing restrictions targeted at Muslim women in Europe has stimulated new forms of globally oriented hijab-activism around the world. British Muslim women have been particularly active in launching and supporting international hijab campaigns and networks, stimulated in part by the comparative freedom they experience in matters of dress, by their concern with international politics and human rights, their enthusiasm for Islam in their personal lives and their sense of solidarity with other Muslims around the world. Whilst to some extent successful in challenging the stereotype of the veiled woman as passive and submissive, hijab campaigners have, at the same time, contributed towards the fetishization of the headscarf, adding yet more weight to the idea that veiling is what Muslim dress, and indeed Muslim women, are principally about.

This surplus of attention to 'the veil' has produced large areas of collective visual and conceptual blindness. Muslim fashions and anti-fashions, in all their diversity, tend to become reduced to a simple binary opposition between veiled and unveiled. If 'veiled', women are perceived to be submissive or dangerous, deluded or transgressive, oppressed or threatening depending on whether their covering is thought to have been forced or chosen. If 'unveiled' they are often uncritically assumed to be progressive, liberated, secular and integrated into modern British or European society in spite of whatever social or economic marginalization some may be experiencing.[7] This reduction of people to one aspect of their appearance has resulted not only in the state sanctioning of cultural stereotypes but also in the shaping of state policies and priorities in particular ways.

In Britain, an important component of multiculturalist policies and agendas from the 1970s and 1980s onwards has been the state's acknowledgement of visible expressions of religious and ethnic difference with the result that Sikh turbans, Muslim hijabs and Jewish Kipahs have become an integral part of the urban landscape and are often incorporated into uniforms in schools and work places. Unlike in France where the mere fact of religious identity being visibly expressed in public is considered a threat to secularism and a matter of collective anxiety, in Britain expressions of intolerance and unease tend to be focused more around particular forms of covering. Hence it is the jilbab and niqab, rather than the more common hijab, that have provoked the most negative attention and debate. The adoption of this particular brand of multiculturalism has meant that alongside the periodic moral panics over Muslim dress in the British media is the simultaneous assumption made by many journalists, photographers and policy makers that those Muslims who wear visible markers of faith somehow represent 'the Muslim community' more than others. This normalization of visible expressions of religious affiliation also plays a powerful role in sustaining stereotypes.[8] Not only does it have the effect of marginalizing those Muslim women who do not wear visible indicators of faith, but it also reduces those who do to a single coherent and monolithic category as if they speak and think with one voice. Failure to acknowledge this means that whenever a controversy emerges concerning any aspect of a Muslim woman's dress, whether at school or in the work place, suspicion becomes attached to all visible Muslims who, by extension, become the focus of public anxiety and condemnation which easily turns to racist abuse.

The aim of this book is not to devalue the significance of the headscarf. To do so would be to ignore the unprecedented popularity this garment has attained in recent years as an object of intense religious, political, aesthetic and emotional investment. It is, however, to argue, that if we want to understand the significance of hijab today we need to move beyond well-worn debates about whether or not it is liberating or oppressive towards a focus both on its form and on the diversity of meanings attributed to it and activities generated around it. These include not only hijab-activism but also hijab-fashion and the burgeoning arenas of hijab-commerce and hijab-chat on the Web.

Second, there is a need to resituate the hijab within the wider context of other clothing worn by visibly Muslim women and those with whom they interact in their daily lives. Too often debates about Muslim dress are so focussed on the presence or absence of the headscarf that the rest of a woman's appearance is somehow invisible, irrelevant and ignored. But scarves are never worn in isolation. They form part of covered outfits which may be loose or fitted, muted or bold, self-consciously fashionable or unfashionable. For some women, looking Muslim is a subtle process, involving the layering of fashionable garments so as not to reveal too much flesh or body shape. For others it may involve choosing to wear a T-shirt with the unambiguous slogan, '100% Muslim', or wearing a full-length jilbab made from track-suit material—both options which combine elements of popular street fashion with Islamic references or ideals. Yet others may favour wearing long black garments imported from the Middle East or new forms of Islamic fashion purchased over the Internet. Many will have wardrobes containing a variety of options. Attention to such details offers the possibility of moving beyond the veiled/unveiled dichotomy to create more variegated and complex understandings of contemporary Muslim dress practices. It also provides a better basis for understanding the new range of fashions currently being marketed as Islamic in boutiques and online stores.

THE IDEA OF MUSLIM DRESS

There is no such thing as a clear-cut category of Muslim dress. Muslims around the world wear a huge range of different garments, many of which relate more to local regional traditions than religious ideas, and some of which are not particularly associated with either. Saris, for example are popular amongst Muslims in Bangladesh, but they are also worn by Hindus and Christians in India. Similarly, the *shalwar kamiz* (tunic and trouser) is a form of regional dress, sometimes considered to have Muslim connotations in North India and Pakistan, but also worn by Hindus and Sikhs. Neither can it be assumed that there is necessarily anything Islamic about the practices of covering or seclusion which were found in ancient Sumarian, Persian, Greek, Egyptian and Byzantian cultural traditions where they were sometimes associated with high status, sometimes with egalitarianism.[9] Today in rural North India face veiling continues to be practised both by Hindus and Muslims but in different circumstances and with different meanings attached.[10] All of this should make us wary of generalizing about Muslim dress. In West Africa, for example some Muslims wear colourful wraps with large and exuberant turbans, whilst others may wear jeans. Both styles of dress contrast strongly with the long, plain black outer garments (abayas or jilbabs) commonly worn in many parts of the Middle East. At the same time, through their participation in Islamic revival movements, substantial numbers of women in different parts of the world have adopted and adapted forms of Middle Eastern dress which they often consider 'more Islamic' than local options. These in turn have sometimes been adapted to create new forms of Islamic fashion. In short, wherever people are located, they are likely to have access to images, ideas, and in some cases, goods, which come from elsewhere, leading to complex reformulations of Muslim clothing practices around the world.[11]

How far religious significance is attributed to particular garments also varies considerably. Some of the stricter forms of covered dress most easily identified as Muslim by outsiders may hold little religious significance for their actual wearers. For example in Saudi Arabia and Iran where the wearing of strict forms of covered outer dress is compulsory for women in mixed public contexts, the women who wear such clothes do not necessarily attribute much religious significance to them. Rather they are conforming, some willingly, others reluctantly, to local dress codes. Hence some young Iranian women wear chic designer headscarves as far back on their heads as possible and choose the shortest and most fitted outer garments they can get away with in order to signal their distance from the government's understanding of Islamic piety.[12] Ironically it is often in contexts where forms of covered dress are not the norm or where their wearing has at some time been discouraged, restricted or prohibited that particular garments tend to become attributed with heightened religious significance.

That British Muslim dress practices should be highly varied is not surprising in view of the variety of regional and cultural backgrounds of British Muslims. According to the 2001 census, there were 1.6 million Muslims living in Britain, more than two-thirds of whom were of South Asian origin. Besides Pakistani, Indian and Bangladeshi connections, there are Muslims of Arab, Albanian, Bosnian, Iranian, Nigerian, Egyptian, Iraqi, Somali and Turkish descent as well as others of mixed backgrounds including white British and European converts and their descendents. Many first-generation migrants from South Asia came to Britain in search of work in the aftermath of decolonization and partition and at a time when the British government was actively encouraging migration to meet the demand for industrial labour after the Second World War. Others have come to Britain for a variety of reasons including economic and political forces and violent conflicts, such as the Iranian revolution (1979), the war in Bosnia (1992–1995) and the invasions of Afghanistan (2001) and Iraq (2003). With different waves of migrants, different clothing traditions have found their way to Britain; some have been reworked and rejected whilst others have contributed to eclectic British fashions.

But it would be wrong to assume that Muslims in Britain necessarily wear clothes which refer to their cultural origins. First, as already mentioned, regional clothing traditions around the world are themselves in a state of flux and have long been caught up in complex histories of colonization, fashion and reform. Second, 60 per cent of Muslims in Britain were born in Britain and their clothing choices have been informed by a wide range of experiences which include not only family histories of migration or conversion but also life in a multicultural urban environment. In a cosmopolitan city like London, interaction with different people, ideologies and artefacts; engagement with the discourses of human rights; identity politics; Islamic revivalism and fashion; experiences of racism and social exclusion; a desire to defy media stereotypes; an interest in personal aesthetics and a concern with international politics and events may all be important factors influencing a person's choice of wardrobe. Added to these is the widening access people have to discourses and products in global circulation whether through international travel, commerce or the Internet. All of these factors make up the context in which new visibly Muslim appearances are being formulated.

In this context new classifications and understandings of what constitutes Muslim dress are emerging, with some regional styles conventionally popular amongst Muslims being classified as 'un-Islamic' and other styles, especially those regionally associated with the Middle East and North Africa, being accorded the status of authentically 'Islamic'. These co-exist alongside more eclectic combinations made up through the layering of assorted garments and new styles of dress being marketed as 'Islamic fashion' designed specifically for the Western market. But on what criteria are these changing classifications and understandings of Islamic dress being made, and how do they relate to religious textual prescriptions?

The central reference point for religious understandings of Islamic dress is the *Qur'an*, the Muslim sacred text believed to be the direct word of God as dictated to the Prophet Mohammed. Some also make reference to the *Hadiths* (reports of the Prophet's sayings) and the *Sunnah* (the example set by the Prophet's life) in their understandings of appropriate dress, although the precise status accorded to these texts varies in different Islamic traditions. Contrary to what is often assumed by outsiders, these textual sources contain more references to men's dress than to women's.[13] The issue of why visibly Muslim men's dress has received so much less attention from the Western media, social scientists and from Muslim men themselves is a matter of considerable interest which merits further research. What is clear, however, is that since 9/11, increasing numbers of young Muslim men in Britain have adopted beards and, to a lesser extent, caps and *thobes* (robes), and that some attempts are being made to develop new visibly Muslim men's fashions adapted to a Western environment. Some of these developments find mention in this book although, as a female researcher, I had far greater access to women's dress practices, which are my primary focus.

Far from being crammed with rules and regulations about women's appearances, the *Qur'an* contains only a few references to women's dress and these leave considerable room for interpretation. Some take them as broad general guidelines advocating the importance of modesty and lack of ostentation; others read them more as indicators or commandments concerning what should be worn and how. This is a subject of much reflection and debate amongst Islamic scholars from different theological and interpretative traditions. Such scholarly debates are beyond the scope of this book. However, given that most contemporary interpretations of visibly Muslim dress for women make reference to a greater or lesser degree to understandings of the *Qur'an*, it is worth taking a brief look at the passages which refer to women's dress and which are widely cited in books, pamphlets, sermons, conversations and numerous online Islamic resources.

The first of these passages begins by instructing first men, then women, in matters of modesty and sexual decorum:

> Enjoin believing men to turn their gaze away from temptation and to restrain their carnal desires. This will make their lives purer. God has knowledge of all their actions.
>
> Enjoin believing women to turn their eyes away from temptation and to preserve their chastity; not to display their ornaments (except such as are normally revealed); to draw their *khimars* (cloth) over their bosoms and not display their finery except to their husbands, their fathers, their husbands' fathers, their sons, their step sons, their brothers, their brothers' sons their sisters' sons, their women-servants, and their slave girls; male attendants lacking in natural vigour, and children who have no carnal knowledge of women. And let them not stamp their feet when walking so as to reveal their hidden trinkets. (sura 24:30–31)

The second passage concerns issues of covering, visual distinctiveness and protection:

> O Prophet, enjoin your wives and daughters and believing women to draw their outer garments around them so that they may be recognized and not be molested. God is ever forgiving and merciful. (sura 33:57)

Interestingly neither passage refers specifically to covering the head or hair, perhaps because all forms of seventh-century Arabian dress likely would have included head-coverings at the time. The first passage is concerned primarily with the regulation of social–moral behaviour in a relational context. Women are advised to avoid the possibility of eliciting sexual attention from all categories of men except those with whom marriage would be impossible by covering sexually charged parts of the body in a context where modesty and decorum is recommended for both sexes. The second is more concerned with the development of a visually distinctive style of wearing dress which enables Muslim women to stand out from those around them. What we have then are different levels of distinction drawn between men and women, between public and private and between Muslim and non-Muslim.

Both verses have been given considerable importance in Islamic reform movements in Egypt, the Middle East, North Africa, Turkey and South Asia from the 1970s onwards.

In these movements dress reform was linked to ideas of cultural resistance, the search for Islamic authenticity, purification and a quest for increased personal and collective piety. Whilst the first generation of women who participated in these movements tended to adopt plain and simple long-sleeved full-length garments and head coverings in imitation of what they perceived as the dress of the earliest Muslims, many women of subsequent generations have gravitated towards more elaborate and fashionable interpretations of Islamic dress, resulting in the emergence and expansion of an Islamic fashion industry catering to their requirements.[14]

In Britain the importance accorded to the wording in these verses varies considerably. Some adhere to austere and literalist interpretations which are promoted both by conservative and revivalist religious scholars as well as by ideologues of radical political groups who are keen to emphasize Muslim distinctiveness in opposition to what they see as Western secular materialist values. By contrast many are more concerned with the ethical principles of modesty, piety and self-restraint than with trying to replicate what they consider outdated and foreign clothing traditions ill suited to contemporary Western contexts. This interpretation offers women considerable room for experimentation. Whilst some women have only a vague awareness of the details of Qur'anic verses, others study them diligently, alongside the *Hadiths* and a variety of scholarly commentaries and interpretations. Some associate increased covering with increased piety, but many argue that what counts is a person's attitudes and intentions rather than their dress or outer appearance. What all of this suggests is that whilst religious prescriptions about dress are an important reference for most visible Muslims, they do not dictate what women wear. Rather, women make choices informed by a wide variety of factors including personal preferences, individual circumstances and questions of social context.

THE ISSUE OF VISIBILITY

One common argument levelled against Islamic dress practices by those who oppose them is that they make Muslim women invisible. This book takes a different starting point. It argues that far from making women invisible, various forms of covered dress actually make Muslim women more visible when worn in Muslim minority contexts. There are many aspects to this heightened visibility. One element is the disproportionate use of images of Muslims wearing distinctive forms of dress in the British press and the Western media more generally. Given that 80 per cent of newspaper stories about British Muslims in recent years associate them with threats, problems or opposition to dominant British values,[15] the use of images in association with these themes is far from neutral. Whilst in daily life the proportion of men wearing distinctive forms of visibly Muslim dress is relatively small, in newspaper images their proportion is high. Groups of men are commonly pictured either in prayer or protest where beards, caps and kurtas act as signifiers of difference in relation to stories which suggest the threat of 'otherness'. As individuals they are frequently depicted either preaching (and by implication, spreading dangerous ideology) or outside police stations (and by implication linked with terrorism). In the case of images of women, hijabs, jilbabs and niqabs function both to indicate (and by implication, confirm) the idea that Muslim cultural and religious values and behaviour are somehow alien and different.

In many cases the images employed have no direct relevance to the story recorded. In others, the items of dress are the focal point of the story as with the coverage of hijab bans in Europe, controversies over school uniforms, disputes and restrictions concerning dress on identity cards or in the work place. Here, too, the greater the degree of covering, the more visual attention it seems to receive. Hence when the prominent British labour politician Jack Straw published his critique and reservations concerning face veiling in the British context, not only did every British newspaper give front-page coverage to the story, but most printed enormous images of women in niqab persistently for days to come as if the size and constant repetition of the images might compensate for how little of the women's faces could be seen. But in blowing up these images to such gigantesque proportions and inflating the longevity of 'the story', newspaper editors also gave the niqab disproportionate presence and status. This created the impression that face veiling was some sort of archetypal Muslim practice, emblematic of a clash between Islamic and British values, when in reality many British Muslims are highly ambivalent towards the practice and actively oppose it in the European context.

The uncritical and misrepresentative use of images of visible Muslims in the mainstream media undoubtedly feeds and sustains negative perceptions of British Muslims as alien, backwards and threatening, and there can be little doubt that the global political context since 9/11 has served to exacerbate this problem. How far such images and stereotypes affect behaviour towards Muslims is difficult to assess. What we do know is that since 9/11 the frequency of incidents of verbal and physical abuse directed at Muslim women in Britain is directly linked to the degree to which they cover, with those wearing face veils reporting high levels of regular abuse.[16] For Muslim men, visible signals of religious affiliation also attract disproportionate attention, whether in the form of surveillance and searches from the police or in the form of suspicion from members of the public.

Heightened visibility is, then, a fact of life for British Muslims who wear distinctive forms of dress and can undoubtedly have negative consequences. But it should also be acknowledged that for many Muslims who choose to wear clothes which indicate their religious belief and affiliation, being recognizable as Muslim is not simply an unfortunate by-product of their appearance but also an essential element of it. The small, but growing, minority of British Muslim men who have in recent years taken to wearing *thobes* (long robes), caps and beards in daily life often do so in an explicit attempt to replicate the actions, example and appearance of the Prophet. For women, not only does dress indicate faith and membership of a wider religious community with all the feelings of sisterhood and solidarity this may engender, but it also plays a vital role in visually signalling that a woman's body and hair are off-limits to men and that she expects to be treated with a certain degree of distance and respect. In other words, through visibly indicating that she is to some degree concerned with issues of modesty, privacy and piety, a woman hopes to control or modify the way others interact with her as well as imposing constraints on her own behaviour. Such understandings of the effects of covering find support both in the Qur'anic verse referring to the separation of the sexes and the one suggesting that Muslim women should be recognizable and, thereby, protected. Some understand the latter verse to mean that being recognizable as Muslim is not only desirable, but is also an Islamic duty and obligation. However, these positive benefits and virtues of visibility are undermined in the British and European contexts by the negative attention many covered women receive from members of the public, politicians and the media precisely because of their visibility as Muslims. Viewed from their perspective, the problem is not visibility as such, but the issue of how best to manage the heightened visibility that wearing certain types of dress engenders.

One means of dealing with this challenge is to develop an alternative range of images and sartorial possibilities which contradict old stereotypes whilst at the same time conforming to perceived Islamic principles and requirements. This representational challenge has been taken up particularly urgently by Muslims in Britain and around the world since 9/11, whether over the Internet, in the print media or through fashion. Britain's first-ever Muslim lifestyle magazine, *Emel*, was for example launched in 2003 partly as an attempt to counter the proliferation and flow of negative images of Muslims in the post-9/11 period. It now has global circulation. The magazine, which is edited by the prominent British convert, Sarah Joseph, projects colourful, upbeat images of cosmopolitan Muslims active in a wide variety of public domains and diverse in their appearances, backgrounds and perspectives. Amongst informative articles on issues of public concern, it includes features on fashion, gardening, cooking and the family in replication of the format found in the magazine sections of Sunday newspapers.

Similarly, fashion designers and entrepreneurs engaged in producing and marketing new styles of visibly Muslim dress in boutiques and over the Web are keen to reverse negative stereotypes by promoting clothes which demonstrate the compatibility of fashion and faith. In doing so, they contribute to the development of a progressive, modernist, visibly Muslim aesthetic, with its own visual vocabulary and material forms.

The effects and resonance of a particular outfit depend, however, not just on the clothes themselves but also the manner and contexts in which they are worn. Dress which makes a person conspicuous in one context may make the same person inconspicuous in another. Mapped onto the complex trans-cultural geography of a city like London is a geography of sartorial expectations which renders the wearing of certain types of apparel easier in some areas than in others, thereby spatially contextualizing the issue of visibility. Whilst some women may feel most at ease by conforming to the dominant sartorial expectations in particular spaces, others develop experimental stylistic strategies which enable maximum circulation and flexibility, at times exploiting the ambiguous boundaries between what is recognizably Muslim or not. Also important are the high levels of emotion invested in particular styles from the perspectives of both wearers and those with whom they interact. Clothes have the propensity to trigger feelings of solidarity and hostility, admiration and disgust, affection and fear, trust and mistrust. Outbursts of emotion in relation to the dress of others often demonstrate the discrepancy between the wearer's intentions and how their appearance is understood. For some, wearing visibly Muslim dress may be principally about signalling membership of a particular taste-community; for others it may play an important role in the cultivation of a pious self; for yet others, it may have strong religious or political connotations. But whatever the personal meanings attached, clothes have important social and material effects which go beyond the intentions of their wearers.

One consequence of the popularity of visibly Muslim dress practices in Britain has been the critique and marginalization of those Muslim women who choose not to cover by those who do. Such women often find themselves criticized or referred to as 'name-only Muslims' as if they are somehow lacking or unworthy of Muslim identity. Whilst some are immune to such criticisms and take active distance from religious definitions of self, others feel insulted by the hierarchies of piety and authenticity implied by such judgements. This is particularly the case when the women concerned are actively religious in their outlook and lifestyle but do not consider the wearing of hijab an Islamic obligation.

In focussing on the visibly Muslim in this book, my aim is not to reinforce the view that 'real Muslims' should look Muslim, but rather to lend insight into the complexities and nuances of visibly Muslim appearances in Britain today. Unlike categories based on regional or ethnic origin, the category of the visibly Muslim is self-chosen. It is based on actions rather than origins. It is about how people wish to be seen rather than how others define them. In this sense it avoids the pitfalls of essentialism characteristic of frameworks which reduce people to their ethnic, regional or religious backgrounds. As many of the examples in this book clearly demonstrate, the category of visibly Muslim is open to anyone who chooses to identify with it, whatever their backgrounds or origins. At the same time some people may in the course of their lives move in and out of the category simply by adopting or ceasing to wear particular clothes.

ABOUT THIS BOOK

Inevitably, when one researches a topic of this kind which is both highly personal and public, one frequently gets asked about one's motivations for doing so. Some have suspected, and others hoped, that my interest in Muslim dress practices might lead me to convert to Islam. Others have been concerned first and foremost to establish whether I am for or against particular types of dress, as if the topic can only be approached from a position of judgement in which research becomes merely a tool with which to prove a foregone conclusion. My own idea of research is very different from this. It is informed by a background in modern anthropology which encourages, where possible, an openness to the existence and validity of different frameworks and perspectives. The aim is not to judge different ways of life but to engage with them and to work against the many easy stereotypes which block awareness and understanding of different perspectives.

There were, however, some factors which triggered my initial interest in the subject. One was the French government's announcement in 2004 of the intention to ban the wearing of religious symbols in French state schools and my growing awareness of the levels of passion this generated amongst many British Muslims. This and various clothing controversies deepened my awareness of the extraordinary levels of discrepancy that persisted between public perceptions of Muslim dress practices and personal experiences of them. A second factor was my long-term anthropological interest in the significance of dress, textiles and material culture, about which I had worked for many years, particularly in India.

The research for this book began one cold January morning in 2004 when I attended a rally in Knightsbridge where women were protesting against the proposed clothing legislation in France. During the five years that followed, it has led me into intimate contact, conversation and debate with many Muslim women, and to a lesser extent men, in their homes. Most of the research has been conducted in and around London but includes the experiences of Muslims from elsewhere who have come to London to study, work, visit relatives and participate in Islamic commerce and events. The extent to which Muslim clothing practices are dynamic has been brought home to me by the levels of change I have witnessed during the five years of this study. Within this period not only have fashion practices in the street diversified at a considerable rate but there has also been a spread in online Islamic fashion commerce with a global outreach, including the emergence of hijabi fashion blogs and commentaries oriented towards and written by Western Muslims.

Like all books based on ethnographic research, this one is a collective product that would not have been possible without the time, co-operation and generosity of the many people who contributed to it by sharing their experiences and insights. Their voices and images feature prominently in the text which is, above all, intended to place people's personal experiences at the heart of public debates and understandings of Muslim dress practices.

The book opens by introducing the sartorial biographies of three successful professional women: the textile artist, Rezia Wahid; the comedian, Shazia Mirza and the social activist Humera Khan, illustrating the variety of factors that have influenced their clothing choices at different stages of their lives. It highlights the extent to which visibly Muslim dress practices cannot be reduced simply to ideas of religious community, politics or ethnic group but involve complex aesthetic, ethical, social and political choices made in the context of cosmopolitan milieux which offer a variety of possibilities. These three biographies are not intended to represent Muslim women in general, but rather to indicate the complexity and variability of individual life histories and experiences and how these become incorporated into particular modes of self-presentation and styles of dressing.

The issue of the geography of dress practices in London is introduced in chapter 3 through the experiences of a white British convert who adopts hijab. This chapter explores how ideas of multiculturalism are played out differently through dress in different areas of the city, highlighting the unwritten dress codes and sartorial expectations which operate in particular spaces and are sometimes at odds with wider multiculturalist discourses. The chapter also raises the issue of the agency of hijab—that is its effects both on the wearer and those with whom she interacts. It also shows how the symbolism and resonance of hijab is shaped not only by spatial factors but also by international political events such as the 'war on terror' and the spread of hijab restrictions across Europe. Whilst this chapter highlights the symbolic boundaries of dress practices and expectations in London, the next (chapter 4) illustrates how some young women are able to transgress such boundaries through their inventive experiments with style. Here attention shifts away from the fact of hijab towards the issue of personal aesthetics, showing how women experiment with colours, textures, techniques of layering and tying which demonstrate both their fashion competence and their religious, ethical, social and political affiliations and concerns. Many of the women introduced in this chapter come from complex backgrounds which do not conform to simple ethnic categories. For them, looking Muslim is a question of invention rather than conformity to inherited tradition. The chapter explores how they create new Muslim looks which tally with their multicultural backgrounds and enable them to navigate complex cosmopolitan relationships and contexts. Here dress is seen as an embodied work in progress, brought out most clearly through the complex sartorial reflections and performances of the two Muslim hip-hop artists, Sukina and Muneera, of Poetic Pilgrimage who are black British Muslim converts.

Whilst many young people seek to expand new possible ways of looking Muslim, there are some individuals and groups who seek to close down the options for Muslim women by promoting a more austere and homogenous collective self-image. Focussing on what became known as 'the jilbab controversy' over school uniforms which dominated British media headlines for a period of two years, chapter 5 introduces the dress politics of the minority radical political organization, Hizb ut-Tahrir, and its attempt to place Muslim women's dress at the centre of a mythological 'clash of civilizations'. The chapter highlights the collusion between media stereotypes and different strands of political discourse including those of Muslim radical and conservative groups and right-wing British racist extremists.

Media controversies also feature in chapter 6 which focuses on the emotive issue of face veiling, viewed from the perspectives of those who cover their faces and those who do not. By outlining different scenarios of encounter, the chapter examines the visual effects of niqab in relation to different actors, asking why face veiling arouses so much passion and controversy both amongst British Muslims and others. It explores why internal Muslim debates on niqab rarely get aired in the mainstream media where face veiling is commonly represented in terms of an opposition between Islamic and Western values. Like other chapters, this one warns against simplistic readings of particular dress forms, unpacking the different repertoires of meaning associated with niqab, including ideas of privacy, protection, religiosity, piety, politics, obedience and self-restraint. Different women's experiences of face veiling are articulated both through conversations and through analysis of online discussions.

The focus on the Internet is further taken up in chapter 7 which explores the relationship between religious and commercial concerns through an in-depth focus on the popular online store, thehijabshop.com, and some of the innovative new products advertised there, including hijabs for sports. Through tracing the development of this Web site and the histories of products on it, the chapter looks at some of the representational challenges posed by hijabi fashion commerce and examines the role played by the Internet in linking the local activities of one British Muslim entrepreneur to the personal preoccupations of individual Muslims scattered in diverse circumstances around the world. What is suggested here is not that religion becomes debased through commerce but that religious and commercial enterprises are mutually supporting and that both find new possibilities for expansion over the Web. This theme is further expanded in the final chapter which documents the emergence of Islamic fashion designers and retailers in Britain, tracing the many different ways ideas of the 'Islamic' are translated into material form by individuals interested in developing new 'culturally relevant' styles of dress for Muslims living in the West. Here we can trace the distinctive features of an emerging Islamic fashion scape oriented towards Western Muslims around the world which draws selectively from different regional styles and from British and global mainstream fashions. It is suggested that far from signalling a challenge or threat to Western values, British Islamic fashions are evidence of the emergence of new cosmopolitan material forms born out of the British Muslim cultural experience.

NOTES

1. Following popular English usage of the term, the word *hijab* is used throughout this book to refer to the headscarf. Descriptive words like *hijabi* to refer to hijab wearers and *hijabic* to refer to styles of dress considered compatible with hijab form part of a new vocabulary emerging amongst young Muslims in the West. However, in the original Arabic usage of the word, *hijab* refers, not to a piece of cloth, but to a set of ideas about separation, screening and keeping things apart (see El Guindi 1999 for a wider discussion of terminology).

2. For further discussion of the blanket use of the term *veil* to refer to a huge variety of different garments, all of which have distinct Arabic names, see El Guindi (1999: chapter 1).

3. There is of course a vast literature on this theme, much of it inspired by Said's seminal book, *Orientalism* (1978). For works dealing specifically with Muslim women's appearances in art, literature, photography and colonial and academic writing, see Bullock (2003), El Guindi (1999), Lewis (1996) and Graham-Brown (1988).

4. See Ahmed, L. (1992) for Egypt and Naghibi (1999) for Iran.

5. See Wallach Scott, J. (2007) for discussion of French feminist opposition to hijab.

6. There is a substantial literature on 'new veiling'. For Egypt, see Ahmed, L. (1992); El Guindi (1999) and Mahmood (2005). For Turkey see Göle (1996, 2003); Navara-Yashin (2002); Sandikci and Ger (2005). See also special thematic issues of the journals *Interventions* (guest edited by Donnell 1999) and *Fashion Theory* (guest edited by Tarlo and Moors 2007) for discussion of this issue in different locations.

7. Figures from the 2001 census show that Muslims in Britain are extremely poorly placed in terms of education, employment, housing and income, with Pakistanis and Bangladeshis (more than 90% of whom are Muslim) representing some of the poorest ethnic populations of the country (see Peach 2005).

8. For example, in the well-meaning 'Diversity Tool Kit' issued to staff and students of the Open University, we read on page 106, 'Muslims believe that modesty and correct behaviour between men and women are very important. Therefore men must be covered from the navel to the knee and only the face and hands of women should be visible.' Such statements reinforce the stereotype of the Muslim woman as covered whilst implicitly suggesting that those who do not cover are not doing what they should.

9. See El Guindi (1999: chapter 2).

10. See Tarlo (1996: chapters 5 and 6), for a discussion of Hindu face-veiling practices in rural Gujarat.

11. See Moors and Tarlo (2007).

12. See Naghibi (1999) and Balasescu (2003), Balasescu and Niessen (2007).

13. See El Guindi (1999).

14. Islamic fashion commerce is particularly well established in Turkey where it is thought to have played a powerful role in the spread of Islamic revivalism amongst the middle classes (Navara-Yashin 2002; Sandikci and Ger 2005, 2007) but is also fast developing in other countries (see Tarlo and Moors 2007) and on the Internet (Akou 2007).

15. See Moore, Mason and Lewis (2008) in 'Reports' in the Bibliography.

16. See Ameli and Merali (2006).

2   BIOGRAPHIES IN DRESS

How do we look the way we do? Is it our upbringings and cultural backgrounds that somehow determine how we present ourselves, or is it the life we lead, the people with whom we mix, the values we acquire, the tastes we develop, the contexts in which we circulate, our responses to changing fashions and the roles we play at different stages of our lives—in short, the experiences we accumulate that influence our clothing choices? Most people living in the West would probably plump for the latter argument—that background influences are significant but they are merely a starting point from which we develop and often depart rather than an all-determining force which dictates our clothing trajectory throughout our lives. Yet a curious thing seems to happen in outsider perceptions of women who are visibly Muslim. Suddenly the idea that clothing preferences are fraught with complex individual, political, economic, social and aesthetic choices and concerns is replaced by the idea that dress is somehow either dictated by cultural tradition and religious prescription or a form of political flag waving.

This chapter tells a very different story. It introduces three successful, professional Muslim women who are not afraid to display their religious identity but whose appearances cannot in any way be reduced to simplistic ideas of cultural origins, political ideology or religious dictates. This is not to say that religion and politics are irrelevant to the way they look but rather to argue that their dress preferences have grown out of complex biographical experiences in which religion, politics, fashion, memory, environmental concerns, aesthetic preoccupations and a sense of global awareness all play their part. They may look Muslim, but looking Muslim can be as complex as looking anything else.

What is striking is how all three women resist slotting into pre-existing sartorial niches either by forging distinctive new 'Muslim looks' or by bringing apparently familiar styles into new public spaces where their meaning is re-assessed and re-negotiated. Far from demonstrating the introverted conservatism so often associated with Muslims by outsiders, all three lead lives characterized by high levels of trans-cultural interaction, whether through travel and histories of migration or through their participation in the multicultural environment of contemporary London. What emerges from a focus on their sartorial biographies is that their clothing choices are a direct product of their cosmopolitan lifestyles and attitudes. This leads us away from a whole minefield of stereotypical oppositions (religion vs. fashion, traditional vs. modern, Islam vs. West) towards a focus on the complexity and transformative potential of personal experience in the creative and symbiotic relationship between people and their clothes.

I would like to introduce the three women in question through the cultural products in which they deal in their professional lives, namely textiles, comedy and opinion. The fact that I first came across these products in the contexts of an exclusive London gallery, a television show and the House of Lords, respectively, is an indication of the extent to which these women are successful actors in British public life.

My initial encounter with the textile artist, Rezia Wahid, was through her delicately hand-woven textiles which were on display in a Christmas exhibition of designer arts and crafts held in the up-market OXO Tower in Central London in November 2004. Rezia's semi-transparent ethereal, predominantly white, textiles with names like 'Istanbul' and 'Topkapi Palace' were prominently displayed in the window of the exhibition. From outside, one could look in through this diaphanous cloth (hand-woven using hand-spun Egyptian cotton and Japanese silk) to see the rich array of coloured felts, pictures, pottery and jewellery made by the other artists whose work seemed somehow grossly material by comparison. From inside one could look out through her sheer veil-like textiles to see cold Londoners strolling along the banks of the River Thames. Rezia's cloth, with its pure and almost sacred aura, floated like mist between these scenes, visually modifying both and providing some sort of alternative lens through which to view the approach of Christmas on a cold winter's evening in London.

My first glimpse of Shazia Mirza was through her comedy. I was watching television some time in 2002. I no longer remember the programme but what I do remember was the unusual sight of a stand-up comedienne with an explicit Muslim look. Shazia was wearing what was her self-chosen professional uniform at the time—an austere black shirt, loose black trousers and a plain black hijab (headscarf). She was staring blankly at her audience and reciting in a deadpan voice the audacious joke which had accelerated her rise to fame just three weeks after the terrorist attacks of 11 September 2001 when two planes were flown into the World Trade Center with catastrophic effects:

> Hello. My name is Shazia Mirza. At least, that's what it says on my pilot's licence!

The third woman I would like to introduce is Humera Khan—councillor and advisor on Muslim affairs, social activist and founder of the pioneering Muslim organization, *an Nisa*, established to offer advice and support to Muslim migrant women and families. My first vision of her was in 2004 at the House of Lords in Westminster where I was attending the roundtable discussion and launch of a newly published book on Muslims in Britain. The discussants around the table were predominantly Muslim men, dressed in dull grey suits and expressing reverent praise and admiration for the book in question. Then in walked a woman dressed in highly patterned colourful cotton prints with a large and exuberant turban-style hijab folded and draped to one side. It was Humera Khan. When she opened her mouth to speak, the room went silent. Within seconds she had transformed the atmosphere from one of genteel diplomacy to one of heated and impassioned debate.

I introduce these women in the public contexts of their work in order to give a sense of the disruptive impact of their visual appearances, the nature of their artistic interventions and a taste of their individualistic styles. What links them is not what they 'wear' or 'do' but rather the ways in which they contribute towards the re-configuration of the largely implicit sartorial maps of London—a city which, in spite of its multicultural pride and ethos, has surprisingly well-maintained ethnic and religious geographies of dress. Humera's bold prints and colourful turban are not what you expect to see in the House of Lords. They command attention. So too does Shazia Mirza's austere black hijab in the context of the comedy club where its wearing is guaranteed to shock. Rezia's textiles, which exude a pure and sacred aura without necessarily evoking Islam as such, make a more subtle, but no less striking, intervention in the context of the visual landscape of British contemporary designer craft. But it is when Rezia herself enters the exhibition space that one gains a fuller sense of how she stretches and challenges sartorial expectations. Despite her well-chosen and elegant choice of hijab cloth, and her trendy tailored coat, she finds herself looked upon by the gallery staff as if she has somehow wondered into the building 'by mistake'. Rezia's visibly Muslim appearance is unexpected in the notoriously white middle-class environment of British designer craft, even in cosmopolitan London. Rezia is aware that in a way her textiles circulate with greater ease than she does. But she is also aware that where her textiles go, she goes too, for her textiles are none other than her autobiography in woven form.

The second element that links these three women is the extent to which their clothing practices are informed by a particular set of feelings, preoccupations and experiences: all have experienced displacement or its aftermath and the feelings of difference it engenders; all are religiously active and politically concerned; all have social lives characterized by a high degree of trans-cultural interaction; all have visual and sensual memories and curiosity which encourage a global outlook and orientation. A biographical focus on their lives gives access to the significance of these factors and enables us to begin to plot the contours of their sartorial inspiration and inventiveness.

REZIA WAHID: AN AUTOBIOGRAPHY THROUGH CLOTH

Rezia Wahid's biography demonstrates the breadth and combination of ideological, sensual and visual resources on which she has drawn in the development of her personal aesthetic in dress and textile art. It is an aesthetic born chiefly out of the creative interplay of distant memories of Bangladesh and concrete experiences of Britain and Islam.

Rezia Wahid was born in a village in the Sylhet district of Bangladesh where she spent her first five years, cared for mainly by her grandparents. Her mother, still in her late teens at the time was busy giving birth to and caring for Rezia's younger siblings whilst her father, who ran a restaurant business in London, divided his time between the two countries. For Rezia, her parents' decision to move to London when she was five represented a sharp and painful rift—away from the Bangladeshi countryside she loved, from the freedom to run about in the wild and from her grandparents with whom she had spent most of her time. Life in a high-rise apartment off the Edgware Road in Central London was a shock to her and the trauma of it used to surface regularly at night in the form of a recurrent dream. In

Figure 2.1   Rezia Wahid in her studio, South London.

this dream she would be running free in the fields around her natal village with her grand-parents watching over her, smiling. Then, all of a sudden, their faces would just melt away and Rezia would wake up in a state of panic, crying.

In the area of London where they bought their apartment, Rezia and her family were very much in a minority, having deliberately chosen to avoid the 'Bangladeshi areas' of the city. Her mother, who still today speaks very little English, continued to wear saris, adding

Figure 2.2 Family portrait taken in Bangladesh with Rezia (standing) and her younger sister (seated) dressed as boys.
Courtesy of Rezia Wahid and family.

a long black outer garment and scarf when out of doors—all of which marked her out as 'foreign'. Rezia was never particularly disturbed by this and was herself accustomed to looking different. In Bangladesh she and her younger sister had from the start been marked out as different from other girls by being 'dressed as boys'. This was apparently a deliberate strategy introduced by their paternal grandfather who did not want them to be treated 'as girls' or limited to the restrictive roles placed on Bangladeshi women. Both Rezia and her sister remember how he was opposed to their dressing up in saris, even for special occasions or for fun. Rezia's mother went along with this sartorial strategy in Bangladesh, but when they settled in London, she introduced a feminine aesthetic, informed by her own love of colourful and silky fabrics. 'She used to love tying our hair up in ribbons and bows and dressing us up ... She still loves to dress us up even now!' laughs Rezia.

Although there is a photograph in the family album in which Rezia and her sisters wear trousers under their skirts in line with Islamic concerns with modesty, this was not common practice in their upbringing. In fact, once in Britain, Rezia's childhood was characterized by an emphasis on fitting in with the local environment, whatever that was. The family moved frequently around the country following her father's business, and the children were often sent to schools where they were the only pupils from Asian or Muslim backgrounds. Rezia continued to be 'the only Asian' and 'the only Muslim' when she took the unusual step of doing a foundation course at the Chelsea College of Art, followed by a post-graduate course in textiles at Farnham College.

Rezia's textiles and personal aesthetic are perhaps best seen in terms of a creative re-engagement with Bangladesh, with memories of her grandfather and with Islam. But this re-engagement was not direct. In fact Rezia and her sisters were deliberately kept away from Bangladesh throughout their childhood for fear that they would have to be promised in marriage to friends and relatives if they returned. As a result, Rezia's Bangladesh existed in the form of remembered images, sensations and projections, as did the image of her grandfather as a holy man, reminiscent of 'a Persian mystic', whom she remembers seated peacefully on the ground, draped in shawls and reciting prayers.

Rezia's re-connection with this imagined Bangladesh came about, not through travel, but through her experiences in England—in particular through an art and textiles training which encouraged a high degree of personal self-reflection and through her discovery, love and appreciation of the English countryside—both of which led her almost inadvertently to look anew at her mother's saris.

A brief discussion of three of her woven textiles—'Feather', 'Woven Air' and 'Istanbul'—gives a sense of how these different elements are inter-woven in her work. Each textile represents a different stage of her autobiographical development in cloth.

'Feather', like many of Rezia's textiles, was inspired by her detailed interest and engagement with nature—something she explored in the Surrey countryside when she was at college. It was here that she began to experiment with the possibilities of translating the feelings of natural elements into woven forms.

> When we studied printing at Farnham my printing was always very simple, very abstract. I was more texture-oriented than print. It was always the *feeling* of the fabric that interested me most. Then we started weaving. We had this project where we had to pick something from nature. We had to go into the woods in Surrey and find something that interested us. I found a feather.

Rezia's sketchbooks bear witness to a refined sensitivity to the relationship between colours and textures in nature, as well as a remarkable propensity to translate these into woven form. But it was when she found a feather that Rezia had, in more than one sense, found something she could relate to—a sensual affinity between the feeling of the feather and the feeling of silk. After analysing the properties of the feather through touch and sketches, she eventually sought to evoke its 'featheriness' in silk cloth, weaving a feather scarf or hijab.

The feather textile represented the first in a series of textiles which sought to capture a feeling as much as a look. The more she studied the details of natural forms, the more she found herself relating to existing textile traditions and techniques that were bringing her closer, though she didn't realize it at the time, to South Asian textile traditions. Her study of a shell for example led her to look more closely at the merging of colours in ikat cloth and to experiment with this technique. But it was when she began to work on the properties of wispy white dandelion flowers that had gone to seed that the connections with Bangladesh and Islam began to emerge more explicitly.

> We were supposed to be doing something called the Personal Project. It was different from anything else we had done and was meant to be really personal. I was a bit lost. Then I found myself in this field of dandelions. I knew at once that that was what I really wanted to do—to create that light and floaty sensation of those dandelions—the soft and airy feeling of floating. When I told my tutor I wanted to capture this floatiness,

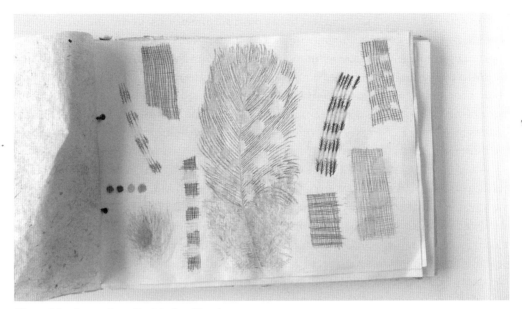

Figure 2.3   A page from Rezia's sketchbook.

she said 'Go and take a look in the resource centre. You might find some saris in there.'
I said '*Saris*!?' And then it clicked.

So it was dandelions in the Surrey countryside that pointed Rezia in the direction of South Asian textiles. She soon found herself leafing through the catalogue of an exhibition of Bangladeshi textiles that had been held at the Whitechapel Gallery in East London several years earlier, and was entitled 'Woven Air'. It was precisely this sensation of airiness that she so desperately wanted to reproduce. It was then that she began to look through her mother's saris with new interest and even set about unpicking the border of one particularly fine jamdani sari with a view to better understanding its composition. And it was through this process that she began to develop her own aesthetic and technique of producing ultra-fine woven textiles with unfinished edges and delicate weft floats based on a re-interpretation of the jamdani tradition. But her attempt to capture the essence of the floatiness of dandelions through a re-working of jamdani techniques was also an attempt to capture a certain feeling of sacredness and holiness that she associated both with her grandfather and with Islam:

> I wanted to portray the atmosphere and feeling you get when you enter a mosque, to convey the sense of purity and tranquillity. I want the light to travel without being distracted by the colour...

So it was from the establishment of aesthetic affinities between a dandelion in Surrey, her mother's sari and her experiences of mosques that she eventually wove the textile piece she calls 'Woven Air' (a translation from the Bengali *Bafthana*).

Since graduating from college more than a decade ago, Rezia has continued to weave her autobiography, till now rejecting attempts to tailor her skills to the fashion industry and rejecting the offer of a scholarship to work in Japan on the grounds that she did not wish to be distracted by 'another culture' before 'discovering her own way'. This has not, however, made her culturally narrow. On the contrary, her visual and religious curiosity have taken her to France, Spain, Turkey, Italy and Japan where her camera delights in small details of Islamic architecture and natural forms, some of which get transposed into subtle floating weft inserts in her textiles—as with 'Istanbul'.

When I visited her studio for the first time in 2004, Rezia was laying the warp for a textile entitled 'Mosque in Rome' in preparation for an exhibition of hijabs aimed at conveying 'how beautiful the hijab can be'. Her focus on hijab had come about in response to her own positive feelings about wearing the hijab—something she has only been doing on a daily basis since October 2001. The date, of course, is not incidental. Although she feels that her adoption of hijab was part of a 'natural spiritual progression', she is also clear that the timing was provoked by the political situation:

> September 11th was some kind of trigger. The media was portraying Muslim women as oppressed and making out that Afghan women were desperate to rip off their burqas, and that infuriated me.

Rezia's active engagement with the anti-war movement and with the charity, Islamic Relief, far from being contradictory to her aesthetic journey, were very much part of her neo-Gandhian philosophy which links weaving, beauty and simplicity to notions of peace and meditation. These are ideas she attempts to convey not just in her weaving and personal conduct but also in her job as a teacher of textile technology in a boy's school in East London. Her contributions to multiculturalism, Islamic charities and the arts were publically recognized in 2006 when she was awarded an MBE (Member of the Order of the British Empire) for her work.

One feature of Rezia's work is her determination to maintain a creative space which engages with Islam and her past without ever being defined or restricted by it. Her commitment to multiculturalism is less about holding particular political views than about the reality of her own life experience. In 2007 for example her textiles were displayed simultaneously in a solo exhibition at the Crafts Study Centre in Farnham, a multicultural fashion show for Charity in South London and the opening of a photographic exhibition on images of British Muslims at the Rich Mix Centre in East London. Here she challenged the conservative views held by many members of the predominantly Muslim audience concerning the display of hair and body form by inviting professional British dancers to dance her textiles on stage. She was more interested in experimenting with the expressive potential of swirling cloth and exploiting the fertile relationship between different art forms than conforming to what she perceived as narrow and confining definitions of the Islamic. A wariness of being pigeon-holed or confined to restrictive ethnic and religious categories is something she has maintained throughout her artistic career.

Figure 2.4 'Istanbul', hand woven by Rezia Wahid.
Photo: Elisabeth Scheder-Bieschin.

Figure 2.5   Dance performance of Rezia's textiles Rich Mix Centre, London, 2007.

By her early thirties, Rezia had developed a clearly defined visual aesthetic not only in her textile art but also her clothes. This involved a subtle layering of garments—perhaps a gypsy-style skirt, dress or top worn, for reasons of modesty, over trousers. By wearing fitted polo neck sweaters or tops underneath short-sleeved shirts and dresses, she is able to cover her arms and front whilst at the same time wearing fitted and tailored clothes. On her head, she often wears two over-lapping scarves in contrasting colours or textures. Though now increasingly common as a style, at the time when she first adopted it, it used to provoke comments from some non-Muslim friends that she looked 'too Islamic', and from Muslim friends that she looked 'too arty' and 'bohemian'. Most of her clothes she buys from regular fashion shops in the high street and from market stalls. It is not the particular items of clothing that make her look Muslim, but the particular layered ensembles that she creates with them. It amuses her that the custom of wearing trousers under skirts has become a street fashion as it is something she herself has been doing since childhood, motivated by a desire to cover her legs. Fashionable, Islamic, distinctive and modern are perhaps the best words to describe her appearance.

Rezia's dress and textiles pose many questions: about the relationship between memory and experience, between individual creativity and collective resources, between autobiography and history, between personal journey and cultural heritage, between feeling as touch and feeling as emotion. It has been through the process of unpicking and re-ordering the different cultural threads of her background that she has been able to create something distinctive and new.

SHAZIA MIRZA: THE ART OF SARTORIAL PROVOCATION

The comedian Shazia Mirza's creative play with dress and textiles is radically different from that of Rezia Wahid, though no less autobiographical. Shazia is probably the most high-profile of the three women discussed here. She is someone who features regularly in the media, whether television, magazines, radio interviews and of course live performances for which she has won numerous awards. She has a commercial agent and a packed professional itinerary which takes her on the global comedy circuit in Britain, Europe, India and the United States, though her plans to perform in Pakistan were cancelled out of fear of the reactions her comedy might provoke. As well as doing stand-up comedy, she also performs in plays, has presented a taboo-breaking TV show on female body hair and writes a regular witty column for the *New Statesman*.

Unlike Rezia, Shazia generally maintains a sharp division between her public and private appearance. In everyday life she dresses in casual 'Western' clothes, favouring smart trousers or jeans with shirts and tops. She has a street-wise quality about her and is someone who in everyday life chooses to 'blend in' rather than 'stand out'. In TV interviews and special events she often appears chic and glamorous, dressing in bright colours and copious amounts of red lipstick. She wears her hair loose around her shoulders, is far from Spartan in her make-up and admits to having a secret penchant for eyelash curlers. But the stage image for which Shazia Mirza became best known is very different. From 2000 to 2003 she routinely performed her comedy wearing austere black clothes with a black hijab—an outfit which acted as an obvious visual shorthand for and stereotype of 'Muslim'.

A pink fitted T-shirt with Shazia's hijab-framed public image printed on the front is perhaps the most apt medium for capturing what Shazia Mirza is about. The ambiguity of the T-shirt is made more apparent by the fact that she herself claims that she does not like wearing T-shirts in public because she feels 'uncomfortable' exposing her arms.

> And that's just habit. It's the way I was brought up. If you were brought up with that
> for twenty-two years and then you left home, you wouldn't feel comfortable either …
> Part of it is that I would probably feel a bit guilty. A feeling that I'm not meant to be
> doing this. And I'd probably think, 'Oh God, men are looking at my arms.' I mean they
> probably wouldn't be but that's what I've had instilled into my mind—that men look
> at every part of you that's on display—they are even looking at your hands—they'll be
> turned on by your hands—so that's what I have in my head.

Figure 2.6 Shazia in New York.
Photo: Paresh Gandhi.

Much of Shazia's life and comedy is about exploring taboos linked to her own experiences as a woman, as a British Asian, as a Muslim and as a comedian—an exercise that offends as many as it excites.

Born in Birmingham to parents who migrated to England from Pakistan in the 1960s, Shazia's childhood was not an easy one. It was not that she experienced racism but that she found her parents' strict 'Pakistani' attitudes and codes of conduct oppressive and inappropriate to the cultural environment in which she was growing up.

> My father was endlessly concerned with what his relatives would think about everything. The Asian community is very racist and judgemental. People accuse whites of being racist and judging us but it's nothing compared with how we judge each other and the racism among Asians.

Figure 2.7   Shazia Mirza dressed for performance, 2001 with T-shirt version.
Available online; courtesy of Shazia Mirza.

Her father's preoccupation with honour and appearances, his desire to maintain respectability according to his image of what was acceptable in Pakistan at the time he left and his fear of the effects of Western culture on his children, particularly his daughters, have all played an important and formative role in Shazia's life, dress and comedy; all of which are, of course, inter-related.

> I hated the restrictions as a child. I wanted to be like Madonna. I wanted to be able to wear ankle socks and dress like a white girl. I used to wear long socks with my school uniform and roll them down once I got to school. I wanted to have patent shoes and pleated skirts like my friends, but I was made to wear trousers under my school uniform and wasn't allowed to do things other girls did, like ballet and going to parties.

Throughout her childhood and still now, Shazia's mother generally wore saris for special occasions and the Indo–Pakistani shalwar kamiz outfit for everyday wear, including swimming. The shalwar kamiz and dupatta combination was what Shazia was expected to wear for festive occasions and weddings, and Shazia recalls having 'hated' it. 'I thought Asian dress was really backwards and boring.'

Brought up in this atmosphere which she clearly experienced as culturally conservative and confining, Shazia longed for escape and dreamed of entering the world of theatre. But a sense of duty led her to study bio-chemistry at University and to take up a post as a chemistry teacher in a school in East London. At night, however, she began to make appearances

Figure 2.8   The Mirza family with Shazia (front left).
Courtesy of Shazia Mirza.

in comedy clubs and pubs where, unbeknownst to friends and family, she was performing stand-up comedy and using her background as her main material.

> When I was young my father said I had to wear trousers under my skirt because if I didn't, men would all want to sleep with me. I tried that, but it didn't work!

Despite her Madonna fantasies, Shazia chose to dress on stage in conservative black trousers and an enveloping long-sleeved black shirt or tunic because, she says, this made her 'a blank canvas'.

> I want people to listen to what I am saying rather than be distracted by what I look like or by my body.

But the canvas did not remain blank for long. It was soon to be framed by a black hijab which became her most identifiable feature and which visually announced, if not screamed, 'Muslim'.

If Shazia is to be believed (and when interviewing her, one always has to remember that embroidering everyday life experiences is both her passion and her profession), her adoption of hijab came about in response to audience criticisms and perceptions of her performances.

When she first stood on stage weaving humour around Asian Muslim experiences in Britain, she found herself accused of being a Hindu making 'anti-Muslim' jokes.

> *My mum keeps a huge list of Muslim men suitable for marriage. It includes height, weight and size of beard!*

By donning a hijab, she was at one level simply claiming the right to speak about Muslims 'as a Muslim'. But in doing so, she was of course picking up on one of the most sacred and semiotically saturated contemporary symbols of our times and taking it into the very spaces it was least expected to frequent—the tainted macho beer-swilling world of London's pubs and clubs from which 'good Muslims' were by definition self-excluded. Furthermore, to make life more complicated—because that is how her life is—Shazia was claiming that she herself was a 'good Muslim'. Several of her jokes revolved around her complete avoidance of sex, drink and drugs and the complexity of circulating in environments where they were most obviously apparent.

> Basically, I joke about myself and allow people to join in. I give them permission to laugh. There's lots of blokes out there who've never even spoken to a Muslim woman. My humour breaks barriers.

From 2000 to 2003 the black hijab became an essential element of Shazia's comedy uniform and there is little doubt that it aided her meteoric success. It got her noticed both by Muslim and non-Muslim audiences, offending many of the former, surprising many of the latter, and shocking both! But the other catalyst in her career was undoubtedly the terrorist attacks of 11 September. Her famous 'pilot's licence' joke was just one element of this; the international media's hunger for Muslim footage was the other. The image of Shazia in hijab became hot property and she had the wit, guts, intelligence and ambition to make the most of it. It was, then, through the inter-play of hijab and 11 September that Shazia, already a successful rising performer, was propelled to international fame.

In effect Shazia used the hijab as a direct and powerful means of exposing and reflecting back to her predominantly white audiences 'Western' stereotypes of Muslims at a time of extreme political tension and sensitivity. When she stared dolefully at her audience and said reassuringly, '*Don't worry, I won't blow you up!*', she was using her hijab-clad image to highlight the escalation of suspicion and fear that had become attached to Muslims in the aftermath of 11 September. Similarly, asked in a television interview where she thought Saddam Husein was keeping his weapons of mass destruction, she replied, '*Up his wife's purdah because no one's thought of looking there!*' It was a comment, not just on the futility of the whole weapons search, but also on the absurdity of how all Muslims were somehow expected to be able to answer such questions.

In effect, the hijab was for Shazia an extraordinarily powerful working tool. It was 'her material' in every sense of the term. But this tool was by no means passive. What she soon found was that the hijab was exercising as much agency over her as she was over it and the relationship was a volatile one which became increasingly difficult to control.

Figure 2.9   Shazia experimenting with hijab, 2003.
Photo: Steve Ullathorne.

In the Western media, Shazia's hijab was good copy. Newspapers and magazines filled with images of this 'brave and devout Muslim woman' but often failed to recognize the irony and nuances of her jokes. The subtlety of her hijab style which, by the standards of many hijab-wearing British Muslims, was 'revealing' in leaving the neck and ears exposed, was never even noticed. Meanwhile the humorous caricature she painted of her British Asian upbringing tended to be taken at face value. She was framed as the Muslim woman stand-up comedian performing against the odds, and although this was the image she had chosen in donning the hijab, she began to feel trapped and restricted by it.

> I didn't want to be THE Muslim female stand-up comedian. I wanted to be Shazia Mirza. But I was trapped in a role. I'd totally lost my identity in all this ... I felt as if I was in prison. And I don't know if that's because people made me feel that way or because I felt that way.

In effect, she began to feel that her hijab was hindering rather than enriching her performance.

> In a way, people were scared to laugh. I was inaccessible. There was definitely a barrier between me and the audience. You know, white laddy blokes on a Saturday night—they wouldn't know how to laugh at that … And I found that when I wore the headdress none of the white male comedians would talk to me at all. They were all scared of me.

As far as conservative Muslim audiences were concerned, Shazia's hijab, and indeed her comedy, had always been controversial, if not problematic. Although many younger-generation Muslims understood what she was trying to do and found her both funny and inspiring (especially her female fans), there were many who accused her of hypocrisy, saying that if she wanted to wear hijab, she should wear it all the time and not just as a 'prop' on stage. Others claimed the hijab was tainted by the alcohol-sodden environment of the comedy club, and yet others objected to a Muslim woman performing on stage at all. Many were deeply suspicious of her jokes, fearing that they encouraged people to laugh at Muslims. In Brick Lane, sometimes popularly known as 'Little Bengal', she was physically lynched by three young Muslim boys and had to be rescued from the stage before she had even finished her opening lines. To accusations that her jokes are anti-Muslim, Shazia makes the complicated claim, 'I never make jokes about my religion, only about my culture.' She also claims that for her religion is a personal thing in which she believes '100 per cent' but which she does not feel obliged to show. 'It's between me and God. I don't have to prove to people that I'm a good Muslim. I only have to prove that to God.'

In late 2003 Shazia made the decision to stop wearing the hijab on stage. She said it felt like 'stepping out of a box'. The burden of 'representing Muslims' which the hijab embodied had been even greater than she had anticipated. At any rate, the weight of the hijab on her head had become too heavy for her to bear. She claimed to have experienced a huge relief at stepping outside the strictures of the hijab and no longer being obliged to perform the role it seemed to dictate. Interestingly her entire style of delivery changed in the process. She no longer performs in the deadpan voice of her earlier days and has developed a more dynamic and fluid stage presence in line with the feeling of 'release'. Shazia no longer performs the Muslim woman stereotype, though her writings and performances continue to deal with cultural taboos and global politics as well as racial, gender and religious prejudice and intolerance.

HUMERA KHAN: THE SOCIAL LIFE OF DRESS

Humera Khan, in her mid forties, is the oldest of the three women introduced here and the only one who was married with children at the time of the research. She has a highly distinctive appearance, the most noticeable element of which is a large, usually brightly coloured and patterned hijab which she wears bound around her head turban-style and hanging loose over her left shoulder. She confesses to possessing a vast number of 'sarongs' and never enters the public space without one tied in this particular manner, though she does introduce further covering when entering a mosque in recognition that her dress might cause offence to some people. Humera's bold hijabs (usually selected from what she considers an Islamic colour palate dominated by rich earthy reds or blues, greens and turquoises) are teamed with long-sleeved, loose high-necked shirts or tunics usually made from natural fibres and worn with loose trousers. The colours and cuts of her clothes are selected to suit the occasion with some in subtler tones for formal professional contexts, though she confesses to always wearing something bright and 'feeling dead' in dull colours. Like Rezia Wahid, she rarely wears black, not because she does not like black but because it has become associated with a particular type of austere and dreary interpretation of Islam with which she does not identify. On the several occasions I have met her I have been struck by the extent to which her appearance commands attention, not just through the colours, forms and fabrics she chooses to wear but also through their capacity to evoke some sort of generalized aura which might be termed *Eastern* or even *exotic* but which cannot be attributed to any particular cultural source or location.

Humera's sartorial biography reveals the extent to which her personal aesthetic and distinctive style have emerged through a whole combination of factors which include reaction against the cultural traditions of her parents, a cosmopolitan city childhood in Central

Figure 2.10   Humera Khan at home, 2005.
Courtesy of Humera Khan.

London, social and political awareness on issues of gender and identity, interaction with people from other cultural backgrounds in both professional and non-professional contexts and religious and visual curiosity concerning Islam.

Though born in Pakistan to parents who had migrated there from India at the time of partition (1947), Humera moved, in the early 1960s at the age of one, to London where she was brought up in an unusual household. The move to London involved a shift in the family's social status. Her well-educated mother, who had never needed to work in Pakistan, took up the live-in job of housekeeper at the Nigerian Embassy in Belgravia, one of London's most exclusive and central locations. Humera's family lived in the basement flat of the embassy residence which made her experiences of growing up unconventional in many ways. On the one hand, she was privileged in living in an exclusive central locality inaccessible to all but the richest of migrants; on the other hand, she was brought up 'below stairs' in a household which was unusually multicultural. Despite status divisions amongst the adults, Humera remembers that the children of the household (consisting of herself, her siblings, the children of the Nigerian ambassador and the Spanish cook) played together all the time. Humera's early childhood was as a result extremely cosmopolitan. She lived in a multicultural household, attended the local Church of England state school, whilst at the same time receiving what she describes as a 'culturally Pakistani' upbringing from her parents.

Where clothes were concerned, Humera's family were not particularly conservative. Her father's sisters had 'shed their burqas' without any particular fuss when they came to Britain and her mother's family had always been more Westernized and 'progressive' in their tastes. In general Humera feels that clothes in those days were not 'the big issue' they have become today. Whilst her mother followed fashions in shalwar kamizes and saris, the children were brought up in Western styles for everyday wear. It was only when their bodies developed as teenagers that their father expected Humera and her sister to discard their dresses in favour of the shalwar kamiz. Humera was unwilling.

> The shalwar kamiz for the sub-continental psyche represented religion at one level, culture, respectability and *udab* (etiquette) which was very important both in the Islamic tradition and in the Pakistani tradition as well. I always rebelled against that and thought, 'I'm not wearing it.' Of course I did sometimes wear it for special occasions, but otherwise not. It was an ongoing source of conflict.
>
> It [the shalwar kamiz] wasn't relevant to me. Also you have to remember that the shalwar kamizes available in the sixties and seventies were horrible. There was that too. I don't think I thought much about it consciously at the time, but if I thought hard about it, I think subliminally I felt that it singled you out. Also, in my mind it represented a type of person who was 'traditional' and all that and I didn't see myself like that. I didn't want to be put in that box.

The family's sartorial tensions were made more complex by the fact that Humera's sister, who was three years older, took an altogether alternative route which was equally distasteful to her parents:

At secondary school my sister got into religion in a big way. It was the early to mid seventies and she started wearing a hijab. It was not at all common then. In fact it was very unusual and my family were dead against it. They said, 'You're never going to get married dressed like that. You are looking ugly. Do you think you are being clever doing that?' etc.

By this time the family had moved out of Belgravia and were living in a more multicultural and less central location in West London. Her sister challenged the school about the uniform on the grounds that it exposed too much flesh and she got a special concession to wear a longer-than-usual grey skirt. Both sisters were, in effect, departing from what they saw as the 'Pakistani' values and aesthetic sensibilities of their parents. Like Shazia Mirza, Humera is adamant that in Pakistan the hijab is still much less common than it is in Britain and that it was never worn by their mothers who simply used their dupattas to cover their heads loosely in modesty-demanding contexts.

Humera's rebellious streak never led her into sexually revealing clothes but she was experimental, fashion conscious and flamboyant. As a young woman, she and several of her friends had casual jobs in fashion boutiques in Oxford Street and they used to pool together their resources and take it in turns to buy something new. Humera's school friends, with whom she has remained close to this day, were not on the whole Pakistani, but neither were they white British. They were from a wide range of cultural backgrounds, black, mixed and white. What they shared in common was not the same ethnic or religious heritage but the experience of being the children of first-generation migrants, of dealing with cultural and generational conflict within the family, of knowing first-hand the financial pressures of life in London and of experimenting with the music and fashions of the sixties and seventies. Humera was particularly into Soul music in her late teens and early twenties and her tastes in fashion were strongly influenced by the fashion aesthetics linked to this scene.

At University in Portsmouth she had her first somewhat alienating experience of being surrounded by a predominance of white British people with whom she made friends at the time but with whom she later lost touch. She describes this period as the 'turbulent years' of her life when she was unsure of her direction, adding 'from the age of eighteen to twenty-five I was not a Muslim.'

Figure 2.11   Humera (far left) and friends as teenagers in their 'Soul' days.
Courtesy of Humera Khan.

It is difficult to say whether it was Islam that brought Humera to the hijab or whether in a funny sort of way, it happened the other way round. In their mid twenties Humera and her sister began to get involved in community work with Muslim migrant women and children in the multicultural outer London borough of Brent. By this stage her sister was no longer a hijab-wearer, having married and moved to Pakistan for a few years where she had found herself 'unable to be the type of conscientious practising Muslim' she had been in Britain. 'She went to Pakistan wearing a headscarf and came back without it.' Nonetheless she remained idealistic and both sisters shared a strong sense of the need to do something to help new Muslim migrants adjust to life in Britain. It was in this context that they began to wear hijab—not for reasons of spirituality, modesty or religious obedience, but out of a desire to fit in and be taken seriously by the Muslim families with whom they worked, many of whom were from less educated and more culturally conservative backgrounds.

> I must admit that I started wearing it for quite vested interests really. I was working with the community and I didn't want to create any barriers, and I thought if wearing the hijab is going to help, then why not? But in a way I felt a bit bad about it because I was only doing it part-time, in the context of my work with people or if I went to a mosque. I never felt very comfortable in it at that time. It was only as I got older that I grew in to it.

So for Humera the hijab was initially an enabling device in the context of her interaction with Muslims from a range of different backgrounds in the multicultural borough of Brent. She and her sister used to tie it in various ways, but generally flat on the head as a scarf. It was some years before they became attached to the style which now forms such a distinctive element of their look and this too was through an interactive engagement with others:

> I saw an English Muslim woman [a convert] wearing this style and I really liked it. It was the late eighties and early nineties. Women were looking for ways they could dress Islamically which were also fashionable and which we could control ourselves rather than being controlled by the fashion industry. We used to go off to Tie Rack and look for interesting Islamic-looking prints like Paisley patterns or whatever we could find. Nowadays I buy cotton sarongs ... I just find it [this style] comfortable. I think its origins are probably more African than anything else. You see, in a shrinking planet you have the opportunity to draw from a lot of different things, and the key to it is to take it back to the root, to the essence of what it means.

Although 'what it means' is something very important to Humera now, at the time of her sartorial experiments, it was not. What was more important was the combination of being acceptable to other Muslims with whom she mixed whilst at the same time being fashionable and innovative and exploring the possibilities offered by various different Islamic traditions. It was through organizing a massive celebration of Islamic culture at a major exhibition hall in Brent that Humera became aware of just how diverse and rich these traditions were. The exhibition helped her cultivate what might be termed an Islamically oriented vision and was influential in forging her own clothing choices and aesthetic preferences.

I was the one who went around all over London collecting stuff for the exhibition. We
had bought loads of stuff—Turkish pottery, textiles, African stuff, Pakistani stuff, Indian
stuff—whatever. And going out searching for all this stuff made me really look around
and see things I hadn't noticed before. I realized what an incredible heritage this was
… The event included a couple of lectures, a fashion show, an exhibition and sale for
women only…

Humera was part of a newly emerging generation of active young Muslims in London
who recognized the need to value the social, political, aesthetic and religious backgrounds
of new Muslim migrants whilst at the same time recognizing the importance of adaptation and transformation. Together with her husband, a political journalist, she set about
establishing a magazine called *Muslimwise,* which was the first-ever magazine dealing with
the concerns of British Muslim youth. The emphasis was not on cultural authenticity or
conservatism but on establishing cultural affinities shared by Muslims from around the
globe and forging something new in the British context.

It is perhaps not surprising that this outward-looking global orientation should have
taken material form at Humera's wedding where she chose to dress, not in Pakistani or
British attire, but in what she describes as a 'Turkish outfit' whilst her husband, who
was born in Mombassa and of Yemeni extraction, wore what she describes as 'Arabic
Robes' and a 'Yemeni turban' ('tied 'wrongly' because no one could remember how to tie
it right!').

It was part of the forging of new styles of British Muslim marriage and I think quite a
few couples were influenced by our event.

Effectively Humera was involved in what is an ongoing process amongst religiously active Muslims in the West of selecting and re-coding clothing, textiles and material culture
from around the world, and classifying them as 'Islamic'. When I first interviewed her she
was wearing a blue and turquoise tie dyed bandhani turban from India. When I asked her
if she had a particular preference for textiles with an Asian look or origin, she said, 'I don't
like the term *Asian.* I tend to go for more Islamic patterns. These blues are very Islamic.
That's my inspiration and I'm a bit of a purist in that respect.' What was to me an Indian
design and textile technique was to her, first and foremost, Islamic and her wardrobe contains many such Islamic garments, some of which have been collected from the numerous
Muslim countries she has visited on her travels.

This desire to separate out what she calls 'the cultural' from 'the religious' is something
Humera shares with Rezia and Shazia and with many other women I have interviewed in
London. In this context, Bangladeshi and Pakistani traditions are often perceived as distor-
tions of some purer Islamic tradition to which the new generation look and which they
perceive to be more compatible with gender equality.

One thing I really didn't like when I was growing up was the clash of colours that people
used to wear in the Pakistani community—you know, that over-done brocadey, silky,

Figure 2.12 Humera's wedding.
Courtesy of Humera Khan.

over-the-top, doll-like thing. It was too much ... And I think it represents putting women in their place. Women, when they are obsessed with their looks, their dress, are not thinking about anything else. It represents something rather sinister from the gender point of view.

Humera also considers that 'the Muslim world' is guilty of distorting women's roles by promoting either 'the self-sacrificing mother' or 'the Barbie-doll thing', both of which she feels miss the essence of Islam's real emphasis, which is on gender balance and complementarity. Her own interpretation of an attractive but Islamically appropriate appearance does not require that the clothes come from Muslim countries but rather that they have what might be called Islamic affinities through their colour, pattern, motif or form. Though she does have several outfits she has picked up on her travels, most of Humera's clothes are in fact purchased from British fashion boutiques and a large proportion of her hijabs are sarongs from the popular chain store, Tie Rack, which is found in most British high streets and at British airports.

It is difficult to say whether Humera eventually grew into her hijab or if in fact the hijab grew onto her. Certainly, what began as an enabling device has become her habitus to the extent that she can no longer imagine herself in public without it.

> It's funny. I went away on holiday with a friend of mine who was not Muslim. This was some years back. And we were out one evening and she said, 'Why don't you take your hijab off here? No one will know.' So I tried not wearing it for one evening and it just felt weird. I'd got so used to it. And I realized it had become a part of me. So after that I wore it without any problems.

Humera's distinctive hijab has not just become an extension of her body, a material component of her public self, but it has also gradually become saturated with spiritual meaning as her religious engagement and conviction has in recent years increased.

> I realized over the years, it's not about how you look, but conceptually about your spirituality. The hijab is about protecting your spiritual self. It also creates an important divide between the public and private. Sexuality is an incredibly powerful thing. It is sacred. You contain it within a sacred space. At the same time you are protecting your energies and remembering that only God is above you … That's how I've come to understand it at a deeper level.

Interestingly even Humera's spiritual understanding of the meaning of her dress is informed by her international orientation. One of the religious specialists she most looks up to and with whom she studies every year is a German woman convert and scholar of Islam who has taken her through all the instances of the use of the term *hijab* in the *Qur'an* with a view to better understanding the concept in context. Many who meet Humera might see her hijab primarily as a form of social and political activism which publically declares her allegiance to Muslims and her desire to assert Muslim interests and rights. Whilst these aspects are not irrelevant, they are combined with personal, religious and aesthetic concerns which make the symbolism of her dress far richer than might at first be assumed.

CONCLUSION

A focus on the sartorial biographies of three exceptional and successful Muslim women shifts the emphasis away from concerns about whether their clothes are Western or Eastern, religious or secular, traditional or modern towards an understanding of the wide range of experiences and concerns that inform the clothing choices of contemporary British Muslim women. Humera, Shazia and Rezia are not 'typical' to the extent that they are highly successful, educated middle-class professionals, but their biographies give a sense of the wide perimeters within which clothing experimentation is taking place amongst progressive, religiously active Muslims living in Britain. In all three cases, far from blindly perpetuating the cultural traditions of their parents, they have sought to distance themselves from what they consider 'ethnic' dress in favour of clothes they consider fashionable, modern and Islamic. Brought up in contexts where saris and shalwar kamizes were associated with both foreignness and restrictive roles for women, they have rejected these clothing forms as 'too traditional', wearing them only occasionally in festive contexts. Meanwhile, in the case of Humera and Rezia, their religious involvement has led them to cover their heads in ways their mothers never did. Whilst their mothers are bare-headed much of the time, and loosely cover their heads in contexts which require modesty, Humera and Rezia have adopted tighter fixed styles of hijab which totally conceal their hair and which they put on in the morning and do not remove until they arrive back home at the end of the day. Their understanding of the degree to which women should cover stems, not from their backgrounds, but from their interpretative readings of the *Qur'an,* their individual spiritual journeys, their commitment to being identified as Muslim and their conviction of the hijab's social and religious benefits.

But if Humera, Shazia and Rezia have rejected the clothing choices of their mothers in favour of a more religiously oriented dress, this new religious dress is informed both by their experiences in Britain and by their global orientation and cosmopolitan sensibilities. In Rezia's case, memories of Bangladesh, of her grandfather and her mother's saris resonate with feelings evoked by the natural forms she discovered in the British countryside and by her religious engagement. In her textiles, all these elements are inter-woven using cotton which comes from Egypt and silk which comes from Japan. For Humera, it is her cosmopolitan upbringing and work with Muslim migrants from diverse backgrounds that have informed her breadth of vision and which have taken on material form whether in her choice of wedding outfit, her African-inspired turban-style hijab (copied from a British convert) or the overall ensembles she creates. Their 'Muslim looks' are concerned not just with issues of modesty but with particular aesthetic sensibilities to colours, textures and patterns which they consider to have an Islamic resonance. At the same time, their choices are also informed by global political awareness and engagement. Shazia's hijab gained increased potency in the context of 11 September and became a powerful medium of political commentary whilst Rezia's decision to wear hijab was directly triggered by the terrorist attacks and the war in Afghanistan.

Finally, what these sartorial biographies reveal is the assertive power or agency of clothes in people's lives. This is most clearly demonstrated in the cases of Humera and Shazia. For both, the hijab was at first a working tool, a means of communicating and enabling specific forms of interaction in specific spaces. In Shazia's case, it was a powerful visual medium for exposing and challenging stereotypes about Muslims literally head on; for Humera, a means of easing her relationship with Muslims from more conservative backgrounds. One was challenging the hidden geography of hijab by thrusting it into public view in the very spaces it was least expected—pubs, theatres and night clubs. The other was subscribing to its geography by adjusting to the values of the Muslim migrant communities concentrated in Brent. But for both women, the hijab ended up playing a more powerful role than they had anticipated. In Humera's case it grew to become a part of her in such a way that she no longer 'feels herself' without it. In Shazia's case, the weight and expectations attached to it became unbearable, leading her eventually to remove it. In both cases the logic of hijab seemed to supersede their capacities to control it. Meanwhile for Rezia, who chose to wear the hijab for her own religious and political reasons, the problem has been not the hijab's effect on her but its effect on those around her. Her greatest fear was that the art/craft-world would reject her in hijab, and she has had to deal with silent hostility to her dress from the headmistress of the school where she teaches textiles.

The three women discussed in this chapter provide a useful starting point for thinking about Muslim dress practices in Britain for they help us break outside the veiled/unveiled dichotomy to get a taste of how complexity, variety and individuality may be expressed in new visibly Muslim looks. Shazia, Humera and Rezia do not know each other and may well disagree on many things if they did, but one thing they share in common is a desire to step outside the boxes into which others try to put them. This applies as much to the expectations of non-Muslims as it does to the conflicting expectations of other Muslims. Whilst their sartorial biographies demonstrate a high degree of performative creativity, they also remind us that clothing choices are never entirely free. They are always made within specific social, spatial, historical, interpretive and interactive contexts and constraints. It is to some of these that we turn in the next chapter.

3   GEOGRAPHIES OF HIJAB

In July 2004, London's City Hall, a spectacular state-of-the-art glass building on the banks of the River Thames, opened its doors to a conference entitled 'Hijab: A Woman's Right to Choose'. The conference was organized by the then–newly established Assembly for the Protection of Hijab (otherwise known as Pro-Hijab), a London-based international network and lobbying group which formed in response to the French proposal to ban the wearing of religious symbols in state schools—a ban which took effect in September of the same year. The conference brought together on one platform an unusual mix of hijab-wearing Muslim women activists from Britain, Belgium, Holland, France, Turkey and Tunisia as well as Muslim academics, legal specialists, human rights activists, left-wing politicians, a Catholic priest, a Sikh dignitary and a German feminist, conspicuous for her short blonde spiky hair and her 'F*uck Racism' T-shirt. The guest of honour was a well-known Muslim cleric from Quatta, Sheikh Yusuf Qaradawi, whose robed presence caused outrage in some sections of the popular press which, perhaps for the first time, found themselves siding with gay rights activists who opposed the cleric's entry into Britain owing to his negative views on homosexuality. A small group of gay men stood outside the entrance of City Hall waving banners with slogans such as 'Unveil your mind' and 'Qaradawi forces Muslim women to veil'. These messages read strangely in relation to the confident and professional-looking hijab-wearing women striding into City Hall and taking their places on the podium and in the audience with a determination to defend the wearing of hijab as a 'human right'.

One theme that was both highlighted and celebrated throughout the conference was the role of London as an exemplary multicultural city. 'London', stated Ruby Mahera, representative of the London Muslim Centre, 'is like a Beacon for other world cities to follow.' This theme was most eloquently developed by London's then-mayor, Ken Livingstone, who was both hosting the conference and speaking in it. 'London', he proclaimed ' … is a city with an underlying creed—that we live by the laws of tolerance, that we accept the differences of the people around us. And that is why every religion exists in this city. Every community from every nation has its outpost in this city. And the city works well. The city works, not just because people tolerate each other; people enjoy the diversity of the city.'

In this sunny, idealized portrait of multicultural London, clothing diversity plays a significant part, acting as visual proof of British acceptance of ethnic and religious differences whilst, at the same time, naturalizing and reifying these differences in the process. Such differences are visually inscribed in the streets where various forms of ethnic and religiously inspired dress from around the world mingle with a huge variety of street styles and hybrid fashions with apparent ease. Such differences have also become formally institutionalized

Figure 3.3   Oxford Street, 2005.

This chapter introduces some of the complexities of the relationship between dress and multiculturalism in London, taking as its starting point attitudes to hijab at a hairdressing salon in a quiet residential area of North West London where hijab-wearing is classified as 'other'. It goes on to explore how the meaning and resonance of hijab is articulated very differently in different spaces, suggesting that despite the trans-national character and multicultural ethos of the city, the adoption of hijab is rarely ever entirely unproblematic for the wearer. For the hijab, more than any other form of religiously connoted dress, is semiotically over-charged. Not only is it subject to the differing logics of particular spatial norms but also to the diversity of interpretations by different individuals and groups (both Muslim and non-Muslim, locally and globally) who try to shape and control its meanings. Such meanings are in turn constantly re-framed by on-going political events and the sensational media coverage of these. Having to contend with the multiple resonances of hijab is an important element of hijab wearing as women negotiate the complexities of living in a city marked by uneven pockets of acceptance and tolerance and by a plethora of competing perceptions and interpretations of their dress. The chapter also explores some of the contrasting emotions attached to the hijab by those who wear it and those who do not and raises the awkward question of the extent to which markers of religious faith may have unintended segregating effects.

HIJAB AT THE HAIRDRESSERS: A STORY OF CONVERSION

A hairdressing salon in a quiet residential neighbourhood of North West London may not seem an obvious place for thinking about hijab, for this is a neighbourhood more noticeable for the whiteness of its inhabitants than for its multiculturalism. But hairdressing salons are interesting places for the easy flow of interaction and conversation they encourage. What follows is an account of how, why and to what effect the hijab became a topic of interest and concern in one particular neighbourhood salon in an area where the only visible Muslims are non-English-speaking mothers taking and fetching their children from a nearby state primary school at particular times of day. The names of individuals and places have been altered with a view to respecting requests for anonymity.

There are three people of interest in this tale: Jane, the owner of the salon, a woman in her forties from an Irish Catholic background; Nicole, a young glamorous Spanish woman employed in the salon and Loraine, a white British girl of Anglo-American parentage, who, along with her mother, is a long-time client of the salon. Each of these women has a connection with hijab, not through their backgrounds but through people they have met in the multicultural environment of the metropolis.

In the case of Nicole the connection to hijab is largely accidental. Nicole left Spain for London some eight years ago when she was in her early twenties. Like many young migrants to the city, she came in search of a mixture of fun and financial remuneration. She settled in a multicultural neighbourhood where rents were cheap and soon found herself mixing with people from a variety of backgrounds. When she split up with her Afghan boyfriend, she met a young man of French Algerian extraction who was working in a local nightclub. Pierre, the young man in question, was from a Muslim background but was not particularly religious. The two fell in love and within a year were married. The Muslim aspect of Pierre's identity was not particularly relevant either to him or to Nicole and might never have become so had he not been diagnosed a few years later with a severe life-threatening disease. In distress, he turned to his local mosque for support, which he found at the hands of a group of devout young Muslim men who convinced him that if he devoted his life to Allah, he might be saved. When Pierre survived a series of life-threatening operations, he felt he had been granted new life from God. This young man for whom Islam once occupied a minor place soon set about re-defining his life according to what he now considered correct Islamic principles. He changed his name to Mohammed; grew a beard; started to dress in long, loose robes on a daily basis; took to praying five times a day, keeping strict dietary rules, spending large amounts of time in the company of other devout worshipers and withdrawing from anything he considered 'un-Islamic', including his wife's friends and, to some extent, his wife.

Nicole's attitude to this was one of stoic acceptance and plucky resistance. She performed what she saw as her wifely duties by supporting Pierre through eighteen months of severe illness but refused to transform her lifestyle to harmonize with his, resisting his attempts to convince her to dress modestly and cover her head and neck. Her initial line of defence was that Pierre's own sisters did not even wear hijab and they were Muslim, so why should she? In response to this, Pierre succeeded in persuading two of his sisters to adopt hijab in order to set a good example to his Spanish wife. But Nicole remained resistant, refusing to attend Muslim social events where she feared that people would 'suck her in', as she put it. Her only sartorial concession was to wear a cardigan over her overtly skimpy tops when in the house so as not to offend her pious husband. But her vibrant, conspicuously fashionable and extrovert clothing habits otherwise remained unchanged. She continued to favour skin-tight trousers, short skirts, high heels and tops which revealed a heavily be-jewelled navel. Meanwhile Pierre (now Mohammed) withdrew increasingly to the sanctity and safety of what became his private room (newly decorated and sanctified with Islamic prescriptions), particularly when Nicole's non-covered female friends came to the house.

Various popular interpretations of all of this circulated in the salon, ranging from 'Pierre has been brainwashed by extremists when he was near to death' to 'He has reverted back to his original roots' and so forth. But the fact is that Pierre was not religiously active before his illness and neither were his parents. It is not that he had returned to his roots but that he has chosen a particular *route* from the wide cultural repertoire of possible ways of being Muslim in London—in this case precipitated by personal trauma and exposure to a stricter, more pious way of life. But in contemporary multicultural London, such a repertoire is open, not just to people from Muslim backgrounds, but also to others. Whilst Nicole was not attracted to the possibilities for personal transformation opened up by her encounter with and exposure to an Islamic lifestyle, there are others who find such trans-formative possibilities appealing.

Loraine is in her early twenties. She has blonde hair and a pale complexion and could, until recently, be seen wearing the jeans and track suit tops ubiquitous amongst her gen-eration. She was raised just around the corner from the salon by her British mother and American father. At the age of seventeen, however, Loraine met and fell in love with a Muslim boy—a student from a Gujarati Kenyan background who had come to England to attend sixth-form college which is where he met Loraine. Until this point, she had not to her knowledge had any direct contact with Muslims, having attended a rather sheltered private school in a largely white middle-class zone of North London. 'When I was at school I didn't know anything about Islam', she told me, 'I mean nothing at all. If you'd asked me what a Muslim looked like I wouldn't have been able to tell you.'

Like Nicole's boyfriend before his religious re-birth, Loraine's boyfriend was not particu-larly religious. He was the sort of person who made an effort to attend Friday prayers from time to time and participated in Eid feasts but not much more than that. But through him, Loraine met other members of his family and was particularly impressed by the women who seemed to take their religion more seriously. In particular, she remembers having felt attracted to the 'rules and regulations' by which they lived their lives and the sense of order, hierarchy and solidarity in their home. This encounter spurred an interest in Islam which

Loraine fed initially through reading and surfing on the Internet, and later through inter-action with religiously active Muslims she met during her first year at University in West London. Here Loraine found herself welcomed by enthusiastic members of the University's Islamic society who encouraged her towards Islam. What appealed to her was the level of their dedication and 'the complete way of life' that Islam seemed to offer which, she said, 'made sense to her', offering 'a whole logic to believe in'. In February 2004 she said the *Sha-hada*[3] and took to wearing the hijab the following day. It was, she said, 'part of the package of becoming Muslim'. Like many other converts, she was keen not to miss anything out and, if in doubt about matters of worship and deportment, she consults an online imam. For the past few years, she has been sharing a house with other young Muslim women from various backgrounds (two Jordanians, one British Asian and one other British convert). All wear the hijab and long-sleeved full-length outer garments (*abayas* or *jilbabs*) when out of the home (though Loraine wears something that looks 'less foreign' when she comes back to visit her mother[4]) and all consider the covering of arms, feet and hair an un-negotiable Islamic requirement. In addition, her house mate of British Asian origin, who teaches in a Muslim school, adds a *niqab* (face veil) when out of doors. For Loraine, what began as a trans-religious encounter has become a means through which to transform her life.

I mention these two cases in the context of the hairdressing salon because the salon provides a micro-environment in which different attitudes and experiences intersect with interlocking and accumulative effects. This can be seen most clearly when we examine the actions and responses of Jane to Loraine's hijab. Jane, as mentioned earlier, is the owner of the salon, a woman in her early forties of Irish Catholic extraction. Her relationship to hijab is far more tenuous and remote than Nicole's or Loraine's and it is precisely for this reason that it is in some ways the most interesting. She began as mere witness to the experiences of the others: of Nicole's resistance to hijab-pressure from her husband and Loraine's deci-sion to embrace hijab—something she learned about from Loraine's mother who deeply resented her daughter's conversion to Islam and devoted a number of hairdressing sessions to publically expressing her horror and disgust. In the summer of 2004, just a few months after her conversion, Loraine's mother booked her a hair appointment at the salon. But Jane was not to meet Loraine in hijab for she rung up to cancel at the last minute—an act which every one in the salon attributed to the hijab. And in a sense, they were right. When I asked her why she had not kept the appointment, Loraine explained that it was not that 'Islam wouldn't let her have her hair cut' as her mother supposed or that 'she mustn't be touched by a non-Muslim' as the hairdresser suspected, but, rather that she did not want to run the risk of a man walking into the salon and seeing her hair uncovered.

What is very clear talking to Jane is that although her encounters with hijab have been indirect, they have had a profound impact on the way she feels about her environment and projected future. Loraine's hijab (though she has only ever seen it at a distance) affected her in significant ways. To her it not only suggested that Loraine had been 'led astray' or 'brainwashed' as she put it, but it also acted as some sort of personal warning. Hearing Loraine's mother's accounts and seeing 'what has happened to Loraine' made her anxious about her own child (then aged four) who was attending the nursery attached to her local state school in the multicultural multi-religious neighbourhood of Finsbury Park in North London. In the past, whenever we discussed schools, Jane had always said she wanted her son to be exposed to as many different cultures and religions as possible. She thought it was 'healthy' in contrast to her own strict Catholic upbringing. 'I hated all the Catholic stuff I grew up with in Ireland', she confessed, 'but this business with Loraine has got me thinking. I mean maybe children need to grow up with a religion in order to have something to rebel against [she laughs, aware of the irony of what she is suggesting]. And perhaps if you don't give them anything, they'll go off searching for something, like Loraine.'

Loraine's hijab had, in effect, become to Jane proof of the potential perils of multiculturalism (although she would never have consciously perceived it like that). It triggered anxieties which not only got her thinking, but also, acting. Despite declaring quite openly that she is 'a complete atheist', she started attending her local Catholic church with the explicit intention of securing her son a place in the safely closeted environment of the local Catholic school and—more to the point—pulling him out of the multi-ethnic, multi-religious local school to which he was already attached. Her efforts were successful. What is interesting is that Jane, far from being some right-wing conservative with entrenched racist views, is, on the contrary, a classic example of the sort of liberal Londoner of Ken Livingstone's description—the one who appreciates ethnic diversity in friends, food and clothing, who mixes freely with people from different cultural backgrounds, employs an Indian nanny to look after her child and people of different cultural backgrounds in her salon (including a British Bengali Muslim girl who does not wear hijab).

To say that Loraine's adoption of hijab *caused* Jane to withdraw her son from the state education system would perhaps be to over-state the case. Yet Jane undoubtedly did succumb to fears and anxieties triggered by Loraine's hijab, the sight of which made her nervous about the number of visibly Muslim mothers standing outside the school gates at her son's nursery—women whose clothing seemed to suggest alternative values and a lack of shared norms. She explicitly links her decision to attend the Catholic church to Loraine's conversion and visual transformation. And it is worth noting that had Loraine simply converted without transforming her appearance, it is unlikely that Jane would have reacted in the same way. It was the material presence of hijab, and the way it made difference visible, that made Loraine's conversion unpalatable, both to her mother (for whom it signified distance and rejection) and to Jane (for whom it signified both warning and threat). Jane did not wish to expose her son to a hijabi environment for fear of what such exposure might unleash. Here we have not the forging of new hybrid identities, about which we read so much in post-colonial theory, but rather the re-enforcement of difference through fear. It is likely that much of the ethnic and religious segregation so visible in London's schools and neighbourhoods is explicable partly in terms of this type of fear—a fear, not so much of encounter or interaction but of the transformation that such interaction might engender. It is, of course, a fear which works in more than one direction, as the proliferation of religious schools to some extent testifies.

TYING HIJAB

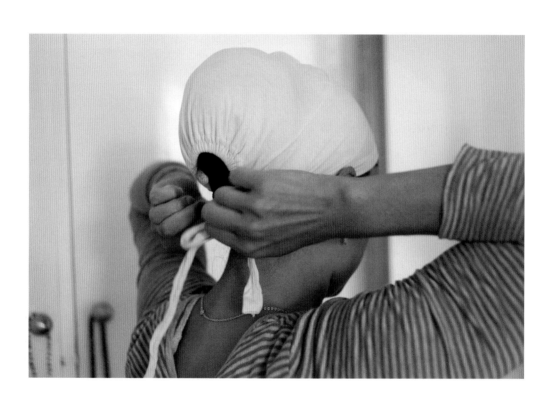

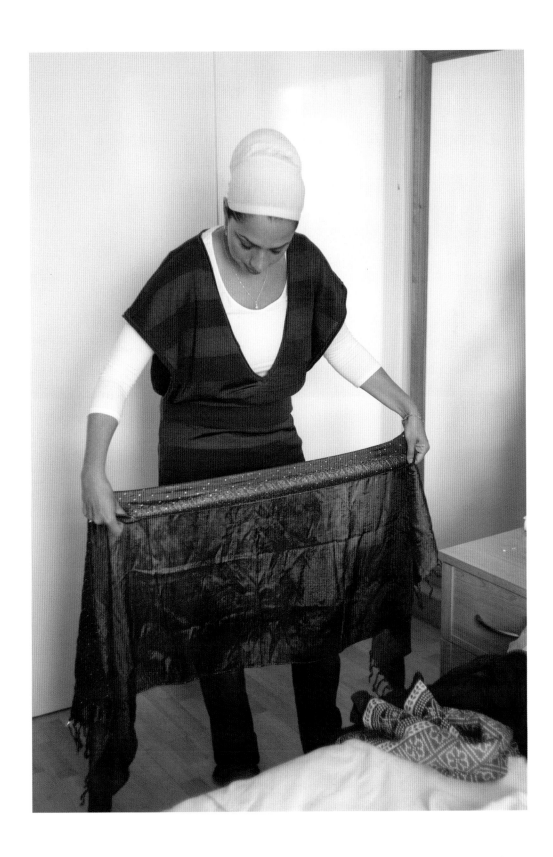

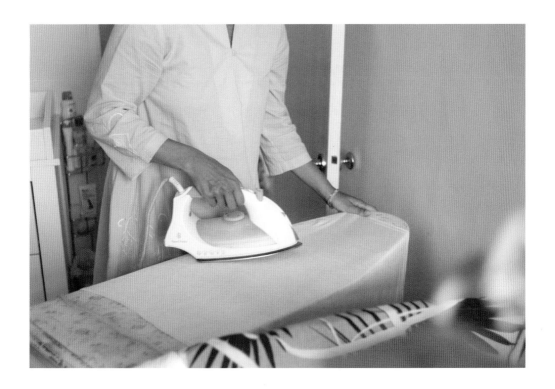

To give an example, both Hasidic Jewish and traditionalist Muslim parents in the Stamford Hill area of North East London recently expressed their desire to keep community services in the area separate even for children of pre-school age. Foremost amongst their anxieties about mixing was the fear that their dress codes might become compromised or diluted through interaction with others. In this locality where visible expressions of religiosity are the norm, the majority of Muslim women (many of whom are of Gujarati origin) wear full-length black jilbabs (long-sleeved full-length outer coats) with hijabs and a significant number have in recent years taken to wearing *niqabs* (face veils) outside the home. Where visual difference is so densely inscribed in the local environment, it can exert a powerful normative pressure which is difficult to resist. A young religiously practicing Muslim couple, Iqbal and Aisha, who moved into the area three years ago from Delhi, found themselves frequently questioned by their neighbours about why they did not visually display their religious identity. Aisha, who had never seriously contemplated wearing hijab when she lived in a conservative Muslim area in Old Delhi, now found herself constantly having to justify her decision not to wear it, not only to other women in Stamford Hill, but also to her six-year-old son, Ahmed. He saw his mother dressed differently from the other Muslim mothers in the area and wanted her to conform to type. She also found that not to wear hijab in such a space was to make herself conspicuous and to attract unwanted attention and disrespectful comments from local Muslim men who perceived the absence of hijab as a sign of dubious sexual morality. Aisha said she did not wish to encourage 'such a mentality' by submitting to a logic which implied that women are essentially the root cause of sin and that it is up to them to conceal their tempting powers rather than up to men to cease viewing women as sexual objects. At the same time Aisha found her decision not to cover difficult, partly because she felt she would like to be visibly identifiable as Muslim, particularly after the events of 9/11 and 7/7, but also because of the collective pressure of her surroundings:

> It affects you when you see so many people around you wearing hijab and niqab. It makes me constantly have to think about it and have to justify my position. I did at one point think maybe I should wear it but I can't. I just can't. Doing something that goes against your ideology is actually very depressing.

How the hijab is perceived, then, is dependent both on the particularities of specific interactions and on the sartorial norms prevalent in particular spaces. In the largely white residential area surrounding the hairdressing salon, the hijab is perceived as something alien, retrograde, foreign and potentially threatening, but in other spaces it may simply symbolize conformity. In Somerstown, a poor area of Central London with a significant British Bengali population, most local married women wear black headscarves and long outer garments (*abayas* or *burqas*). When I asked a number of first-generation migrants, some of whom had come to Britain in the last few years, how they felt their dress was perceived by people in Britain, I soon realized that they all assumed that I was referring to the attitudes of other Bengalis in Somerstown. The women in question were leading socially and geographically restricted lives. Lack of language skills, poverty, child care pre-occupations, limited education and conservative social attitudes conspired to make them unlikely to find or indeed seek work outside the home. Many rarely left their homes at all except to visit local relatives or the local Friday street market or South Asian Women's Community Centre. None of these first-generation migrant women I spoke to had ever had a sustained conversation with a white person, let alone entering into a white person's home. Their circulation within London was in effect restricted to an ethnically, linguisti-cally and religiously coded space which meant that the attitudes of other Londoners were largely irrelevant to them. Their principal concern where dress was concerned was to look respectable amongst other Bengalis and not attract too much unwanted attention, gossip or speculation. To achieve this, black outer garments and headscarves were perceived as a safe option because they deflected attention, although most had not felt them necessary when they lived in Bangladesh. Asked what they thought about how British people dressed in London, they responded with a mixture of amusement and embarrassment and con-fessed that they had been shocked at people's nakedness. Their stereotypes of Westerners were no more or less crude than many of the stereotypes of Muslims that circulate in areas dominated by white secularist norms.

What all of these examples seem to suggest is that a hijab-wearing lifestyle is just one of a huge repertoire of possible lifestyles open to people—both Muslim and non-Muslim—in the multicultural city of London. It is a lifestyle far more prevalent in some areas than others according to the distribution of different ethnic and religious groups. Whether a person's hijab attracts or deflects attention is heavily dependent on these spatial factors. What is also clear from these examples is that one person's dress may affect another person's actions: Jane, a self-declared atheist and advocate of multiculturalism, withdrew her child from the local school to keep him away from the perceived threat of hijabi culture; Pierre, a re-born Muslim, felt obliged to retreat behind closed doors to avoid the provocative sight of his wife's uncovered friends; and Ahmed, a six-year-old Muslim boy from India, sur-rounded by British Muslim women in hijab, jilbab and niqab, was doing his best to try to persuade his mother to do likewise.

POSITIVE AND NEGATIVE RESONANCES OF HIJAB

How can we understand Loraine's decision to defy the sartorial expectations of her friends, family and local environment by adopting hijab? At one level her decision can be explained in terms of micro-interactions—her meeting with a Muslim boy, her personal spiritual quest and eventual conversion. At another level her decision cannot be divorced from a much wider set of discourses and practices concerning the positive meanings attached to hijab by religiously inspired hijabis. It was at University where she met dedicated, prac-tising hijab-wearing Muslim women that she was exposed to a whole set of positive dis-courses about the meaning of hijab. Despite her mother's fears to the contrary, Loraine was not attracted to the aggressive political ideology of radical Islamic groups (whom Loraine classifies as 'nutters') but rather to the idealized notions of modesty, privacy, protection

Figure 3.4   Pro-Hijab activist protesting outside the French Embassy, London, September 2004.

from the male gaze, rejection of consumerist values and, above all, religious duty that Islam seemed to promote and the hijab seemed to enable and embody. These are the same ideas that Pro-Hijab activists are keen to promote through their explicit comparison of the ideal Muslim woman with the Christian ideal of the Virgin Mary and with nuns. The primary association is with modesty, goodness and virtue. Why, such women ask, when nuns are respected as a good example and positive moral presence in Western society is the woman in hijab regarded as suspicious and oppressed? Abeer Pharaon, head of the Pro-Hijab campaign when it started up in 2004, even went so far as to argue that the hijab would be the 'natural attire' of all women of every religion were they free to choose—something she tried to prove in a lecture delivered at the first-ever women's only FOSIS (Federation of Islamic Students) conference held in Leicester in the summer of 2004. In a remarkable PowerPoint presentation she juxtaposed images of scarf-wearing women from different historical periods, religions and cultures as 'proof' of the 'natural affinity' all women have with hijab.

The positive resonance of hijab is something felt very strongly by many of the hijab-wearing women in London I have met over the past few years, most of whom are from Muslim backgrounds where their mothers did not wear hijab. They too have often come to the hijab through encounters with people they have met in a multicultural urban environment. One such example is Jasmine, a woman of South Indian origin, who had a somewhat itinerant international childhood before settling in London in her student years. As a child and adolescent she wore what she describes as 'Western dress' and used to shock relatives back in India with her short hair cut and jeans. Now she shocks them even more by wearing the hijab. The person who convinced her of the Islamic necessity of adopting the hijab in daily life was a woman she describes as a Spanish feminist whom she met on an Arabic course in London.

What many hijab-wearing women speak of are the feelings of community they have when they see other women in hijab. Jamila is a thirty-six-year-old woman who was born and brought up in the north of England, but now lives in North East London. She adopted hijab a few years back, following the example set by her daughters who attend an Islamic school in Stamford Hill and who had been inspired to adopt it by school friends. Although she never used to wear such attire, Jamila now regrets not having worn it earlier. She speaks passionately of the extraordinary sense of respect she felt when she first went out into the streets of Stamford Hill in hijab, and of how suddenly other scarf-wearing women greeted her with 'salaam' making her feel that she really did belong to one big community. Others tell of how, through their hijabs, they are able to greet complete strangers when they travel abroad, marking their collective recognition of belonging to a global Islamic community or *umma*, and contributing towards the creation of such a community in the process. As one young woman put it, 'The whole sisterhood thing is really powerful. A friend of mine was shocked when she first started wearing hijab. She said she kept getting greeted by complete strangers. I said, "You'd better get used to it, cos that's all part of it. For some sisters I think it's the most important aspect."'

In and Out Razanne comes with a two-piece fashion set for wear inside and outside the home. At home Razanne loves to dress in all the latest fashions. In a minute she can be ready to go out with this traditional jilbaab coat.

Razanne helps Muslim girls understand that in the home they can be the ultimate fashion statement yet still have attractive attire while dressing modestly outside the home.

NEW

Figure 3.5 Razanne doll, popularly known as 'Islamic Barbie', as advertised on the internet by the American Company. Noor Arts, 2005.

The hijab acts as a collective affirmative device, not just in the physical world and through acts of looking, but also in the virtual world where the 'sisters' forums' of Islamic Web sites are literally over-flowing with hijab stories and discussions in which Muslim women in Britain and around the world share their trials and tribulations relating to dress and recount the momentous moment when they first decided to wear hijab, often against the wishes of their parents. So ubiquitous are such discussions in the British context that in 2005 a Web site entitled cheatnet.com was actually advertising a pre-written essay for school girls entitled 'My Hijab Story'.

Closely linked to the positive feelings of community engendered through hijab is the popular idea that the hijab plays an essential role in maintaining the social and moral order.[5] Several women have told me that they feel the hijab helps prevent marital break-down, stopping men from being led astray and preventing women from leading them astray in the first place. One woman even went on to suggest that it saved taxpayers' money in social services bills as a result![6] These 'benefits' of hijab are propagated in a variety of forms—whether through inspirational teachings, casual conversations, dolls, children's books, popular songs, private blogs and online hijab chat.

For example in a multimedia computer screen saver entitled *Hijab,* verses celebrating the virtues of a hijab wearer are intermingled with messages concerning the power of hijab to protect women from exploitation, bring psychological peace to men and women, improve the moral character of society, guard women from the lustful looks of men, prevent people from being distracted from constructive social work, prevent social corruption and im-morality, bring confidence in social participation as a human being rather than as a sexual

Figure 3.6　Three friends dressed up for the Global Peace and Unity event, London, 2008.

commodity and save time and money by preventing people from flaunting themselves and worrying about clothes. These messages are flashed on screen along with Islamic prescriptions from the *Qur'an* and *Hadith* and cut-out images of veiled women to the background of the uplifting sound track of world music singer, Dawud Wharnsby (a Scottish convert to Islam), singing his song, *Veil,* in which a Muslim girl living in the West defends her decision to wear hijab in response to an imagined Western observer's sceptical and critical interrogative comments.

For some women, the act of wearing hijab also has an explicit proselyzing intent. They speak of wearing hijab as an act of *dawah* (the duty of spreading the faith), attracting the curiosity of non-Muslims and thereby potentially drawing them towards Islam. This they see as part of the duty of being a 'good Muslim'. For others, it is principally a matter of religious obedience and modesty not unlike that traditionally expressed in other monotheistic religions. Many point out that both Christian and Jewish women used to cover their heads and, in some sections of both communities, still do. Rezia Wahid, the textile artist discussed in the previous chapter, described with good humour her experience of entering the Vatican in Rome and finding herself surrounded by what she described as 'all these women in hijab' who welcomed her, assuming from her skin colour and headwear that she was a follower of Mother Theresa. Such tales indicate the potential for solidarity amongst religiously oriented women pre-occupied with issues of piety, modesty and belonging. Occasional examples of such solidarity surface in Internet chat rooms. For example on one right-wing Jewish Web site where negative perceptions of Muslims were the norm, I came across some postings from orthodox Jewish women expressing their support of Muslim women's rights to wear hijab and drawing parallels between how Muslims are treated today and how Jews were treated historically. Recognition of potential points of convergence also feature in some online clothing stores such as the American online store, Headwear Heaven, which in 2004 was advertising a range of inspiring headwear options without reference to any particular religion.[7] Several of the many online Islamic fashion stores that have emerged in Britain and the United States in recent years welcome clients of other faiths, some removing all references to Islam in favour of advertising 'modest' or 'faith friendly' fashions.[8]

However, these positive and extrovert interpretations of hijab are constantly undermined by the more dominant negative resonance encountered on the streets and in the press—resonance fed by the complex legacies of Orientalist, imperialist, secular and feminist discourses as well as by the contemporary political situation. This negative resonance, in which the Western-dominated global media invests a great deal,[9] builds upon a whole other set of associations which tie the hijab to ideas of patriarchy, oppression, victimhood, ignorance, tradition, barbarism, foreignness, fundamentalism, suspicion and the threat of violence—associations which have been greatly inflated by 9/11 and through subsequent events such as the London bombings of July 2005 and the 'Danish cartoon controversy'.[10] It is no coincidence that the cartoon which caused the most outrage was the one which reasserted the association of Islam with violence and terrorism, using dress—the prophet's turban—as the link. Reactions to this cartoon by European Muslims should be understood not only in terms of the fraught political situation and Islamic preoccupations with iconography, but also in relation to the fact that since 9/11, people who look Muslim are constantly having to fend off the association of their dress with terrorism and oppression. This applies both to visibly Muslim men and women.

There has, in the past few years, been an undeniable media hunger in the British and European press for images of covered women whose concealment seems to serve as a visual shorthand for lack of integration, oppression and threat. For example at the Pro-Hijab Conference in London, there were only 4 women wearing niqab in a female-dominated audience of 200, yet there was an obscene conglomerate of photographers gathered around these 4 women like a pack of bloodhounds in pursuit of the image that would cause the most sensation—and all of this against a backdrop of earnest speeches about how to combat stereotyped perceptions of Islam.

Living at the receiving end of such stereotypes is a constant challenge for many Muslim women. A nation-wide survey conducted by the Islamic Human Rights Commission revealed the extent to which specific forms of dress attract different levels of discrimination and intolerance. Muslim women who did not wear religiously connoted dress reported

Figure 3.7   Niqab hunting. Press photographers at the Pro-Hijab Conference chasing after images of women in face veils, London, July 2004

far lower levels of harassment than women who were visibly identifiable as Muslim. Discrimination against the latter had also increased substantially since 9/11. Furthermore the frequency of mockery and insults experienced seemed to vary in direct proportion to the degrees of covering worn. Whereas the proportion of hijab wearers who reported experiencing racist comments on a weekly basis since 9/11 was 5.9 per cent, the proportion of jilbab wearers was 9 per cent and the proportion of niqab wearers as high as 25 per cent.[11]

Any individual adopting visibly Muslim forms of dress in London, whatever his or her intentions and beliefs, is likely to have to engage with some of this negative attention. In Loraine's case, she puts up not only with her mother's extreme reservations but also with strangers speaking to her slowly as if she were either foreign or stupid (a problem many Muslim women speak of). She has also received comments along the lines of: 'Poor thing! Her parents must have forced her!' (a comment she finds particularly ironic given her mother's hostile attitude to hijab). 'My mum's convinced I'm a fundamentalist,' she muses, 'she thinks that if I go on holiday with her to Florida wearing the hijab I'll be arrested at the airport!'—a joke which might have been funnier were it not for the extent to which Muslims have been criminalized both in the United States and Britain since 9/11.[12]

It is of course this negative resonance that the comedienne, Shazia Mirza, was trying to confront and re-direct by performing stand-up comedy in a hijab. It is the same attempt to confront the associations made between Islam and terrorism, and to face racism and suspicion head on, that we find in a slogan printed on a sixth-form college student's T-shirt: 'Don't panic, I'm Islamic.' Yet so sensitive is the hijab issue that attempts to expose 'Islamaphobia' often get interpreted as anti-Islamic gestures. For example when the contemporary

Figure 3.8   Censored images from the series, 'The Witness of the Future', Islamic Project, AES Art Group, 1996.
Copyright AES Art Group.

Moscow-based art group, AES, displayed their digitally manipulated photographs from the series, 'The Witnesses of the Future', which showed Islamicized versions of iconic buildings in famous Western cities, they found themselves accused of producing anti-Islamic art. The series was produced in 1996 but became more controversial in the light of September 11th. Their defence of the project was that their art was intended as a psychoanalytic interrogation of Western paranoia about Islam. Nonetheless, at the Rutger's Maison Gross School for Arts exhibition in the United States, T-shirts portraying the image 'New Liberty', which showed the Statue of Liberty wearing a burqa and holding the *Qur'an,* were withdrawn from sale for fear that 'the T-shirts would spread the very fears they purport to deconstruct'.[13] This, along with an image of Islamisized London, was also excluded from an exhibition of their work in Walsall in the British West Midlands for fear that the images might act as 'an incitement to violence' given 'the current political climate'.[14] Certainly their proximity to images produced on some right-wing fascist Web sites is undeniable.

Within this highly charged environment, every action and image with potential Islamic resonance comes under scrutiny. When in the summer of 2004 the London Metropolitan Police published a poster encouraging people to ring a terrorist hotline, they found themselves accused of re-asserting the link between Islam and terrorism. The poster showed a woman's eyes peering from behind a black screen which was presumably intended to evoke notions of vigilance. To many Muslims, accustomed to having to defend elements of their clothing practices, the image seemed a direct sleight to Muslim women in niqab.

It would be wrong, however, to imply that tensions concerning hijab are restricted to relations between Muslims and non-Muslims. The issue of women's dress occupies an important place in internal debates amongst Muslims both in Britain and around the world concerning different interpretations of Islam. For example the peaceful protests of Pro-Hijab activists opposed to the French ban on religious symbols in state schools in September 2004 were, to a large extent, undermined by the aggressive tactics of militants in Iraq who kidnapped and threatened to kill two French journalists unless the French ban was revoked. Their forceful tactics were entirely at odds to the discourses of peace and respect for human rights expressed by the British protesters outside the French Embassy in Knightsbridge. As a result, alongside banners expressing the virtues of hijab and the rights of Muslim women to wear it, they also carried placards demanding the release of the French hostages. Meanwhile, on the other side of the street, a small group of Muslim protesters (some Iranian) gathered to express their hostility to hijab and to declare its oppressive effects on young girls who, they claimed, are forced to wear it.

The wearer of hijab does, then, expose herself to a whole host of positive and negative projections from others. Just as her act may be respected and admired by some Muslims, it may be criticized and reviled by others. The inspirational meanings attached to hijab by many young British women who have come to it as a matter of personal choice and

Figure 3.9a Metropolitan Police 'Anti-Terrorist Hotline' Poster in the London Underground, 2004. Photo by Jenny Newell.

Figure 3.9b   Fatima in niqab, posing with her granddaughter at a community centre in North London, 2006.

perceive it as a gesture of liberation are radically different from the oppressive associations attached to it by those Muslim women who were once forced to wear it, particularly those who moved to Britain to escape the restrictions of the Islamic regime in Iran where covering the head, hair and body is compulsory for all women.[15]

But Muslim opposition to hijab is not restricted to those who have fled oppressive state regimes. There are some Muslim women in Britain who find the increasing popularity of hijab disturbing and perceive it as a backwards and divisive step. Whilst most uphold the right of women to wear it if they wish, they resent being considered lesser Muslims and often criticize hijab wearers for being judgemental and over-pious, for getting their priorities wrong, for falsely co-opting the language of human rights, for failing to criticize gender inequalities in Muslim countries and for refusing to put the *Qur'an* in historical or cultural perspective. They also emphasize the extreme sexualization of the woman's body implied by the idea that she must cover and complain that it is not up to women to cover but up to men to exercise self-restraint and stop viewing women in a sexual way. Their responses to friends who adopt hijab can at times be hostile. Whilst visible Muslims often maintain friendships with women who do not wear hijab, there are cases where a person's adoption of hijab or jilbab has triggered a noticeable cooling of friendships.

What all of these examples show is the overwhelming polyphonic resonance of hijab which individuals and groups try their best to shape but are ultimately never able to control. Being visibly Muslim in London means engaging with the different shades of this resonance, whether in the form of racist abuse; suspicious, pitying or condescending looks; failed job applications; misunderstandings between friends or the person sitting close by on the bus leaning ever so slightly the other way. As one young woman put it in relation to her work colleagues' reactions to her decision to wear hijab, 'It is not that anybody said anything. But it is like racism. If you feel it, it's there.'

THE AGENCY OF HIJAB

Closely linked to the issue of the resonance of hijab is the question of its effects—both on the wearer and on observers. In a provocative editorial entitled, 'Please Don't Rub Your Religion in My Face' (*Guardian,* 17 June 2003), the British journalist, David Aranowich, provided an ironic account of the rant that goes through his head when confronted by turbans, kipahs and hijabs as he sits on a London bus taking his children swimming on a Saturday morning. His argument is that he does not know how he is supposed to react to such visual displays of religiosity. Concerning the Jewish kipah he writes, 'This apparently helps to remind the wearer of the existence of a higher authority, as well as making him an ambassador for the faith. But you can't help feeling that the kipah-man is really saying, "I have a relationship with God which, by the way, YOU don't."' Concerning the hijab, he asks, 'Is it saying "Don't look at me" or "Look at me"?' The interest of this lies not so much in the answer as in the question, for it highlights the extent to which one person's dress enters another person's visual field, not only altering that person's perception of the urban landscape but also provoking new thoughts and feelings (perhaps of solidarity, perhaps of hostility, curiosity, bemusement, irritation). How this process works is skilfully captured by Ian McEwan in his novel, *Saturday*, when his surgeon hero, Henry Perowne, finds himself both distracted and repulsed by the sight of three veiled women, described as 'three black columns', entering a Harley Street clinic. 'He can't help his distaste,' writes McEwan. 'It's visceral,' and one wonders if it is the author or his character whose views are expressed here. At any rate, the sight of the women's dress in the streets of Central London plunges the hero into a darker mood, triggering an existing set of stereotyped associations and feeding his preoccupation with the perceived threat of 'Islamic terrorism'.

These feelings or emotions associated with dress often have a significant impact on people's relationship to public space. I have heard both hijab and niqab wearers expressing their reluctance to visit areas where they will be in an extreme sartorial minority—not so much because they fear attack (though at times, some do) but because they feel over-conspicuous, ill at ease, 'out of place'. Equally, I have come across non-Muslim women who feel uneasy going to areas of London where large numbers of women are covered. For example an Italian woman who has been resident in London for seven years claimed to feel so depressed at the sight of covered Arab women in Regent's Park that she would rather stay in her flat on a sunny day than subject herself to this vision. Having been brought up on the Italian coast where sunshine is associated with peeling off the layers and the feelings of freedom that come with this, she found the presence of women in long black robes and, in some cases, face masks, oppressive. She is one of a number of non-Muslim women who have expressed unease at their own bare legs and arms when in the presence of covered Muslim women. What is at stake here is the recognition of a lack of shared norms. Writing of the Turkish context, Nilufar Göle argues that it is the public visibility of Islam and the corporeal, spatial and ocular aspects of this that create a feeling of malaise to secular liberal modernists.[16] But it should be pointed out that the malaise can be a two-way process. On the other side of the coin are earnest young Muslim men wondering if they should avoid visiting public parks in the summer owing to the abundance of naked female flesh to which they are bound to be unwittingly exposed. On the Quatta-based Web site, IslamOnline. net, it was helpfully suggested that parks in Western countries should be visited by Muslim men either early in the morning or in the evening when hopefully women would be wearing more clothes owing to reduced temperatures. Men were also advised to lower their gazes and say a prayer if confronted unexpectedly with female nakedness in the British streets. More generally it was recognized that the summer was a time when men should be especially on their guard against the increased temptation to which they were exposed.

Returning to Loraine, it is clear that the logic of hijab affects her movements in a variety of more or less subtle ways, discouraging her not only from going to the hairdressers, but from doing a whole range of other things she previously enjoyed, such as mixing freely with members of the opposite sex, going to bars, going swimming and hanging out on the beach in Florida where her family spend their annual holidays, but these are constraints that she herself has chosen. So whole-heartedly has she taken up the logic of hijab that, like so many other hijab wearers, she now claims that she would feel utterly 'naked' if she went outside without it. The hijab does in effect impose limits on the types of places she can go and the degree of interaction she has with others. But many hijabis see such constraints as a benefit. As one twenty-three-year-old woman from Watford commented in the IHRC survey, 'It doesn't stop me doing anything that is good for me.'[17] Indeed many more religiously oriented hijab wearers see it as a physical reminder of the importance of moral restraint and a tool through which to cultivate a more pious self.[18]

The pressure of living up to the virtues and expectations of hijab—'of being worthy of it'—is a common theme in many women's accounts. Some who do not wear it speak of 'not yet being ready to adopt it'; many perceive it as a stage in their spiritual development and talk of the sense of responsibility it brings with it, of how it makes them representatives of Islam and acts as a constant material reminder of how they should and should not behave. One talkative middle-aged woman who used to work in her father's news agent's shop commented, 'I realized [when I adopted hijab] that others saw it as a barrier, but more to the point it stopped *me* from being so extrovert which was good for me because that was what I wanted.' In such comments one can sense the powerful drive towards self-discipline of some hijab wearers. The woman in question has since imposed an even stricter form of restraint upon herself by adopting niqab. Another woman spoke with passion about how her adoption of hijab was based on a realization that she needed to create a signal to men that she was not available. She saw this both as a duty and responsibility not only in relation to the opposite sex but also to God.

What such examples suggest is that the hijab not only to some extent guides who can interact with whom but also regulates the nature of those interactions. This contextual interactive aspect of Islamic dress makes it different from other religious dress codes, leading Pro-Hijab activists to argue that the hijab is not a religious dress at all but rather a requirement of the Islamic way of life based on the separation of the sexes and submission to God. If it were 'merely a religious symbol', they argue, it would be worn by Muslim women all the time on a permanent basis, but instead it is worn only in public situations or situations where non-family males are present. In emphasizing this aspect, hijab activists build on the original Arabic meaning of the word *hijab*—which is concerned with screening and separation rather than a particular form of dress. It is of course precisely such potential separating effects that many European governments are anxious to diminish.

But if the hijab makes certain interactions less likely, it also enables and encourages others. As mentioned earlier, it encourages feelings of belonging, sympathy, trust and shared community. If it has prevented Loraine from doing certain things and entering certain spaces, it has also given her access to environments from which she was previously excluded: prayer rooms at University, the Islamic society, a shared house with other Muslim women of various ethnic backgrounds and a female Muslim social world characterized by levels of intimacy and trans-nationality she had never previously experienced.

At the same time the hijab allows space for individual interpretation and there are many different styles and nuances to hijab wearing. Differences in fabric, styles of tying, textures and patterns of cloth and accessories such as hijab-pins leave ample room for individual experimentation and engagement with fashion as we shall see in the next chapter. Many women have extensive collections of hijabs to match a wide range of outfits and invest a considerable degree of time and effort in maintaining them. In one online discussion forum a young woman asked chatroom participants how many scarves they owned. Whilst some said they possessed 15–20, one found to her horror that she had 356, whilst two others claimed to have more than 500.[19] This provoked the suggestion from some other participants that those with excessive numbers of hijabs should give some to Oxfam. Whilst some women favour one particular style, others experiment with a variety of styles which they vary according to context, mood and what they are wearing. Jasmine, for example who works as a teacher in higher education, took to wearing a simple gypsy-style hijab to work in response to some of her male students from Muslim countries who, she felt, undermined her when she wore a more 'traditional' style. However, with all of this variety comes the critical gaze of more pious Muslims who assert that many women wear the hijab as a fashion accessory and that, in doing so, they misunderstand its true meaning. Almost everyone I have interviewed at some point stated that the hijab is really 'an attitude of mind' or that it is 'in the heart' so that if a person does not have the right attitude, then the headscarf becomes ineffective. Stories abound about the errant hijabi girl who tries to attract attention in the tight see-through blouse, or the one plastered in make-up or caught sitting on a boy's lap, thereby letting down hijab and, by association, other Muslims. Young women do in fact police each other's dress to a considerable degree, exploring the boundaries of what is or is not acceptable in hijab. Those who expose their necks or leave some hair visible often become targets of censure.

The amount of online chat dedicated to these subjects suggests that young Muslim women in Britain are just as preoccupied with their appearances as their non-Muslim counterparts. However, the claim that they are escaping the pressures of competitive consumerism and obsessive bodily preoccupation is powerful and attractive. Certainly, in venerating modesty and piety over visual displays of flesh and overt sexuality, they seek to present an alternative role model for young women which puts them on a moral high ground in relation to their non-Muslim peers. The Canadian singer, Dawud Wharnsby, captures this in the following lines from his lyrical song, *The Veil*:

> See the bill boards and the magazines that line the check out aisles,
> With their phoney painted faces and their air-brushed smiles?
> Well their sheer clothes and low cut gowns, they're really not for me.
> You call it freedom, I call it anarchy.
> This hijab, this mark of piety,
> is an act of faith, a symbol for all the world to see.
> A simple cloth, to protect her dignity.

To the claim put forward by the French government that the hijab puts unacceptable pressure on young girls to conform to oppressive religious norms, hijab-wearing women

Figure 3.10   Fashions in hijab tying, Oxford Street, 2007.

Figure. 3.11   Anonymous cartoon in circulation on Islamic Web sites, 2005.

are quick to point out the pressures placed on young girls in the West to conform to the unrealistic body images peddled in the media, and the low self-esteem and proliferation of eating disorders they see as a result. To them, the hijab is lived as a form of resistance to these pressures even if, in the process, they re-assert the identification of women with sex and submit to another set of discourses and disciplinary regimes concerning the female body.[20]

CONCLUSION

In his seminal work on the micro-dynamics of social interaction, Erving Goffman speaks of what he calls the rules of the social order, by which he means the implicit moral norms that govern all forms of social communication, however casual. Individuals do not have to follow such norms but they do have to take them into consideration, choosing whether or not to abide by them, circumvent them, challenge them and so forth. He was particularly interested in the bodily idiom through which we exchange and anticipate levels and modes of interaction before words are ever exchanged. The main rule of behaviour common to all situations is, he argues, that people are obliged to 'fit in' to some degree but how they do this is both culturally specific and contextually variable.

Much of Goffman's research was about American society in the 1960s and 1970s when the dominant social and moral norms were those set by white Americans, and where blacks, Jews and other groups who did not conform to the ideal type were stigmatized. Often, he noted, they responded to their stigmatized condition by self-consciously adopting precisely the very stigma symbols that marked them out, in other words by visually accentuating their difference and investing it with heightened meaning. It is within this framework that he understands the wearing of Hassidic Jewish dress or Afro hairstyles in the American context. Nilufar Göle draws on Goffman's work to argue that the adoption of hijab by young Muslim women in Europe and the West should also be understood in terms of the voluntary adoption of stigma symbols—an attempt to reverse the stigma by converting it into a self-chosen object of sacredness and desire. Certainly the high levels of both negative and positive attention accorded to hijab in the West would seem to endorse such an interpretation. But what interests me in particular is how we might use Goffman's work to think about the relationship between dress and multiculturalism in a city such as London.

What is clear from the examples given in this chapter is that the rules of social behaviour in a multicultural city with a heterogeneous population are by no means clear-cut. Particular norms prevail in particular spaces but the movement of individuals across spaces lends a considerable degree of diversity concerning the expression and interpretation of appropriate bodily idiom. This is not to suggest that there is no social order but rather to suggest that the social order is a dynamic work in progress. It is under negotiation, as it were, through human interactions and the attempts of different groups to re-write and expand the normative possibilities. Malaise and misunderstanding occur precisely in those situations where different ideas of appropriate behaviour come into tension. By adopting hijab and investing it with so many meanings, young women not only seek to make their faith visible, but they also attempt to manage the way others perceive and interact with them. Many of the difficulties they experience lie in the mismatch between the messages they seek to convey and the interpretations made by others. For some, the simplest option is to withdraw from spaces which make them vulnerable to misunderstanding or to retreat to or remain in spaces where they are in a visible majority. But there is also a new generation of young visibly Muslim women in Britain who do not wish to be restricted to religious or ethnic ghettos and for whom stylistic experimentation and engagement with fashion have become an important means of contributing to the establishment of a new cosmopolitan social order. It is their multicultural lives and hybrid appearances that form the main focus of the next chapter.

NOTES

1. The most significant of these struggles took place in the 1960s and 1970s when a number of Sikh men suffered dismissal from work for refusing to remove their beards and turbans. Some of them underwent lengthy legal struggles which lasted several years against a backdrop of racial intolerance and narrow nationalist ideologies. Eventually under the Race Relations Act of 1976, dismissals of this kind became classified as acts of indirect discrimination against an 'ethnic group'. However, because Muslims were classified as a 'religious' rather than ethnic group, their dress codes were not covered by the same legislation (cf. Poulter 1998: chapter 8).

2. The comparative ease with which the hijab was incorporated into the uniform of the London Metropolitan Police Force in 2004 demonstrates the extent to which the logic of multicul-

turalism has been institutionalized. Representatives of the Muslim Association of Police had approached the Commissioner with a proposal for a hijab option, expecting to have to justify their request with reference to the Sikh case and other arguments. Instead they found the Commissioner approved their proposal right away and asked them to put forward some suggestions of designs (interview with Chief Inspector Richard Varley of Scotland Yard, 2004).

3. The *Shahada* is the Muslim declaration of faith: 'There is no god but God and Muhammad is the Prophet of God.'

4. For example on the day I interviewed her, she wore a light-coloured hijab with a knee-length pale pink coat rather than a full-length jilbab or abaya in concession to her mother's sensibilities and the sartorial expectations of the area.

5. See Suzanne Brenner for a perceptive analysis of how women who adopt Islamic dress in Indonesia perceive this as part of an attempt to reconstruct both themselves and the whole society around them (Brenner 1996).

6. This view is not shared by all hijabis, some of whom remark that they find they get more attention from men since adopting hijab.

7. Interestingly, during the two-year period in which I was consulting this Web site (2004–2006), it changed its advertising strategy from a general one aimed at 'all women' including religious women and those experiencing hair loss and 'bad hair days' to an explicitly Muslim-oriented strategy in which it refers to 'Islamic inspired Hijabs' and displays different headwear options in pointed dome-shaped frames, cf. http://www.headwearheaven.com/

8. See for example the Leicester-based online store, Imaan, discussed in chapter 8.

9. For discussion of portrayals of Muslims as victims and terrorists in the British media since 9/11, see Ahmad (2003). See also Moore, Mason and Lewis (2008) in 'Reports' in the References.

10. This controversy revolved around the Danish newspaper *Jyllans-Posten*'s decision to publish irreverent cartoons of the Prophet Mohammed in September 2005 and Muslim responses to this which, in some cases, turned to violence.

11. Ameli and Merali (2006: 30–40).

12. For example in 2004 both the singer, Yusaf Islam (previously known as Cat Stevens), and the Muslim philosopher, Tariq Ramadan, were refused entry into the United States despite the fact that both are respected public figures with important contributions to make to debates concerning Islam in the West.

13. Cf. Blake Eskin (1998), 'Soros-Sponsored Visions of Islamic Future Irk ADL were Meant as Irony', cited in www.aes-group.org/critics.asp (accessed 15 March 2007).

14. Cf. inIVA press release (2003, April), 'Walsall Council Ban Photographs', www.universities-in-universe.de.islam/eng/2003/01/veil/index/html (accessed 15 March 2007).

15. The difficulties of growing up with the sartorial dictates and pressures of the Islamic regime in Iran are superbly captured in Marjane Satrapi's book and film *Persepolis*.

16. Göle (2002).

17. Ameli and Merali (2006: 23).

18. For discussion of the role of veiling in the cultivation of a pious disposition, see Mahmood's excellent work on the piety movement in Egypt (Mahmood 2005).

19. 'AhlulBayt Discussion Forum>Sisters Forum>Hijab and Clothing Discussions>How Many Scarves (Hijab)', (2004), http://www.shiachat.com (accessed 17 January 2006).

20. As Abu-Lughod put it in relation to the overlapping fields of power in which Bedouin women's lives are located, 'If the systems of power are multiple, then resisting at one level may catch people up at other levels' (Abu-Lughod 1990: 53).

4   NAVIGATIONS OF STYLE

In June 2007, Rich Mix, a new multicultural arts centre in Bethnal Green in East London, opened its doors to a photographic exhibition by Peter Saunders, a British photographer who, since converting to Islam in the 1970s, switched from photographing famous pop stars to focussing on visual subjects of Islamic interest. His exhibition, entitled, 'The Art of Integration', was a collection of photographs of British Muslims aimed at capturing the positive contribution they make to British society. The image advertising the exhibition showed an attractive white girl, apparently a Muslim actress, wearing a Union Jack flag as hijab. This was, however, a rather literalist and contrived interpretation of 'integration' and Britishness compared to the more inventive and visually arresting appearances of most of the people attending the exhibition opening. For here was a creative mingling of styles with Western, Eastern and Islamic resonance which, when combined, seemed to defy the boundaries of each category to suggest some sort of new trans-nationally oriented British Muslim aesthetic.

This creative mélange was particularly apparent in women's dress. Here the latest season's fashionable strappy dresses could be seen worn over long-sleeved blouses and trousers and teamed with chiffon or silk hijabs, held in place with sparkling broaches and worn with well-chosen earrings and elegant shoes; jeans and long tops were worn with multiple hijab cloths, twisted and layered into bold and impressive silhouettes which highlighted rather than diminished the beauty and stature of their wearers whilst at the same time keeping their hair concealed. Further cloths were draped over shoulders and around necks as shawls and scarves by some who favoured additional covering or who simply appreciated the effects, feel and elegance of flowing cloth. Others wore long-sleeved kurtas in wild silk or linen over long, flared skirts or trousers, matched with draped or backwards-tied hijabs which encircled their hair. Some outfits seemed to play on Victorian elegance; others evoked some sort of layered gypsy chic. The small minority of non-hijabi women present were also elegantly dressed in contemporary fashionable clothes often with a global twist. The Minister, Baroness Uddin, who had been invited to make one of the opening speeches, looked rather old-fashioned and conventional in a dark coloured shalwar kamiz with matching dupatta. More visually arresting was the outfit of a make-up artist who wore a jilbab emblazoned with embroidered messages and a face veil made out of camouflage-printed cloth.

Taken collectively, this was an aesthetic which placed high value on the covering of skin and hair, but which was also characterized by skilled dexterity in the manipulation of cloth, a clear appreciation of colour and an obvious engagement with mainstream fashion.

Figure 4.1   Zarina Saley (centre) with her brother, Mohammad, and friend, Arige at an exhibition opening at the Rich Mix Centre, London, 2007.

fashion
the styli
that sor
feelings
how vi:
down-
or poli
visibili
this vi

THE P

The I
pecta
the s
clotl
of tl
time
ovei
to v
acte
suc
sia
coi

cl
ar
fa
p
r
r

There was undoubtedly an Eastern feel to many of the clothing combinations, but with the exception of the conspicuously South Asian shalwar kamizes of Baroness Uddin and her companions, most of the outfits worn could not be traced back to any particular cultural tradition or origin. These were hybrid and contemporary fashionable, visibly Muslim outfits which suggested simultaneously a globally informed aesthetic repertoire, an Islamic orientation and a preoccupation with personal style.

Two women who stood out from the crowd for their noticeably grittier urban Muslim look were the young black rappers, Sukina and Muneera, who perform under the name, Poetic Pilgrimage. As part of the cultural entertainment of the evening, they took the stage with a confrontative rap-poetry dialogue about the plight of British Muslims, and in particular hijab-wearers, shunned and abused by mainstream British society and told to 'go back home'. The main point of the poem was that there was no 'back home' for them to go to. These were British Muslims who belonged exactly where they were and whose ultimate orientation was not some imaginary far-off homeland but their faith in Allah. The repeated rephrasing of an old Marvin Gaye classic of the 1960s made this point succinctly:

Wherever I lay my prayer mat, *that's* my home! Sister,
Wherever I lay my prayer mat, *that's* my home!

Poetic Pilgrimage cut through the atmosphere of bourgeois refinement typical of exhibition openings, not only with their socially, politically and religiously charged lyrics, but also by their rap-style delivery and their entire body idiom. Both had teamed their full-length spangled Indian skirts with metal-buttoned faded denim jackets with rolled-up sleeves. Sukina wore several chunky bangles which, on her powerful arms, produced an almost armour-like effect. On their heads thick Indian shawls glittering with silvery lurex were tied to form hijabs of considerable bulk, under which plainer cotton coloured hijab cloths framed the face. Both wore bright eye make-up, glossy lip stick and conspicuous earrings. These were not women prepared to fade into the background or blend into the crowd. Their bold message was announced as much through their dress, body language, stature and deportment as through the words of their poetry. But it would be wrong to assume that Poetic Pilgrimage's bold street style stemmed from life in some black British Muslim hood in inner-city London—not least because the performers had only converted to Islam two years back and had been raised in Bristol. Like so many people I met at this cosmopolitan Muslim event, finding an appropriate look had for Sukina and Muneera required navigating a complex range of issues and attachments in relation to questions of race, religion, politics, class and geography. Just as there was no obvious 'place' to which they might return, so there was no obvious dress for young, black, British, female, Muslim convert rappers to wear. Their look, as we shall find out, was the result of considerable experimentation and reflection as they tried to reconcile different identity strands that many might assume to be incompatible.

This chapter is about the stylistic navigations of a group of fashionable young hijabi women, many of whom I first met at the exhibition opening at the Rich Mix Centre.

Ta
tha
an
w
ar
as
to
s
v

Figure 4.10   Laura in East Africa.
Courtesy of Laura Blizzard.

Coming from a white non-Muslim British background, she was particularly aware of the various stereotypes associated with hijab by outsiders and was keen to avoid giving people the opportunity to make negative assumptions about her. For this reason she still tends to avoid wearing the hijab in a conventional style immediately identifiable as Muslim. When I met her in the hall of residence where she was working during the summer holidays of 2007, she was wearing a minimal bun-style hijab which left her neck uncovered. She explained that she had not wanted to reveal her Muslim identity at the job interview for fear that it might stand against her or that people would make negative associations. However, this later put her in a difficult position in relation to the uniform she was expected to wear which had short sleeves. She has got around this by wearing a long-sleeved top under her uniform blouse and keeping her hijab to the minimum bun style—a compromise she is not entirely happy with but which saves her from attracting 'unnecessary attention'. Laura strives to maintain a British identity with an internationalist outlook which is based on the blurring of boundaries. In this way she seeks to minimize the hijab's potentially alienating effects in relation to friends and family as well as strangers.

For Fatima from her tight-knit Bengali background in Luton, the aim is to down-play what she considers 'ethnic dress' in favour of styles she considers more British on the one hand and more Islamic on the other. This has meant stepping out of the shalwar kamiz, popular amongst Bengalis in Luton, and wearing long flared skirts and fitted tops which declare her affinity with British high street fashion.[10] These she matches with conspicuous brightly coloured hijabs tied so as to conceal the hair and neck but teamed up with large jangly earrings and eye make-up. Whilst her mother considers Fatima's skirts 'too Western', Fatima considers her mother's saris 'un-Islamic' on the grounds that they cling to the shape of the body and reveal the midriff. When back in Luton Fatima returns to wearing a shalwar kamiz so as to 'fit in' and not attract unnecessary comment, but in London she goes for a trendy British Muslim look which amplifies her Muslimness and down-plays Bengaliness. The tension between religious and ethnic sartorial expectations is a common theme in online discussion threads and was amusingly highlighted by one girl in a comic

Figure 4.11   Laura, teaching in East Africa.
Courtesy of Laura Blizzard.

Figure 4.12   Soumaiyah in the underground.
Photo: Kharunya Paramaguru.

Figure 4.13   Soumaiyah (right) with a friend.
Photo: Kharunya Paramaguru.

Figure 4.14   Soumaiyah's 'Egyptiany hijab'.
Courtesy of Soumaiyah Forbes.

Figure 4.15   Soumaiyah pops to the local shop in an abaya.
Photo: Kharunya Paramaguru.

e-melodrama entitled, 'The Hijab Chronicles', in which she invited other online participants to add different episodes. In episode 9, written and posted by someone under the
name 'ya Rahman', Shazia, a glamorous University student and self-acclaimed 'Bengali
Bimbo of the Year', finds to her horror that she has accepted to attend a 'deep and mean-
ingful' organized by the ISoc (Islamic Society) on the same evening that she is supposed to
be singing in the Bengali talent show organized by the BanglaSoc (Bengali Society) to raise
money for flooded villages in Bangladesh.

> But what would the ISoc say if they found out? Dancing in a sleeveless spaghetti strapped
> fuscia pink shalwar singing an Aqua classic was certainly off the cards as hijab, right?

Her solution was to borrow a black oversized jilbab and waist-length hijab which she
wore with a bright pink niqab (cut out of her fuscia-coloured shalwar) and to stand on
stage performing a hijabi number:

> I'm a Hijabi girl, In a Wahhabi world
> Hijab is Drastic, is Fantastic,
> You can't see my hair, unless mahrams everywhere
> Life in segregation is Emancipation.
> Come on Hijabi let's go party?
> No! No! No! No!

Come on Hijabi let's go give dawah?
Yes! Yes! Yes! Yes!,
Come on Hijabi, let's go party?
No! No! No! No!,
Oh sorry, come on hijabi let's study Bukhari?
Yes! Yes! Yes! Yes!

After this stunning act of impression management, the fictional Shazia receives fifteen marriage proposals from the brothers in the executive committee of the ISoc, leaving long-term female members of the society to 'gather dust on the shelves of spinsterhood'.[11]

This tongue-in-cheek tale beautifully captures not only the pull between ethnic and religious affiliations but also many of the ironies of the cosmopolitan University hijabi scene where wearing hijab, ostensibly to ward off the male gaze, often has the adverse effect of enhancing a woman's desirability to men, especially religiously oriented Muslim men. Many of the girls I have interviewed are aware of the aura of virtue and mystery attached to their hijabs by some men, and it is something they consciously and unconsciously play on whilst at the same time maintaining the official Islamic discourse that the hijab protects them from the male gaze and prevents them from having inappropriate relations with men. That sexuality may be as much revealed through hijab as concealed by it is of course a recurrent theme in much Eastern literature.

For Soumaiyah, a Jamaican convert, the challenge is not to escape her cultural roots but to dress in a way that makes sense both in terms of her Rastafarian upbringing and her Islamic attachment. For her Poetic Pilgrimage's poem, 'The Weight of Two Worlds', feels like a description of her own life. Everything about Soumaiyah's appearance, from her cool baggy ensembles and experimental hijab styles to her striking green eyes, speaks of both hybridity and ambiguity. On a recent trip to Paris, she was standing outside an exhibition on Diaspora when she was approached by a bloke who asked, 'Where are you from? Are you from Diaspora?!' And in some ways his question is not as stupid as it sounds! In Nottingham, where she grew up, the only Muslims she met were Pakistani, but for Soumaiyah, wearing the 'triangular hijabs with lace and stuff' would have felt false. She picks and chooses garments with a diverse range of cultural associations and then, as she puts it, 'I give it my own twist.' One of her favourite hijab styles involves twisting or plaiting cloth across her forehead to create an effect which many say is 'Egyptiany'. She also favours African wraps and frequently finds herself mistaken for a Rasta. It is an ambiguity about which she feels both happy and slightly guilty. She is adept at creating new effects from twisting, layering and wearing multiple scarves which she might wear with baggy denim dungarees one day and a Moroccan kaftan the next.

Soumaiyah's flat mate, Shireen, is also a skilful wearer of different styles and a good source of inspiration. Her hybrid international background means she feels relatively unrestricted in the range of garments from which she can pick and choose. On her computer she has a picture gallery entitled, 'My Beautiful Hijab' in which she collects together digital

Figure 4.16 Shireen.
Photo: Kharunya Paramaguru.

images of hijab styles she particularly likes. In the folder are pictures of friends and strangers as well as images culled from various Web sites. The folder acts as a source of visual inspiration when the flat mates are trying out new styles. In this way Soumaiyah and Shireen participate in the emergence of a cosmopolitan Islamic aesthetic which is inclusive rather than exclusive in what it draws on. The look they develop is cool and flexible, earning the name of 'hijabi *it* girls!' in certain circles.

CONCLUSION

A focus on styles of hijab and their integration with other items of dress shifts attention away from the question of whether or not a young Muslim woman wears hijab to the wider question of how she manages her appearance. What emerges is how through engagements with fashion and experiments with style young cosmopolitan visibly Muslim women in London manage the impressions they exude in complex ways by emphasizing and de-emphasizing different aspects of their identity in different contexts. Whilst visible Muslims are often blamed for their supposed 'lack of integration' into Western society, the sartorial biographies of the young women represented here seem to tell a very different story. Their wardrobes and outfits could in many ways be read as material manifestos of integration, not in the sense of slotting into an existing frame but in the sense of expanding

5   DIVERSITY CONTESTED

The colourful and eclectic clothing combinations worn by young visibly Muslim women in Britain bear witness to the diversity of ways Islamic clothing prescriptions are interpreted and to the fact that their wearers are not alien or other but rather ordinary people scouring British high streets and other outlets, selecting clothes and composing outfits which correspond to their personal and social lives. However, these hybrid and eclectic styles visible in the streets are rarely represented in the mainstream media where British Muslims are often pictured wearing long black garments (*jilbabs*), with tight face-grabbing black hijabs often accompanied by face veils (*niqabs*). Over the past two decades, and particularly since September 11, these austere and uniform images have acquired high currency in the British media where they function as some sort of visual short hand for 'lack of integration' or 'threat'. Playing both on a desire for and fear of 'otherness', such images have become standard fare for illustrating a whole host of Muslim-related news stories, most of which have nothing to do either with the women concerned or their dress. The accumulative effect of the perpetual reproduction of these images is the creation of a standardized normative idea of 'the Muslim woman' as swathed in dark and shapeless garments, if not semi-effaced by an additional face veil. It is an image of uniformity which serves both to emphasize and to prove otherness. Some Muslim women do, of course, choose to wear long dark jilbabs and abayas in various styles but the impression often given in newspaper reports and TV coverage is that these represent some sort of standard Muslim dress.

From time to time, however, such images, already so familiar, seem to acquire additional legitimacy through news stories which actually involve the very items of dress they illustrate—hijabs, jilbabs, niqabs. Some of these news stories focus on attempts made by various governments to restrict the wearing of such items in various institutional or public contexts (the ban of hijab in state schools in France, the restrictions on niqab wearing in Italy or Holland, controversies over school uniforms and employment issues in Britain). Others focus on the struggle of individual Muslim women to retain particular forms of dress in a range of public contexts (schools, sports grounds, hairdressing salons and so forth).

The high level of publicity accorded to such cases and the volume of visual imagery attached to them serves to further reassert limited and monotone perceptions of Muslim women as essentially alien and covered. It also provides disproportionate space for the voices, ideology and propaganda of both radical political groups and conservative religious authorities, both of which present themselves as representatives of Muslims in general and are often equally intent on propagating a uniform, homogenized and restricted interpretation of what

Shabina in a jilbab amounted to 'constructive exclusion' and breached both domestic law and the European convention of human rights as it denied her both the right to an education and the right to express her religious beliefs.

The head teacher and governors of the school defended their position by suggesting that the available uniform was already culturally and Islamically sensitive, that they were opposed to the introduction of the jilbab both on health and safety grounds and on the grounds of wishing to protect pupils from minority interpretations of Muslim dress held by some extremist groups who were active in the local area. They also pointed out that some non-Muslim pupils had expressed that they felt intimidated by women in jilbab and some Muslim pupils had made it clear that they did not want to feel under pressure to wear it. Shabina initially lost her case but went on to take it to the Court of Appeal where she was represented by Cherie Booth, wife of the then British Prime Minister, Tony Blair. Booth successfully argued that Shabina's fundamental human right to express her religion was being violated and that a policy of respecting diversity and inclusion should be upheld. The judge ruled in Shabina's favour, arguing that she had been unlawfully excluded from school, unlawfully denied the right to manifest her religion and unlawfully denied access to a suitable and appropriate education. Standing outside the courtroom wearing a well-cut coat on top of her jilbab, and ushered forward by her brother, Shabina rattled off a defiant statement to the press which was broadcast in news bulletins in Britain and world-wide: 'As a young woman growing up in post 9/11 Britain, I have witnessed a great deal of bigotry from the media, politicians and legal officials. This bigotry resulted from my choice to wear a piece of cloth. It is amazing that in the so-called free world I have to fight to wear this Islamic dress …'

The controversy attracted an extraordinary amount of media attention both before, during and after the case with the image of Shabina in a jilbab featuring in news papers, internet forums and television documentaries. For right-wing journalists, it was presented as an iconic example of how Muslim demands are uncompromising, unreasonable and ultimately at odds with 'Western liberal values' which they threaten to destroy. They also pointed out Shabina's reported links to the radical Islamist group, Hizb ut-Tahrir, suggesting that the girl had been forced to wear a jilbab by her brother who was said to be heavily involved with the organization. A number of feminist writers argued something not dissimilar, producing well-worn uncompromising and unnuanced interpretations of the 'hijab' and 'jilbab' as fundamentally patriarchal and oppressive. On the left end of the spectrum, some journalists proclaimed the court judgement to be a victory for human rights, diversity and tolerance, a view also held by many human rights activists and legal specialists. The *Guardian* newspaper gave prominent front-page coverage of the court case victory, under the heading, *I could scream with happiness. I have given hope and strength to Muslim women.* The article that followed offered an exclusive interview of a school girl's 'battle to wear Islamic dress'. It quoted Shabina arguing, 'Today's decision is a victory for all Muslims who wish to preserve their identity and values despite prejudice and bigotry.'[3]

The best Mother's Day gifts for EVERY pocket

WIN A DREAM COTTAGE IN THE SUN
TOKEN COLLECT · SEE PAGE 44

THURSDAY, MARCH 3, 2005   www.dailymail.co.uk   40p

GO ON, SPOIL HER THIS SUNDAY

FEMAIL MAGAZINE: PAGES 58-59

As judges rule that a girl has the human right to wear head-to-toe Islamic dress in the classroom, heads ask:

IS THIS THE END OF SCHOOL UNIFORM?

A MUSLIM schoolgirl controversially won the right to wear head-to-toe Islamic dress in the classroom yesterday.

The Appeal Court ruling was seen as effectively ending the current right of each school to decide its policy on uniforms.

Shabina Begum, 16, argued that her school breached her human rights by sending her home when she arrived for lessons wearing a jilbab. After a case costing £70,000 of

By **Gordon Rayner** and **Tahira Yaqoob**

taxpayers' money in legal aid – in which she was represented by Cherie Blair – three judges ruled that the teenager's school had acted unlawfully in excluding her.

Their decision came despite overwhelming support for the jilbab ban from other pupils, staff, parents and governors at Denbigh High School in Luton, where 79 per cent of students are Muslims and 43 different languages are spoken. Local councillors also backed the policy.

Headmistress Yasmin Bevan –

herself a Muslim – permitted girls to wear a skirt, trousers or a shalwar kameez and headscarves.

She made clear that the main reason she did not want the jilbab worn was to protect vulnerable pupils from being exploited by Muslim extremists.

At one stage, an extremist group had picketed the school gates and distributed leaflets to pupils exhorting Muslims not to send their children to secular schools. But yesterday's decision by the Appeal Court effectively decrees that the human rights of one pupil

Turn to Page 8, Col. 1

Shabina in jilbab at the High Court yesterday

Figure 5.1   The Jilbab controversy in the headlines.

My own encounter with Hizb ut-Tahrir came about, not in relation to the jilbab contro-versy, but in relation to protests against the French proposal to ban the wearing of religious symbols in state schools. It was a cold winter's day in January 2004 and protestors had congregated at Marble Arch. There were various groups participating in the rally, including the Stop the War Coalition, The Muslim Association of Britain and the Muslim Women's Society, but Hizb ut-Tahrir protesters with their standardized orange banners and placards were particularly visible and vocal. In contrast to the placards wielded by supporters of other organizations, which were phrased in the language of liberal democracy, carrying such messages as, *Hijab—our choice, Hijab—our right, Where is French Liberty?*, the plac-ards wielded by women members and supporters of Hizb ut-Tahrir bore messages fraught with challenge and confrontation:

> Secularism dishonours women.
> Hijab ban—who are the fundamentalists?
> Hijab ban symbolises war on Islam.

Marching through the fashionable streets of Knightsbridge, these women temporarily transformed the visual and auditory landscape with their dark-covered dress, their orange banners and their aggressive chanting, projected through loud speakers. Not many people were about on this dull afternoon, but those who were looked on and listened with be-musement to the collective chanting and responses:

> **No slave to fashion, Yes to Hijab!**
> **No to secular vanity, Yes to Hijab!**
> *Do we want secularism?* **NO!**
> *Do we want liberty?* **NO!**
> *Do we want Islam?* **YES!**
> *What are we?* **Muslim!**
> *What are we?* **Muslim!**
> *What are we?* **Muslim!**

This visual and verbal display was part of a larger public effort on the part of the Brit-ish branch of Hizb ut-Tahrir to define and control the dress and reasoning of the 'Islamic sisterhood'. Later that week, its members held a picket outside the German Embassy and went on to organize seminars and lectures on hijab in London, Nottingham and Derby. As with the jilbab controversy, the French hijab ban was a convenient tag on which to hang and spread Hizb ut-Tahrir ideas through protests, rallies, articles, seminars, leaflets, booklets and tracts which expressed its views on politics through dress and other topics. Accepting some of the leaflets about dress, I went on to attend a one-day seminar on hijab in Willesden Green (West London) and an afternoon of lectures at Queen Mary's Col-lege in East London, the latter organized by Hizb ut-Tahrir under the less-controversial name, QMUL Muslim Women's Cultural Society. This technique of assuming different names in order to retain access to University sites where it has been banned is described by Husain for the 1990s, but was clearly still going on in 2004.[6] The flier advertising this 'sister's intercollegiate event' read, 'In the current political climate in Europe, the Hijab is no longer a religious symbol but a political symbol—shaking the very foundations of Western civilisation.'

The atmosphere in the seminar hall in Willesden Green was studiously joyless. The audience, consisting of 200 women dressed in dreary-coloured plain jilbabs and long enveloping hijabs, listened earnestly to a mixture of fiery and scholarly speeches from four women, one of whom, a French lawyer, spoke of the terrible oppression experienced by French Muslims. The French 'hijab ban' was presented as a war on Islam and a reminder of the urgency of establishing the *Khilafat* (Islamic state). Women were reminded of their essential role in preserving the identity of the global *Ummah* (community).

Hizb ut-Tahrir's ideas on dress, like its ideas on all other topics, are dominated by the attempt to establish and prove a binary opposition between Islam and the West. Much of the literature it was circulating in 2004 seemed to revolve around trying to convince British Muslims of their need to disentangle themselves from 'the West' even as they were living in

Figure 5.3 Audience at a conference on hijab organized by Hizb ut-Tahrir, Willesden Green, London, February 2004.

the West. This meant trying to convince British Muslims that 'the West' threatened every aspect of their 'Islamic identity': it perverted their relationship with God by introducing false and alien values; it perverted social relationships with others by allowing forbidden interactions and surrounding Muslims with the temptations of *Shaytan* (the devil); it perverted their relationship to their own bodies by making women slaves of the capitalist fashion industry which, in turn, led men astray; and it perverted their modes of reasoning by introducing false and seductive ideas of integration—all of which according to Hizb ut-Tahrir distorted and were antithetical to what it called 'the ideology of Islam'.

For men, an important priority was to learn to hold back from the corrupting and distracting temptations offered by the decadent West. In an article entitled, 'Avoiding the Temptations of Western Society', young men were advised on how to defend themselves from the barrage of sexual temptation, drugs, alcohol and pornography that inevitably surrounded them in 'Western society'. People who hung out in city centres on a Friday night were likened to 'a herd of wild animals that can't control their desires'.

For women, dress was the central medium through which this multi-headed threat of Westernization could be tackled. There were three main strands to the HT approach. First, it promoted a particular interpretation of what constituted Islamic dress as a means of asserting the physical and political unity of the Islamic sisterhood and emphasizing its superiority and distance from the West. Second, it used the idiom of dress and fashion as a means of asserting the Western woman's slavery both to capitalism and to patriarchal domination and exploitation. Third, it promoted a particular mode of reasoning in relation to dress, insisting that Muslim women must not only wear 'Islamic dress' but also wear it 'for the right reasons'. This 'correct reasoning' meant defining freedom, democracy and personal choice as 'Western concepts' which did not have any place in Islam. In this way the 'threat' of both physical integration and mental integration could be resisted, aided by considerable borrowing from sociological texts which clearly emanated from Western sources. Many of these ideas are for example formulated in a 40-page booklet entitled, 'The Western Beauty Myth', written and published by Hizb ut-Tahrir in London in 2003. This text appropriated and reworked arguments formulated by the American feminist Naomi Wolf in her book, *The Beauty Myth,* and used her feminist critique of the fashion industry as a means of 'proving' the superiority of 'the Islamic' approach to dress and politics. Details of the three main strands of Hizb ut-Tahrir's argument about women's dress are given below.

VISUAL UNITY OF THE GLOBAL *UMMAH*

By imposing a particular limited interpretation of the Islamic dress code, Hizb ut-Tahrir was seeking not only to establish a politics of presence but also to erode away both 'Western influences' and so-called regional or cultural influences which it perceived as equally alien. The wide range of clothing options worn by Muslims from different cultural backgrounds was perceived as a threat to the global unity of the *ummah* and was therefore in need of elimination. Hence colourful saris and shalwar kamizes, popular particularly amongst many South Asians in Britain and South Asia, were redefined as 'un-Islamic'. It was precisely this argument that Shabina Begum's brother used when he declared in a court statement that the shalwar kamiz was really 'Pakistani cultural dress' that had nothing to do with Islam.

This self-conscious erosion of regional variation in favour of a standardized and sombre interpretation of Islamic dress is the material embodiment of HT's general identity-building project—outlined clearly in a video it produced in 2002 about British Muslims, entitled *Identity Dilemma*. In it, a young man expresses his identity:

> *I am not British even though I was born in this country,*
> *I am not Palestinian even though my parents were born in Palestine,*
> *My children, they are not Pakistani, even if their mother's parents were born in Pakistan,*
> *No. We are Muslim, and our allegiance is not to Britain or to any Arab culture or Pakistani culture. Our allegiance is only to Allah and to Islam.*

For women, the prescriptive side of this Islamic identity lay in Hizb ut-Tahrir's interpretation of *Qur'anic* verses relating to dress. According to its interpretation, only a woman's hands and face should be in view and it was therefore *fard* (obligatory) for all Muslim women to wear the jilbab or equivalent full-length, long-sleeved garment and to cover their hair, neck and bosom with a *khimar* (scarf/hijab). These clothes should be of plain thick material in dark or muted colours since they were intended to cover the beauty and conceal the female body form rather than attract attention to it. The collective visual effect of such dress is clearly visible from a photograph of the audience at the Hizb ut-Tahrir seminar in Willesden Green. Such an interpretation is not of course confined to Hizb ut-Tahrir. A similar interpretation of Islamic dress is found in a number of Middle Eastern countries where jilbabs or equivalent long outer garments were popular amongst Arabs in pre-Islamic times and later became associated with the wives of the prophet and other Muslim women. The re-interpretation and adoption of such dress has played an important role in Islamic reform movements around the world whether in Egypt, Pakistan or Britain.[7] The anti-colonial writings of the Egyptian ideologue, Sayyid Qutb, and the Pakistani ideologue, Mawdudi, form a basis for many of the ideas reworked by Hizb ut-Tahrir.[8]

According to Hizb ut-Tahrir, wearing such dress is essential not only for a woman's relationship with God, but also for asserting a non-Western Islamic identity in the public sphere, thereby converting every Muslim woman into a visible ambassador for Islam:

> *The hijab is one outward manifestation of the Islamic resurgence in Europe and Muslim World.*[9]
>
> *... it is a public expression of Muslim women shunning the Western values and secularism and adopting Islamic values and identity.*[10]

When a member of the audience at the Willesden Green seminar pointed out that rather than diverting the gaze of others, the hijab when worn in the Western context actually had the adverse effect of attracting attention, the speaker replied:

Yes … That is right. We should stand out like a sore thumb … Islam has come not to blend in with everything else around us. Islam has come to dominate.[11]

According to this logic, it was part of every Muslim woman's duty to attract the attention and curiosity of those around her so that she might explain her dress to others and, in doing so, attract the *kufir* (infidels) to the faith. In view of this explicit proselytizing agenda, it is not difficult to see why members of Hizb ut-Tahrir should have been so keen to advise Shabina Begum over the jilbab affair, and it is more than likely that it was their ideas that inspired the controversy in the first place. Shabina's statement that she hoped she had encouraged other girls to make sure that their uniforms conformed to the religious obligations of Islam is entirely coherent with this ideology, as are all the other opinions she expressed. Viewed in this light, the wearing of jilbab and hijab became not just a religious duty but an explicit form of politico-religious activism.

To sum up, for Hizb ut-Tahrir, Islamic women's dress, consisting of jilbab and hijab, represented Muslim identity, purity, solidarity and religious and political activism. As such it was a particularly apt metaphor and material practice through which to express rejection

Figure 5.4   Speakers at the hijab conference organized by Hizb ut-Tahrir, Willesden Green, London, February 2004.

of 'the West' and the restoration of the global *ummah*. It was also one of the key means by which Muslim women living in the West were expected to demonstrate their distance and difference from their polar opposite, the so-called Western Woman—also imagined chiefly in stereotypical sartorial terms.

THE WESTERN WOMAN AS 'OTHER'

At Queen Mary's College in London, I helped myself to a leaflet with the unwelcoming title, 'All Women Are Slaves: The Trials and Dilemmas of Muslim Student Life'. In spite of its title, it was written in a relatively jaunty and intimate style with *Qur'anic* citations left to a minimum. It began with the innocent quotidian question, 'What shall I wear today?', describing a woman's daily rituals as she sifts through her closet, cleanses her face, puts on her make-up and so on. The leaflet went on to explain that readers probably thought they were free to choose what they wanted to wear, but in reality the apparent freedom of women in the West was merely an illusion because such women are forced to conform to sexualized media images and male-dominated expectations which mean they are judged purely on their appearances. The leaflet concluded with the assertion that whilst capitalism enslaves woman, Islam liberates her, giving her status, honour and dignity. Yet ultimately, 'all women are slaves', for 'Islam made the woman a slave to the creator Allah (*swt*)' as opposed to a slave to mere man—yet another argument reproduced by Shabina Begum.

The subtitle of this leaflet, 'The Trials and Dilemmas of Muslim Student Life', was intended to highlight the perils of exposure to Western practices and reasoning faced by students in higher education institutions in Britain. As Ed Husain makes clear, Hizb ut-Tahrir activists know their public and play on the insecurities students from culturally diverse backgrounds may feel when they leave home for the first time and find themselves exposed to a cosmopolitan University milieu. In the leaflet such students were advised to avoid unnecessary contact with non-Muslims, except in circumstances where they had the opportunity to guide the *kufir* (infidels) to Islam.

The leaflet provides a classic example of the ease with which members of Hizb ut-Tahrir draw from the discourses of Western feminism in their critique of the West and 'Western woman's plight'. An important element of this was holding up a mirror to the stereotypical rhetoric most commonly levelled against Muslim women and hurling this back at the 'Western woman' of their imagination. According to this logic, it is 'the Western woman' who is the oppressed and unwitting victim of patriarchy and whose imprisonment can be read from her clothes (or lack of them). It is this Western woman who was enslaved by capitalism and a multi-billion-dollar fashion industry; obsessed with her body image to the point of ill health (anorexia and plastic surgery being the proof); 'imprisoned in a perpetual state of inadequacy' (as evident in high rates of depression and low self-esteem built by the impossibility of living up to media images); victim of false consciousness (deluded into thinking she has freedom of choice when in fact her clothing choices are dictated and coerced by the fashion industry); forced to expose herself to men's desires out of fear of failure should she not parade as a sex object; victim to a succession of trendy diets and judged only on the superficiality of her appearance and on the degree of flesh she reveals.[12]

To boost the argument, various media reports and statistics on anorexia, plastic surgery, depression and other health and social issues are cited as conclusive evidence of the Western woman's oppression. No mention is made of the fact that Iran, where all women are obliged to cover by law, has one of the highest plastic surgery rates in the world and that the record for crimes against women is high in many Islamic countries. Here, rape, sexual harassment and violent crime are instead portrayed as the obvious consequences of the Western woman's bodily exposure with the implication that a culture of overt sexuality is not only accepted in the West but positively enforced. By contrast, the modest Muslim woman is portrayed as a revered, respected and treasured member of the *Ummah*. In this battle of sartorial rhetoric, Hizb ut-Tahrir challenge descriptions of the burqa as a 'mobile prison' by quoting the famous feminist Mary Woolstencraft's passage about women's oppression: '*Taught from infancy that beauty is a woman's sceptre, the mind shapes itself to the body and roaming round its guilt cage, only seeks to adorn its prison.*'[13]

Similarly, they quote Polly Toynbee's alarmist condemnation of the burka:

> The top-to-toe burka, with its sinister, airless little grille is more than an instrument of persecution, it is a public tarring and feathering of female sexuality. It transforms a woman into an object of defilement too untouchably disgusting to be seen … More moderate versions of the garb have much the same effect, inspiring the lascivious thoughts they are designed to stifle …

To this Hizb ut-Tahrir responded with a reference to the Miss World Beauty contest held in Nigeria in 2002 where 'the Muslim *Ummah* rose up' in protest at the degrading treatment and display of women's bodies. Here burka and bikini were pitched directly against each other with a question mark left dangling over which dress reduced women to mere sex objects.[14]

Feminist arguments were, in turn, mixed together with exerts from Islamic texts. So, elsewhere in 'The Western Beauty Myth', we read:

> The Western woman has become an object judged simply on superficialities rather than her thinking and intelligence. Allah perfectly describes this whole reality in an *ayah* [quoted first in Arabic, then in translation]
>> *But the Unbelievers—their deeds are like a mirage in sandy deserts which man parched with thirst mistakes for water, until when he comes up to it, he finds it to be nothing.*[15]

Ultimately it is suggested that the superficialities of the beauty myth were exposed long ago in the *Qur'an*, which provides answers to all things. Similarly, Germaine Greer's lament that she was forced to travel the earth to see if she could glimpse a surviving whole woman who did not exist to embody male fantasies or rely on a man to endow her with identity and social status and who did not have to be beautiful was met by the following response from Hizb ut-Tahrir: 'Our advice to her would be that she ends her travels and save her money by examining the true status of women within Islam and the *Khilafat* system.'[16]

Although much of this discourse is locked into a set of binary oppositions between the Muslim Woman and the Western Woman, Islam and the West, religion and secularism as if these were clear-cut and mutually exclusive categories, it is clear that the real task for HT was to try to convince other Muslims of the validity of this set of oppositions. This was inevitably an uphill struggle since, as we have already noted in other chapters, most Muslims in Britain and Europe live lives that contradict the ideology of Hizb ut-Tahrir and demonstrate the everyday realities of integration, hybridity, adaptation, negotiation, re-invention and so forth. It is perhaps for this reason that much of Hizb ut-Tahrir's attack is targeted at the so-called Islamic thinkers who have propagated false ideas of 'modernism, secularism, the spirit of Islam and the emancipation of the Muslim woman'. The Westernization of the wives of Muslim premiers around the world, the sexually explicit content of Bollywood films and the emergence of the Indian fashion industry are all taken as proof of 'the way the West has effectively demonised the Muslim woman in her normal attire and made her something who, if not extinct, is alienated and unwanted in her society'.[17]

Part of HT's sartorial mission was therefore not only to transform the appearances and behaviour of Muslim women but also their attitudes and modes of reasoning. This was highly explicit in their approach to the French ban on the hijab, which was framed as much in terms of exposing and dismissing 'the incorrect responses of the Muslim community' as it was in detailing the so-called correct response. This was part of a wider agenda of rescuing Muslim minds from the 'extremism of secularism'.

DRESSING CORRECTLY FOR THE CORRECT REASONS

In an article entitled, 'The Attack on the Veil', published in Hizb ut-Tahrir's in-house magazine, *Khilafah*, an account is given of various incorrect responses women may have in relation to proposed bans on hijab. The first of these involved accepting the idea that the khimar and jilbab are symbols of oppression. The Muslim woman who considers herself free to display her beauty as she wishes has 'chosen to join the ranks of the much degraded Western woman, lowering her status to a mere commodity and all the while remaining deluded, believing she is liberated'.[18] She is the first victim of the attack on hijab.

The second victim was the Muslim woman who considered it her 'democratic right' to wear Islamic dress as a matter of 'personal freedom'. This, we are told, is a dangerous argument for if the Muslim woman is free to wear hijab, this implies she is also free NOT to wear it—and, by extension, is free to fornicate, drink alcohol, commit adultery and so forth. 'No', bellowed a speaker at the Willesden Green Conference, 'The call for freedom has no place in Islam. We do not cover because we are free to cover or because we have the choice to cover but because it is an obligation commanded by Allah.' The woman who argues she is free to choose to wear hijab has 'fallen prey to the *kufir* agenda'. Readers of *Khilafah* are warned that the fact that Britain and certain other countries tolerate hijab should not lull people into assuming that they wear it as a matter of 'choice'. Such countries, we are told,

Figure 5.5   Hizb ut-Tahrir protest, Hyde Park, London, January 2004.

are not so much against the Muslim woman's cloth as 'against the very reason motivating her to wear it'. It is therefore all the more vital that this reasoning be kept intact. 'The Muslim woman' is therefore reminded that, 'If she were to cover based on the concept of personal freedom, then her reasoning to do so is on a par with that of the Western woman who wears a mini-skirt.' This logic leads Hizb ut-Tahrir to criticize Merve Kavakci, the Turkish politician who explained that covering her head in the Turkish Parliament was a 'test of democracy', arguing that 'In the 20th century, they must allow us that freedom.'[19]

The third victim of the attack on hijab is, according to Hizb ut-Tahrir, the Muslim woman who thinks she can cover up and be fashionable too, and whose clothes are affected by Western fashions. Such women are incorrect in suggesting that there is any common ground between the Muslim woman's dress and Western fashion, for such a suggestion implies the possibility of integration. Young British Muslims who have spoken out in the press about the compatibility of Islam and fashion are condemned as ignorant, deluded and Westernized. Readers are reminded, 'The motivation to cover for the Muslim woman is the desire to obey and please none other than Allah (*swt*), and is in complete contradiction with the desire to attain a specific appearance based on trends set by the fashion industry. To discuss the divine *hukm* (order) revealed by Allah (*swt*) in the context of the man made, superficial and pretentious concept of "fashion" is most definitely an insult to the rules of Islam.'[20]

The fourth victim of the attack on hijab is the Muslim woman who argues that by wearing khimar and jilbab, she is maintaining her modesty and warding off the male gaze, unlike the Western woman who displays her charms in an explicit manner. This, as we have seen, is a very common argument among many contemporary hijab wearers who feel they attract less sexual attention through covering. According to Hizb ut-Tahrir such reasoning is wrong: first, because it is a defensive form of human reasoning rather than acceptance of a divine command, and second, because it is based on the unstable variability of modesty. Since the measure of modesty can vary from person to person and country to country, it cannot be considered a suitable criteria by which women's dress should be determined, not least because it implies 'that the Islamic dress code can be changed according to the change of time'. Such discussions seek to 'dilute the pristine identity of the Muslim woman and her view of Islamic dress'.[21] Here we return to the notion of the importance of sartorial uniformity for the global *ummah*.

Finally, we are told, the only correct reason for covering is because it is commanded by the Creator, Allah. 'Adopting any other, Western inspired reasoning for wearing the khimar is unacceptable and only lends support to the Attack on the Veil. Each time a Muslim woman allows her Islamic motives for covering to be affected by the *Kufir* concept of personal freedom, she allows the attack to achieve success.'[22]

Although the precise wording and examples vary in different Hizb ut-Tahrir articles and speeches, the basic key features of the argument are consistent. Dress is an important means of defying the corrupting forces of integration, working on both bodies and minds. It is a means of combating the decadent notions of 'liberation', 'individualism' and 'choice' that threaten to dilute the purity of Islamic identities in the West.

In the Question and Answer sessions at the seminars and lectures I attended, a number of Islamic clerics around the world were dismissed for having issued 'dodgy *fatwas*' permitting Muslim girls to remove their hijabs if coerced to do so. And young women who suggested simply dressing modestly in a long skirt, long top and headscarf were told theirs was a very dangerous approach that betrayed a false understanding of Islam's clearly defined dress code. Mention of the emergence of a distinctive 'European Islam' of the type advocated by the philosopher, Tariq Ramadan, was also greeted with dismissal and contempt. One of the slogans chanted on the protest march has been—'We want Islam, Not *French* Islam.' Central to Hizb ut-Tahrir's notion of 'the inevitability of the clash of civilizations'[23] is the notion that these civilizations remain incompatible, distinct and devoid of any trendy post-colonial hyphens.

THE JILBAB CONTROVERSY RECONSIDERED

There seems little doubt that the thirteen-year-old Shabina Begum had imbibed the ideology of Hizb ut-Tahrir—an ideology founded on intolerance and confrontation with an explicit anti-Western rhetoric and agenda which includes fundamental opposition to the values of freedom, democracy, equality and human rights. Whilst her argument in favour of the jilbab was sometimes framed in terms of a desire for increased modesty, it was noticeable that throughout her court appearances she wore well-tailored, close-fitting jilbabs with tight tailored jackets and cardigans which were far more revealing of the female form than the school's comparatively shapeless shalwar kamiz. Her principal objection to the latter outfit revolved around the fact that it was associated with Pakistani culture and could also be worn by Hindus and Sikhs. Whilst she said she did not consider Muslims who wore the shalwar kamiz to be bad people as such, she did consider those who wore the jilbab to be better Muslims. This is not to doubt the sincerity of her religious convictions, but rather to recognize that these convictions rested on notions of inequality and moral superiority which included the religious obligation to encourage others to follow her example.

School uniforms do not of course encourage individuality or creativity and some people oppose them for this reason. The rationale behind them is that they de-emphasize social and economic differences between pupils and instil a sense of collective identity. One of the striking things about the way uniforms have evolved in the British context is that they are relatively sensitive to people's desires to express cultural and religious differences and have often been adapted to suit the requirements of particular groups through a process of consultation between staff, parents, pupils and governors. It is precisely through such a process that Denbigh High School's uniform had been redesigned in the early 1990s. A similar process is apparent in schools up and down the country, many of which have incorporated regulation turbans, skull caps, headscarves and shalwar kamizes into uniforms whilst retaining an overall sense of collective identity through colours and other shared features. It is this combination of inclusiveness and respect for diversity that the Department of Education and Skills seeks to encourage.

Negotiation with Shabina had not been possible, however, because the entire issue was from the start formulated in terms of Hizb ut-Tahrir's logic of confrontation. It was presented not as a request for consideration but as an ultimatum and threat. There is, of course, something disconcerting about a political group which openly rejects notions of freedom, democracy and human rights advising this young girl to fight her case on the grounds that her individual human rights had been violated. This point was eloquently made by Guyuddin Siddiqui, leader of the Muslim Parliament of Great Britain, when, on hearing the Court of Appeal's decision in favour of Shabina, he commented, 'It may be a victory for human rights but it is also a victory for fundamentalism.

THE FALL OUT: A STEREOTYPE RE-INFORCED

Muslim responses to the jilbab controversy were extremely divided. The representative of the MCB (Muslim Council of Britain), Britain's largest umbrella organization for Muslim groups, was vocal in his support of Shabina's right to wear a jilbab to school, arguing that the full gamut of Islamic interpretations of modesty should be respected. The Islamic Human Right's Commission and the Society for the Protection of Hijab also took up the cause with a combination of righteous indignation and religious fervour. But Muslim

Islam Under Threat...

Banning of Hijab

The French President Jacques Chirac has approved a proposal that will ban the wearing of the hijab by Muslim women in French schools and public buildings. The Hijab issue is a vital issue that threatens our future existence in the West. Muslims must understand that there is a dark future awaiting us if we do not hold firmly to Islam. If we surrender the hukm of Hijab today, then tommorow it will be the whole of Islam that we surrender. Muslims must be firm in adhering to Islam and seek help from Allah (swt) to adhere to the haq.

3pm Sunday 8th February 2004

Family Centre, Russel Road, Forest Fields, Nottingham. Brothers and Sisters are welcome.

For further information: east.midlands@1924.org or 07970 256 846

Organised by members of *Hizb ut-Tahrir*

Figure 5.6   Flier advertising Hizb ut-Tahrir hijab seminar in Nottingham, 2004.

public opinion was far more variegated than these official responses implied. Discuss-ing the case with a large number of Muslim women, I have encountered a wide variety of perspectives. Some did indeed perceive the case as 'yet another' example of prejudice mounting against Islam. They felt this was unfair treatment of a girl who had firm beliefs that should have been respected in an education system oriented towards social inclusion and respect of diversity. Others, however, argued that Shabina should have accepted the school's uniform like other pupils. I particularly remember discussing this issue with a group of women, most of whom wore jilbabs and *niqabs* (face veils). I had assumed from their style of dress that they would be sympathetic with Shabina but instead found them arguing that she should either have accepted the school rules and contented herself with putting on a jilbab at the end of the school day, or she should have left and gone to an Islamic school instead rather than expecting her existing school to adapt its rules to suit her requirements. As one woman put it, laughing, 'How far can we go?!!', to which another woman added, 'We can't unscramble the world to get what we want. We have to move ourselves a bit as well.'

There were, however, two points on which everyone with whom I spoke seemed to agree: first, that the issue should never have gone to court; and second, that the media publicity around the case was a negative thing for 'the Muslim community'. This media publicity did not, of course, occur in a vacuum. It was happening against a steady stream of news stories concerning the bloody and unpopular wars in Afghanistan and Iraq, terrorist incidents involving Muslims both as victims and perpetrators at home and abroad, a rise in state security and anti-terrorist legislation with a strong Muslim focus and growing decla-rations about the death or failure of multiculturalism. In the period between the Court of Appeal ruling and the Law Lord's judgement of Shabina's case, Britain had experienced its first suicide bomb attack by British Muslims, and the atmosphere of interrogation, suspi-cion and public scrutiny had escalated. There was much talk of banning organizations like Hizb ut-Tahrir who preached a rhetoric of hatred in spite of the risk that such a ban would pose to the right to freedom of speech. In short, British newspapers were filled with dra-matic headlines about Muslims, most of which portrayed them in a negative or provocative light. The jilbab controversy therefore entered this expanding media coverage of so-called Muslim Problems, adding to its swell.

In view of this tide of mainly negative publicity, it is hardly surprising that most Mus-lims, whatever their personal opinion about the dispute, should have wished for a quieter resolution behind closed doors rather than a public spectacle involving three court cases and several front-page headlines. This desire to avoid media publicity was in turn linked to an acute awareness of how such publicity could turn against Muslims in general, inflating public anxiety at a time when Muslims increasingly felt 'under suspicion' and were increas-ingly targeted for abuse and attack. Whilst there is no way of measuring how this one case may have increased the risk of attack for women who look Muslim, there is ample evidence to suggest that women who wear conspicuous forms of Muslim clothing are subject to more violence and abuse than those who do not.

Equally damaging in the long term is the way this controversy contributed to a re-inforcement of existing visual stereotypes of Muslims already so well-entrenched in the British media and public imagination. Like Muslim opinion, non-Muslim opinion was divided over this case but generally for different reasons and with different effects. At the left side of the political spectrum were many, including people of different faiths, who felt that Shabina should have had the freedom of choice to wear 'her religious dress to school'. But what such a view fails to acknowledge is that there is no such thing as a fixed category of 'religious dress' in Islam, but rather a range of interpretations. To take the jilbab as 'the religious dress' of Muslims is to subscribe to and condone a particular conservative mono-chrome interpretation of Muslim dress. The effect is to further fix a visual stereotype and inadvertently give strength to the view that it is somehow 'natural' for a Muslim girl to wear a jilbab. This is, of course, precisely the view of radical political groups like Hizb ut-Tahrir but also of a number of conservative Muslim organizations and movements, some of which have close affinities with Islamic movements in such countries as Saudi Arabia, Egypt, Iran and Pakistan. Islamic bookshops in Britain sell a number of books offering religiously sanctioned advice and dictates concerning what women should wear—some of them published abroad, many published in Britain. Titles range from the comparatively neutral, *The Obligation of Veiling and Women* (USA 2003) and *Women in Shariah* (Nigeria 1989) to the overtly misogynist, *Women Who Deserve to Go to Hell* (Pakistan 2004), a book which threatens immodest women with the prospect of hell fire as 'an invitation' for them to reform their dress and behaviour. Such books play heavily on a combination of scrip-tural authority, guilt, fear—none of which sit easily with the notion of freedom of choice. The books targeted at children are generally less harsh and unforgiving, but they nonethe-less encourage young Muslims girls to perceive the fashionable clothes of their contempo-raries as 'haram' and to observe strict vigilance in relation to their own appearances. For example *A Muslim Girl's Guide to Life's Big Changes* (London 2005), recommended for girls aged nine to fourteen, contains a centre-page quiz entitled 'Is your Muslim identity safe?' Children are invited to respond to a series of questions by ticking either 'always', 'mostly', 'sometimes' or 'never'. The first of these questions concerns how careful they are about avoiding tight clothes, short sleeves and designer labels. The second is about how often they cover their hair. The book also contains kindly phrased reminders such as:

> I don't wish to scare you but this is what the Prophet (Peace be upon Him) has to say about women who dress inappropriately. 'If you see them (women who dress inappro-priately) curse them because they will be deprived of the Mercy of Allah.' (p. 16)

Such books are targeted at pubescent Muslim girls living in a non-Muslim environ-ment and although not explicitly separatist in their message, nonetheless often discourage unnecessary interaction with non-Muslims. It is not difficult to see why heads of British schools interested in promoting equality in a multicultural environment might feel uneasy about some of the ideological discourses and psychological pressures experienced by some Muslim girls.

Figure 5.7   Children's one-piece hijabs purchased in Whitechapel, London, 2007.

But if those who supported Shabina's case inadvertently contributed to the stereotyped image of the Muslim woman in a dark jilbab, so too did those who opposed it, perceiving the jilbab as a sign of extremism, female oppression, separatism per se when it may be worn by large numbers of adult women for a whole variety of reasons, including personal piety, convenience, cultural conservatism or protection from a perceived threatening environment. There is a serious danger in fixing particular meanings to particular types of dress without comprehension of the context in which particular garments are chosen and worn. Media interpretations of the jilbab controversy which took Shabina's politicized perspective as indicative of the oppressive and intolerant nature of Islam ultimately told us more about the ignorance of certain journalists and commentators than about either Muslims or Islam.

Who, then, benefited from the jilbab controversy? Not Shabina, for although, unlike most teenagers, she got the chance to express her rebellious sentiments on the world stage, she nonetheless lost two years of schooling as well as the final court case, and claimed to have lost many of her old friends in the process. Given that her mother also died during this period, leaving her an orphan, life must have been hard for Shabina Begum. Not the head mistress and governors of Denbigh High School either, for although their decision was ultimately supported by the House of Lords, they had spent three years embroiled against their wishes in a painfully public dispute which they could happily have done without.

But some did gain mileage out of the case and the publicity around it—most noticeably, Hizb ut-Tahrir whose politicized perspective on women's dress was touted all over the national and international media where it was often presented as 'the Muslim view'. More generally, extremists on both sides of the political spectrum found in this case food for inspiration and malice. Against the cry on radical Muslim Web sites of 'jihad through jilbab', came the cry on racist Islamaphobic Web sites, 'Go back to the dusty third world hell hole from whence you came.' Sadly, these were the voices that the jilbab controversy ultimately served to magnify.

NOTES

1. Hizb ut-Tahrir ('the Liberation Party') is an international Muslim political group founded in Jerusalem in 1953 by a Palestinian judge. It calls itself a political party whose aim is to work towards the establishment of the *Khilafat* (Islamic state under *Shariah* law), first in the Middle East, then world-wide. The organization is banned in many Middle Eastern countries and in Germany and has been subject to restrictions on British University campuses following accusations that it propagates anti-Semitic views. The British branch of Hizb ut-Tahrir was established in 1986 and has a significant student following, though estimates of membership numbers vary considerably (Akhtar 2005). According to a report in *The Independent*, the conference organized by Hizb ut-Tahrir in Birmingham in 2003, entitled, *British or Muslim?*, attracted 8,000 people and its 2002 conference was the largest Islamic event ever organized in the United Kingdom (*The*

Independent on Sunday, 7 August 2005).The British government has expressed unease about the ideology of the organization and has contemplated banning it on several occasions but has never been able to prove its alleged links to terrorist activities.

2. This account of the controversy is taken from legal transcripts relating to the cases and judgements of the High Court (2004), the Court of Appeal (2005) and the House of Lords (2006). See http:/www.minorities.org/print.php?IDA=3262, http://www.bailii.org/ew/cases/EWCA/Civ/2005/199.html (accessed 15 March 2005), http://www.publications.parliament.uk.pa.ld200506/ldjudgmt/jd060322/begum (accessed 24 March 2006).

3. Dilpazier Aslam, *Guardian,* 3 March 2005, p. 1.

4. Live dialogue number 569, 17 March 2005, http://www.islamOnline.net/livedialogue/english (accessed 30 June 2005).

5. Shabina's articulate responses were apparently written within the two-hour period of the online dialogue session, and it seems highly probable that she would have had people and/or literature close on hand to assist her.

6. See Husain (2007: 116).

7. See El Guindi (1999: chapter 8), for the origins of the jilbab and its popularity in the Islamic reform movement in Egypt in the 1970s.

8. See Husain (2007) for an ex–Hizb ut-Tahrir activist's version of the connections between different strands of radical Islamic discourses. See also Akhtar (2005) for discussion of the appeal of Hizb ut-Tahrir's rhetoric to sections of young educated British Muslims in response to feelings that Muslims around the world are suffering persecution at the hands of 'the West'.

9. Tajo Mustapha's speech outside the French Embassy in London, 17 January 2004.

10. Imrana Zalloom's speech at Willesden Green Hijab seminar, 24 January 2004.

11. Imrana Zalloom's speech at Willesden Green Hijab seminar, 24 January 2004.

12. Carolyn Pedwell provides an interesting historical analysis of the emergence of a Muslim stereotype of 'the Western woman' as a response both to Western stereotypes of the 'Muslim woman' and Victorian stereotypes of British women. She suggests that Egyptian reformers opposed to Westernizing modernist agendas and policies of the late nineteenth and early twentieth centuries drew strategically on Victorian images of women as weak, frivolous and obsessed with their appearance, and that it was against this image that they constructed the notion of the veiled Muslim woman as strong, modest and pious (Pedwell 2007).

13. Also quoted in 'The Western Beauty Myth', p. 9.

14. This was clearly in line with Hizb ut-Tahrir's dress activism at Tower Hamlets College in the 1990s where a seminar was organized under the heading 'Hijab: Put up or Shut up'. The posters for the seminar juxtaposed the image of a woman in a mini-skirt with a woman in hijab and niqab (Husain 2007: 67).

15. Hizb ut-Tahrir, 'The Western Beauty Myth', p. 19.

16. Hizb ut-Tahrir, 'The Western Beauty Myth', p. 35.

17. Hizb ut-Tahrir, 'The Attack on the Veil', *Khilafah Magazine*, 2003, 16/7: 19.

18. Hizb ut-Tahrir, 'The Attack on the Veil', *Khilafah Magazine*, 2003, 16/7: 20.
19. Hizb ut-Tahrir, 'The Attack on the Veil', *Khilafah Magazine*, 2003, 16/7: 20.
20. Hizb ut-Tahrir, 'The Attack on the Veil', *Khilafah Magazine*, 2003, 16/7: 20.
21. Hizb ut-Tahrir, 'The Attack on the Veil', *Khilafah Magazine*, 2003, 16/7: 21.
22. Hizb ut-Tahrir, 'The Attack on the Veil', *Khilafah Magazine*, 2003, 16/7: 21.
23. Hizb ut-Tahrir (2002) has reworked Huntington's 'Clash of Civilization thesis' into a 64-page booklet of its own entitled, 'The Inevitability of the Clash of Civilizations'.

6   COVERING CONCERNS

OBSERVATIONS ON THE LONDON UNDERGROUND

Russell Square tube station, 9.30 a.m., June 2007. A robed figure steps into the tube train. She is wearing a long free-flowing black abaya which sweeps from her shoulders to the floor. Her head is bound with a tight black headscarf, her face covered with a black face veil (*niqab*), tied at the back. Her eyes briefly scan her surroundings through the narrow slit of her niqab. She carries a large and noticeably stylish grey bag containing books and a file. She is probably a student. A middle-aged man standing inside the carriage looks up abruptly as she approaches, then looks studiously the other way. A row of people seated opposite also register her appearance before rapidly averting their eyes. The young woman in black remains standing near the door. She stares through the glass with a fixed posture which seems to speak of distance, dignity and reserve. Now that he is sure not to meet her gaze, the man who had initially looked away turns to scrutinize the long black figure, his eyes moving up and down her twice as if he is trying to reconstitute the person inside the garments. It is a look of curiosity and slight misapprehension. Two of the seated women also periodically eye the young woman in black as if slowly digesting her appearance. A young woman dressed in jeans with a short jacket and maroon headscarf glances at everyone before returning to her novel. A child further down the carriage stares wide-eyed until distracted by a toy handed to her by her mother. All the while the woman in black keeps her gaze fixed out of the window, watching the dark tunnel spin by. Her stance is upright and self-conscious. She seems aware that she is probably being looked at and at the same time studiously impervious to the fact, as if sheltered from potential stares by the layers of her garments. At Kings Cross station, she swoops out of the carriage without looking at any of the passengers, the drape of her abaya lending a certain gravitas to her determined walk. A series of eyes follow her off the train. The two women exchange quick looks of shared visual acknowledgement, and then continue their conversation.

What is all this looking about? Why does this isolated veiled figure attract this type of visual attention? One reason is, I suggest, architectural. It is about configurations of the body in space. In the context of a tube train in central London where other people are dressed in various forms of fitted apparel which make clear distinctions between the body and the head, the covered woman occupies a different space from those around her. What the man had sensed as she moved into the train was probably not much more than a black form approaching, a form that was not immediately decipherable. It is no doubt this that had made him start ever so slightly as she entered his visual field. His first glance seems to have been a cognitive exercise, an attempt at identification. Having identified that the

figure approaching was first a human being and second a Muslim woman, his second impulse was to look the other way.

The three-stage sequence of glancing, averting the eyes and then staring is not unique
to this one man's encounter with niqab on a weekday morning in the underground. It is in
fact a very common response when covered women make appearances in locations where
their dress flouts the visual conventions dominant in that particular space—whether it is
a tube train, a public park or a shopping street. Here the onlooker seems caught between
a desire to look and the realization that the clothing worn seems designed to discourage
looking. In such circumstances the covered woman is both hyper-conspicuous and hyper-
concealed, creating an impression of being simultaneously present and absent, public and
private. Such conspicuous privacy breaks with the conventions by which visual information is habitually exchanged in such public spaces. It confuses the onlooker. It is not that
strangers on tube trains habitually speak to one another or even look directly at one another. They do not. But they do habitually exchange small fragments of visual information
not only through their dress but also through their eyes and facial expressions. It is in fact
through the arrangement of facial muscles that individuals establish what Goffman called,
'conditions of co-presence'—expressing their aliveness to each other, keeping their 'sensory
portals open' to minimal information flow.[1]

'There is typically', writes Goffman, 'an obligation to convey certain information when
in the presence of others, and not to convey other impressions, just as there is an expectation that they will present themselves in certain ways. There tends to be an agreement not
only about the meaning of the behaviours that are seen but also about the behaviours that
ought to be shown.'[2] Goffman is not implying that all persons share the same normative
conventions, but that in a particular context of interaction, certain norms and expectations prevail, regardless of whether or not particular individuals choose to abide by them,
even if, as we have already seen, these norms are open to contestation and change over
time. A woman wearing a face veil in a context where visual information is habitually
exchanged through facial expression has in effect put up a powerful form of 'involvement
shield' which indicates that she is 'out of play', unavailable for anything other than the
most minimal 'unfocused interaction'. Unfocused interaction in Goffman's formulation
concerns what is communicated between persons merely by virtue of their co-presence in
the same social situation. It is the unavoidable consequence of physically being there. What
the niqab does is block interaction at this unfocused level, denying the possibility of a more
sustained form of 'focused interaction'.

This is not to imply that individuals in the street generally feel free to eye each other up
and down with impunity. Neither is it to assume that men and women look at each other
in equivalent ways. Visual interaction is in fact highly coded and regulated through subtle
gestures of acknowledgement and disengagement. As strangers approach each other in the
street their eyes connect at a certain distance, then disconnect, as individuals show willingness to display 'civil inattention' towards each other. By withdrawing their gaze, individuals
demonstrate that they are not making the other person a target of curiosity. According to

Goffman, the 'proper level' of civil inattention conveys that a person has no reason to suspect the intentions of others or to fear them, feel hostile towards them or to wish to avoid them or draw attention to them. In other words, people show that they have no need to look further whilst at the same time expressing that they had nothing to fear or avoid in having been seen in the first place or in having been seen to be seeing.

When the man in the tube looked away from the niqabi woman, he was, in effect, conforming to the accepted expectations of high levels of 'civil inattention' in the underground. But he was unable to sustain this level of disengagement for two reasons. The first was that he had not received any reciprocal assurances from the woman in question. The woman had avoided visual interaction with him entirely. What he had registered then was her apparent desire to remain disengaged, closed to interaction. Such deliberate disengagement disrupts the feelings of ease that occur when individuals tacitly agree to avoid further visual interaction by mutual displays of civil inattention. Instead, what develops are feelings of unease—the feeling that perhaps there might indeed be something to suspect or fear after all in the absence of the usual messages of re-assurance exchanged between strangers.

So the man now turns to look and, finding that the person he is looking at remains shielded from his gaze, he feels at liberty to stare in ways he would not normally do. But there is something else at stake in his compulsive looking. The long black garments which both attract and repel his vision are not seen in isolation. They have associations, both historic and contemporary, which he brings to his looking at this one woman.

In the European past, the covering of the face is charged with a whole variety of negative associations: ghosts, burglars, prisoners, masked figures, Halloween pranks and untrustworthy

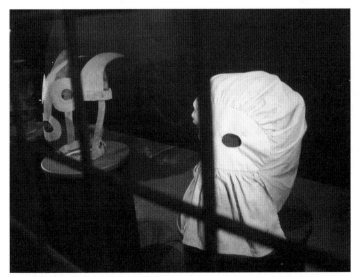

Figure 6.1 The covered face in European history: Prisoner's masks, Nordic Museum, Stockholm.
Photo: Arzu Unal.

disguises of various kinds—associations which seem only to confirm his unease and which contradict his impulse to avert his gaze. Perhaps he even feels he needs to keep an eye on this masked woman just in case she is not quite what she seems. Present in his mind are perhaps other more contemporary associations with covered faces—Hamas militants on TV or in the newspapers. Such images might suggest to him that the niqab is linked to radical interpretations of Islam and to the possible threat of terrorism. Just two years ago, a tube train like the one he is standing in, was blown up by young Muslim radicals. His mind perhaps fills with a series of more or less formulated associations—'trouble makers', 'untrustworthy', 'alien', 'backwards', 'irrational', 'imprisoned', 'brainwashed', 'oppressed', 'extreme'. He no doubt suspects that the woman on the train is just a person going about her daily business, that her bag contains books not bombs, but he may not be able to halt the associations that have flashed like a bad film through his head.[3] And so he cannot quite trust her presence enough to keep looking away. Something seems to be telling him that someone with so much to cover up just might have something to hide.

Having not conversed with the man in question, I cannot of course verify precisely what was going through his head when he stared so intensely at the niqabi woman. My reading is conjectural, but it is also informed by what many Londoners from different backgrounds have told me that they feel when they encounter women in niqab in locations where they do not expect to see them. Feelings of unease, anxiety, misapprehension and sometimes rage are not uncommon and many refer to extremism, oppression and terrorism—all of which seem to exacerbate curiosity and the desire to look. One woman in her forties commented: 'The less you can see, the more you try to see. You somehow need to look harder to reassure yourself that there is a person under there.'

Such responses to niqab are not universal. They are highly contextual. In countries where veiling is common practice (Saudi Arabia, Yemen, Iran), it is not women who cover that are conspicuous, but those who do not. Here it is the uncovered woman who attracts excess visual attention which often comes with highly charged negative associations (loose, immoral, available, sluttish, tempting and corrupting). In British cities too there are spaces where face veiling has become, if not entirely banal, then at least unremarkable.

In London's Whitechapel (East London) and to a lesser extent Green Street (North East London) and Southall (West London)—all areas with a big South Asian presence—many Muslim women cover their faces to greater or lesser degrees whilst purchasing food and clothing in the market. Some wear separate face veils tied over colourful headscarves; some wear black burqas with niqabs; others simply use their shawls to cover their faces. In Whitechapel, in particular, where there is a high density of British Bengali Muslims, face covering has over the past decade acquired some sort of normative status amongst married Muslim women. It signals that they are present for purposive action (the purchase of vegetables) but not for further degrees of unnecessary interaction (casual chat, flirtation, being seen). Here the niqab has become integrated into patterns of looking, enabling rather than preventing displays of civil inattention, allowing women to go about their daily chores without hassle. But the same women may feel hesitant to move around outside the

Figure 6.2   Niqab wearing, Whitechapel Market and Green Street, East London, 2007–2008.

insulated clothed space of Whitechapel for fear that the very dress that protects them in one space will make them a target of negative attention in another. According to a survey conducted by the Islamic Human Rights Commission in 2002–2003, women in niqab have since the terrorist attacks of September 11 become an increasing target of religiously oriented racial abuse. Of the twenty British niqabis interviewed for the survey, eight reported experiencing dress-related abuse at least once a week. Only one of the twenty women concerned reported such a high level of abuse before September 11.[4] The niqab wearers I have interviewed all reported experiencing the humiliation of name calling in the streets and on buses, the most common insults being 'Ninja', 'ghost', 'Terrorist' and 'Bin Laden's Sister'. Some seemed almost to accept this abuse as part of the trials expected of a niqab wearer in 'non-Muslim lands' as if it somehow added to the courage and self-sacrifice which many associated with the practice.

What the niqab signifies and how it is perceived is then dependent on a whole variety of factors: when it is worn, by whom, where and to what effect. It is these questions I wish to explore by describing different people's experiences of encounters with niqab in different circumstances. The material I present comes both from my own encounters, conversations and observations as well as from encounters described or initiated over the Web.

AN ENCOUNTER BETWEEN NIQABIS

Ridzy is a young Muslim blogger who describes herself as 'the crazy one'. In 2006–2007 she kept a blog diary as well as participating in the 'ninja on the loose blogspot'. In her blog she described herself as 'just a 16 year old kid' whose interests include reading, writing, talking, Ahmed Bakhatir [singer], drama, art, dressing up and taking risks. Her favourite books include *Harry Potter*, *Lord of the Rings* and *The God of Small Things*. One day in the summer of 2007, she posted the following comment on her Web site. It was addressed to two niqab-wearing women she had seen in her home town of Leicester. She herself is a niqab wearer so the situation she describes refers to acts of looking between niqabis in a British city with a strong Asian Muslim presence. Her entry is reproduced in full:

> *As Salamu Alaikum* [Peace be upon you],
>
> *I greeted you. Are you going to walk away?*
>
> *You know, today, on my way back from school I saw two niqaabi girls. They were both walking out of a Madressah* [Islamic school], *their lesson for today over. They had big kitaabs* [books] *and folders that contained Islamic stuff in it in their arms. They were covered, head to toe. Under this sweltering heat they were wearing shoes that covered their feet fully. Niqaabs that covered their eyes. Gloves so that men may not see their hands. Shawls long enough to sweep the streets of Leicester. I looked at them with a sense of pride. Wow! Niqaabis! Even more covered than me! I'm niqaabi, but I don't cover my eyes or hands and on hot days I like flip flops. It's great, I thought, as I saw them walking towards me. Alhumdulila* [praise God], *it's amazing how when I started wearing niqaab, I barely saw Muslimahs* [Muslim women] *wearing khimars* [covered dress]. *Like Mujahidahs* [God's warriors], *I thought. Covered up for Allah, from head to toe.*
>
> *I love wearing niqaab. I love niqaabis. I respect them. But not all of them and here's why—*
>
> *I had two text books in my arms. I was holding them against my chest. You could read the title of one of them—'Medicine and Health through Time'.*
>
> *The two girls were walking past me and I thought I'd greet them. 'As Salamu Alaykum, sisters!' I said. No exaggeration, but I said it so cheerfully, someone would think we were long lost friends, meeting again after years. They both stopped. Then slowly one turned around so that she was facing me. She tilted her head in order to read the title of my book properly. Then*

she held out her kitaabs in front of her, read out the title and walked off. I shouted behind her, 'Pride isn't going to get you to heaven!'

My blood was bubbling. Some sense of electrical energy was rushing through my veins. I wanted to turn around and chase after the girl. Beat her up. Turn her to pulp. But I know that's wrong.

So, I'm educating. I'm learning worldly stuff and you're learning Islamic stuff. That doesn't put you a step higher than me. That doesn't make you superior. That doesn't mean you are going to heaven and I am going to hell. You don't become an Alimah [a scholar of Islam] *for the title. You don't become an Alimah so that people look up to you and think you're great. You don't become an Alimah so that you can get a good reputation. You do it for Allah. You do it for Iman* [strength of faith], *to gain Allah's love, to fear Allah and be rewarded.*

Obviously I'm not blind enough to think all Niqaabis and all Alimahs are like that ... But today I learnt that there are people out there that like to hide behind veils, that like to hide behind beards just to look good. What's in their hearts, only Allah knows. What's in everyone's hearts Allah knows.

SubhanAllah [Glory to Allah]

I'll get over this incident, insha'Allah [God willing]. *However, what I learned today will live with me for as long as I'm alive.*

Ridzy.[5]

What is going on in this sequence recorded with so much passion and rage? Clearly we are a long way here from the man on the tube at Russell Square who viewed the niqab wearer with unease. What Ridzy expects is some sort of acknowledgment, if not positive interaction, when she sees another niqab is in Leicester in a context where niqab wearing is a conspicuous minority practice. There is, writes Goffman, an expectation of 'mutual accessibility' between people who visually signal membership of the same group. The examples Goffman gives are of Orthodox Jews, blacks and bearded men who, he claimed in the context of North American cities in the 1960s, greeted each other in spite of being strangers. It is visual recognition of shared group membership that makes such a high degree of focused interaction possible. Written into the 'communication contract' of people whose appearances express shared group membership and by implication, shared values, is the idea that they may interact as friends even if they are total strangers. They have an entitlement to greet each other not only with an exchange of looks but also with verbal exchanges. It is an expectation of shared mutual acceptance and respect.

The rage expressed by Ridzy relates to the fact that in spite of the commonalities she perceives and feels between herself and the two niqabi women who approach her, she finds that she is snubbed by them, treated as if she were invisible, a 'non-person'. Such an extreme form of civil inattention is usually reserved for those considered inferior by the onlooker. Goffman speaks of children, servants, 'negroes', mental patients being treated in this manner in 1960s America by people who considered themselves superior. Such categories of persons were treated as unworthy of acknowledgement, as if they did not exist.

What is clear is that this is not the sort of treatment that Ritzy expects of fellow niqabis with whom she feels immediate recognition, solidarity and admiration. Furthermore she is only too aware that such an improper degree of civil inattention signals a sense of superiority on their part. The two women are carrying and self-consciously displaying religious books and they are more covered than she. Their style of niqab comes replete with an eye veil (a style of layered niqab popular in Saudi Arabia) which renders the eyes of the wearer invisible; their hands and feet are totally covered, leaving not a single patch of body surface visually accessible. They have become walking cloth forms sealed off from the world around them. But whereas such shielded appearances are designed to ward off the gaze of men and unbelievers, to a niqab wearer like Ridzy such appearances are inviting. She reads in their concealed forms a sign of their strength of faith and love of Allah—something she both shares and admires. In her rage there is disappointment—that these two women whom she had been so excited to see and to whom she expresses positive feelings as if greeting a lost friend should shut her out as they would an uncovered stranger. She bitterly resents this snub which she rightly interprets as a performance of superior piety.

What she describes is not a typical encounter between niqabis but an encounter which does not conform to the expected norms of interaction between covered women. Whilst such women deliberately make themselves unavailable to the male gaze, they commonly signal their solidarity with other niqab-wearing women in contexts where they are in a conspicuous minority. What the example also reveals are the different nuances to layers of covering and the ease with which degrees of covering become associated with degrees of piety which further delimit interactions in particular ways. A woman may have everything covered except her eyes, hands and feet, but to a woman with gloves, socks and eye veils, this may not be enough.

SOME LONDON–SAUDI ENCOUNTERS

Yasmin Arif is a fashion designer specialized in the sale of long Eastern-inspired designer gowns (jilbabs, abayas, jelabiyas). Her boutique, Arabiannites, is situated in the London Muslim Centre in Whitechapel just a few doors along from Europe's largest place of worship for Muslims, the East London Mosque. Yasmin was born and raised in this part of East London to parents of Gujarati Muslim origin, but was pleased to move beyond its local confines when as a student she went to study at the Chelsea College of Art and later at the London School of Fashion. Although she returned to Whitechapel to open her boutique in 2005, she lives outside the area and has always looked further afield for her creative inspiration.

Interested in fabrics, design and stitching from a young age, her degree was in Product Development for the Fashion Industry and included a work placement in a North London shop which specialized in bridal and evening wear, where she says she spent six months

Figure 6.3   Interior of Arabiannites boutique, Whitechapel, 2007.

with her head 'buried under ball gowns!' She then went on to work at Selfridges for a period of five years, first on the shop floor and later as a buyer. As a student and young professional, Yasmin did not dress in a visibly Muslim way and resisted what she perceived as
local pressures to wear hijab. She described herself as a stylish dresser, who always enjoyed
experimenting with fabrics and style whilst at the same time avoiding clothes that were
overtly sexually revealing. Asked what led her to enter into the world of Islamic fashion design, Yasmin described how it was the sight of covered women parading through Selfridges
that had initially inspired her.

> When I used to work at Selfridges, I used to see the parade of Arabs gliding in black
> through the store, and I thought, WOW! It's amazing! They are totally covered but they
> still maintain their stylish image whilst looking very Islamic. They looked incredible
> sweeping through the store, and I thought, why isn't that ever explored here?
>
> Then I'd travel to the Middle East—Dubai—and see how the women dress up there.
> Dubai is a great inspiration. People wear mainly black so that can be restrictive but there
> are all these little details. They have black on black—patchwork, sequins, accessories
> that dress it up. They really go out of their way to dress up the black in any way they
> can, and they're very designer led, so they'll wear designer shoes and handbags, make-up

and jewellery to enhance the richness. Sometimes they can take that too far which goes against what the jilbab is about, but I like to take aspects of their dress.

In Dubai I used to stay with a really good friend, who is Hindu, and she really encouraged me when she heard me talking about my ideas. She said, 'You could really do something you know, bringing a taste of the East to the East End of London.' And I thought about it—bringing Eastern fashions to people from Eastern backgrounds who are not familiar with the possibilities. I wanted to get a feel for the East but blend it with what we have here—to be in touch with Western designs as well. What I make are feminine clothes that are practical and elegant for women who want to cover. I want to show how long flowing clothes can be beautiful and stylish, how Muslim women don't have to be dull and dowdy. They can take pleasure in their dress—look better and feel better for it … I use a variety of fabrics, lots of natural fibres and different textures—quite different from what I call the parachute fabric and polyester jilbabs you mostly see in the market round here [in Whitechapel].

What we have here is an example of an aesthetic gaze. When Yasmin looked at the Arab women parading through Selfridges, she was not disturbed by whether or not they were wearing face veils but was attracted to the drama and details of their long and flowing garments and their ability to command visual attention with an elegant and stylish swoop of black. Having had experience working on ball gowns and bridal wear, she recognized the aesthetic potential of covered dress and was aware that this was a niche market that had hardly been explored in the British context where covering was principally associated with modesty and conservatism rather than fashion. Hers was the entrepreneurial eye of an observer spotting a creative and commercial opportunity. London was full of Muslim women who covered but the clothes they wore were generally uninspiring—cheap synthetic imports from Syria and Pakistan.

Yasmin was in many ways unusually placed for her enterprise: she'd been raised in Whitechapel but had been one of the very few pupils in her school who was not Bengali; she wanted to design Islamic clothes but she herself did not wear hijab, jilbab or niqab; she had been pleased to get away from Whitechapel, which she found a restrictive environment, but it was here that she returned to open her boutique in 2005. That year she also began wearing black hijabs and jilbabs to work, partly 'to anchor the image of the shop' and partly to get a better understanding of her customers and their requirements. She had seen pride and glamour in Middle Eastern dress forms and was keen to show British Muslim women that covered dress could be beautiful, stylish, feminine, elegant and designed whilst at the same time maintaining its function as concealing and modest. It could be something people actually wanted to wear rather than merely something they thought they ought to wear. Her boutique contains a number of stylish evening garments as well as some simpler everyday wear. The materials she uses are often sumptuous, the colours sometimes bold with interesting design features incorporated into the sleeves and hem lines, some of which pick up on contemporary Western fashion trends. Asked if she thought it was important for Muslim women to look Muslim, she replied, 'Yes, but not in a political way'. For her, looking Muslim seemed to be more about identity and aesthetics than religion or politics.

But how did local women in Whitechapel view Yasmin and the glamorous covered dress she was promoting? How did they look at her? Whilst Yasmin's boutique was welcomed by many local women, some saw it as their duty to come into the shop to tell her that she should be wearing niqab. Conservative interpretations of Islamic clothing prescriptions are widespread in Whitechapel and the proximity of her shop to the East London Mosque made her an easy target for moralizing discourses. Whilst Yasmin, informed by a training in fashion design, had gained aesthetic inspiration from the stylish clothes of the Arabs she had seen in Selfridges, local Bengali Muslim women, many of whom would not be able to afford to shop in Selfridges, are more likely to have been exposed to Saudi *Wahhabi*[6] teachings than to Saudi glamour. Such teachings are propagated in books, tapes and pamphlets readily available in Islamic bookshops in Whitechapel and elsewhere in Britain and in the sermons of local and foreign imams. One such imam is the Saudi cleric, Shaykh Haitham Al-Haddad, imam of a mosque and Islamic school in Parsons Green, West London, who studied *Shariah* in the Sudan before settling in London where he is apparently completing a PhD at SOAS. A lecture he delivered on niqab at a Sisters' Event at the Brady Centre in Whitechapel in May 2007 is available on YouTube and gives a taste of the ideology and persuasive forces that encourage the spread of niqab wearing.[7]

His lecture begins with the unsubstantiated claim that all scholars agree that the niqab is either *fard* (compulsory) or highly recommended and that many consider it was the practice of all Muslim women to cover their faces in front of non-*Mehrams* (non-family members) throughout history.[8] He dismisses popular arguments that face covering was a

Figure 6.4   Lecture on niqab at the Brady Centre, Whitechapel, as shown on YouTube.

simpler garments, although she is sensitive to their tastes and has increased her production of relatively simple black clothes accordingly. Many of her customers do, however, come from farther afield—Leicester, Luton, other parts of London and beyond, although she does have a number of regular local customers who visit her boutique on a weekly basis. She likes to attract women from a whole variety of backgrounds, including non-Muslims, some of whom are attracted to the exotic Oriental feel of her boutique and the garments and jewellery it contains. Arabiannites, whilst at one level promoting full-length covered dress, stands as a subtle visual and ideological counterpoint to the austere *Wahhabi* interpretation of covering restrictions for Muslim women.

A VEILED CONTROVERSY

In October 2006, Jack Straw, prominent Labour MP and cabinet minister, published an article in the *Lancashire Guardian* in which he expressed his discomfort with niqab wearing which, he noted, had spread in recent years in his local constituency of Blackburn in the North of England. His discomfort was twofold: on the one hand he said that he had difficulty communicating with women wearing niqab and had for the past year been asking them if they would not mind lifting their face veils when they came to speak with him in his office; on the other hand he felt that the veil was a visible statement of separation and difference that made the possibility of good inter-community relations more difficult. Asked if he thought British Muslim women should remove their niqabs, he responded that whilst he did not want to be prescriptive and was against the banning of items of dress as has happened in France, he 'would rather' British Muslims did not wear the niqab and burqa, not least because facial expressions are an important element of communication.

Overnight, Straw's comments were transformed by every British newspaper from *The Guardian* to *The Sun* into an apparent command: 'Take off your veils!,' accompanied by dramatic gigantesque images of the eyes of Muslim women staring out through the narrow slits of black niqabs—images which simultaneously maximized otherness and magnified the presence of niqab. Meanwhile, newspaper columns immediately filled with a familiar set of identities and positions: the outraged liberal concerned about the infringement of human rights, the offended and defiant Muslim crying Islamaphobia, the self-righteous feminist condemning oppressive Muslim practices and various right-wing elements gloating at the controversy which they saw as proof that they had been right about 'the Muslim problem' all along. Some newspapers (*The Mail* and *The Telegraph*) framed the issue in the format of a 'Muslim problem page' in which a diverse range of stories involving Muslims were cobbled together and where even violent attacks against Muslims were somehow represented as further evidence that 'they' were causing trouble. Others filled with personal declarations by Muslim women about why they choose to cover and fears that Straw's comments would serve as a justification for racism—fears which soon appeared justified when a group of white youths tried to pull the veil off a woman in Liverpool. Key themes in the Sunday papers that week were anxieties about multiculturalism, the frustrations and demands of Muslims and feminist 'home truths'. By Monday the focus had switched to

Figure 6.5   Media coverage of 'The Jack Straw Controversy', 2006.

security (news that a British terrorist had escaped under a burqa). By Tuesday, it was talk of bans (should other institutions follow Imperial College's lead in prohibiting students from wearing face veils?), and by the following Saturday, it was concerns about education and employment law (was it right that a teaching assistant in the North of England had been sacked for wearing niqab in the classroom?). Suddenly, the minority practice of face veiling had become a carrier of the nation's ills. Everything from education, multiculturalism, security and the law seemed to hinge on this piece of flimsy fabric which was presented as the ultimate symbol of the incompatibility of Muslim and Western ideals. With this came consistent complaints of overload and excess. 'The rest of us', declared one journalist of *The Sunday Express*, 'are just tired of having Islam thrust in our faces day after day.' Even the publicity around the controversy had somehow become Muslims' fault.

Not surprisingly, the more the polemic was presented as a generalized attack on Muslims, the more Muslims took on a defensive position, many expressing outrage and blanket condemnation at Jack Straw's 'insensitive' and 'incendiary' comments. Prominent members of the MCB (Muslim Council of Britain) issued a statement urging that all Muslims, whatever their difference of opinion, should present a united front on the issue of the veil. Like other boutique owners, Yasmin Arif of Arabiannites found that the demand for niqab rapidly escalated in the days following the controversy as a number of women decided to wear niqab in solidarity with their 'sisters' under attack. Muslim women who had previously confided to me their wholehearted opposition to face veiling now spoke out on radio and television in its defence, expressing shock and outrage at Jack Straw's comments. His point about the difficulty of speaking to someone whose face was obscured was derided as irrational and absurd. Didn't we all communicate on the telephone and by Internet on a daily basis? What need had we of facial expressions in the age of virtual communications?

The media justified its excessive coverage of the story by arguing that it was airing a debate which needed to be had. But in reality, the exposure of the veil to public scrutiny seemed to have the opposite effect. Rather than airing the complex pre-existing debates taking place about niqab amongst British Muslims, it ended up totally obscuring them. What masqueraded as a debate about the veil was little more than a veiled debate which, like the niqab itself, left far more hidden than revealed.

By framing the debate as a sensationalist polemic between 'us' (the 'reasonable' Brits) and 'them' (either 'trouble-making Muslims' or 'victimized Muslims' depending on the perspective), the media not only failed to engage adequately with the very real issues raised by Straw, but also failed to acknowledge that these are precisely the issues that pre-occupy many Muslims in Britain and elsewhere around the world. Far from being an archetypal form of Muslim dress which somehow epitomizes what Islam is about, the niqab is in fact one of the most hotly contested items of dress amongst Muslims in Britain.

To gain access to the nuances of this internal Muslim debate on niqab, I turn to the Internet where, as many pointed out in response to Straw, intimate encounters and exchanges take place between people who do not rely on seeing each other's faces. And it is precisely this point that renders the Internet such a fertile space for discussions on niqab as it brings niqabi women into interaction with people they might otherwise be unlikely to encounter. Many of these discussions take place in the sisters' forums of Islamic Web sites, although they are not exclusive to women. Some men also take advantage of the opportunity to engage with niqabi women on the Web, knowing that they would be unable to have such intimate and frank exchanges with them in the flesh. What makes Internet discussion forums and threads so interesting from an ethnographic point of view is that they represent unmediated conversations between people who voice their opinions far more freely than they would if interviewed by a researcher. They also demonstrate the extent to which new technologies like the Internet assist in the decentralization and delocalization of religious authority as individuals become able to pick and choose from a wide variety of religious sources and interpretations rather than relying on the interpretations of one particular local religious leader or the views endorsed in a particular local mosque.[12] What comes across in this context is not a wall of defence about niqab but a highly complex and heated debate—mostly amongst younger generation educated Muslims from a variety of different ethnic and regional backgrounds, including converts, as they try to give shape to their ideas of Islam in early-twenty-first-century Britain and beyond. Their discussions are informed both by a combination of religious textual interpretations and practices and ideas of democracy, human rights, politics and social responsibility, reaffirming the diversity of contemporary British Muslim opinion.

PASSION, PIETY AND THE FACE VEIL—MUSLIM CONCERNS

One striking feature of discussion threads on niqab is the vehemence of the passion expressed there, both by niqab wearers and their critics. From the perspective of niqabis, what comes across is the intensity of their religious zeal, self-discipline, and in some cases, self-righteousness and their condemnation and misapprehension of those who doubt the correctness of what they are doing. Their emotional investment in niqab is countered by equally impassioned arguments against it put forward by men and women who vehemently oppose the practice. At one level, all of this might be considered just another example of how the anonymity of the Internet enables, and to some extent encourages, expressions of unfettered and heightened emotion, including rage. But the high degree of passion is also linked to the sensitivity of the subject under discussion. Although only worn by a relatively small minority of Muslim women in Britain, the niqab is the most visually distinctive and materially encompassing of all the dress practices associated with Muslims and has taken on iconic representational status, both historically and in the present.[13] For those British Muslims who perceive face veiling as alienating, regressive and detrimental to women, finding themselves somehow associated with the practice by proxy is a cause of great frustration and irritation. What they resent is the way this small minority practice takes on representational status for Islam as a whole, regardless of whether or not the majority support it. And whilst many Muslim women who are against niqab respect the rights of others to wear it, as highlighted by responses to Jack Straw's comments, they resent the inference sometimes made that by not wearing it, they are somehow less pious Muslims. Furthermore, just as many Muslim women oppose the argument that a woman's face is charged with potential sexual temptation and is therefore best concealed, similarly some Muslim men resent the implication that they are incapable of controlling their sexual thoughts and desires to the extent that they require women to cover.

The following critique of niqab posted by a young man who calls himself 'Muslim Democrat' gives a taste of the types of issues discussed by Muslims outside the mainstream media. The extracts here are taken from a discussion thread hosted by MPACUK (Muslim Public Affairs Committee, UK) in 2005, one year before the Jack Straw controversy. The thread begins with a provocative posting from Muslim Democrat:

> To sisters: Is it really necessary to wear veils covering your face? As I understand it, it is not required at all. I'll say sisters, you are making your life extremely difficult, drawing attention to yourself, disguising your identity and generally being a nuisance. Your face, sisters is who you are. When you hide your face, you hide your identity. You are nothing but a blob walking in the street, no personality, no thoughts, a statistic, a symbol of oppression. How can you get a job or anything if you don't have an independent existence, do you want to be the property of your father, your husband, your brother ... It is the antithesis of democracy and it does British Muslims especially Muslim men an extreme disservice.

Most of the women who replied to this posting were highly critical of a man thinking he had the right to interfere in the matter of women's appearances. Many defended niqab wearers on the basis that it was their right to choose such dress. The most heated defence, however, came from a niqab wearer herself—a British convert and senior activist of MPAC whose online identity is 'Hater of the Wall' and who produced principally theological arguments in favour of face covering. Below are some abbreviated extracts of her heated exchange with Muslim Democrat:

MD:	*Face the facts, covering your face in a democracy is not an option!*
HOTW:	*Brother you seem confused … democracy by definition gives women the option.*
MD:	*Another point veiled sisters: we men can control ourselves. The sight of your face, no matter how beautiful it is, is not going to make us want to seduce you, REALLY!*
HOTW:	*Your comments are regarding actual* zina *(adultery, fornication) but there is also the zina of the eyes (looking beyond accidental glance), zina of the heart (desires). Although men may be able to control themselves physically, do they (and u?) refrain from zina of the heart at all times … the wisdom of the Shariah is that all avenues to evil/sin are cut off.*
MD:	*I'm sick and tired of Westerners thinking that I, as a Muslim man, am in some way forcing women to hide themselves.*
HOTW:	*How dare you question any sister who chooses to wear niqab as an act of worship to Allah alone. How dare you question that a sister may choose to follow the Sunnah* [the examples] *of the likes of the mother of the believers, Ayesha RA … Your comments seem as if you are embarrassed … I find it mind boggling that you should question the* ibadah [worship, submission] *of another Muslim … do you fear Allah?*
MD:	*I remember not long ago it was a shock to walk down the street and see a person whose face you couldn't see—now it's just normal. Get with the program guys. We are moving ever faster into the ghetto, towards social exclusion by encouraging prejudices by the indigenous population…*
	For crying out loud—nuns wear scarves, Catholic women wear it, Jewish women wear it. NO OTHER group has women covering their faces … By the way I think you should learn something about freedom of expression … Gagging is not British and I don't think it's very Muslim either.
HOTW:	*I defend your right to speak because Allah gave you free will, but as a Muslim I abhor what you are saying because Allah gave me free will … If someone told me to give up even 1% of my* deen [religion] *to please someone other than Allah I never would even if you gave me all the gold dust on this planet…*
	I ask you to consider the following quote:
	1. Jihad al-nafs (jihad against one's lower self) 2. Jihad al-shaitan (jihad against shaitan) 3. Jihad al-fasiqueeen (jihad against wrongdoers) 4. Jihad al-kuffar (jihad against unbelievers) 5. Jihad al-munaqueen (jihad against hypocrites).

> *An American brother commented on the above on the NSA forum in 1995: '. . .*
> *She* [the covered woman] *is like the mujahid waving the flag of Islam high in*
> *the land of non-believers, in the land of Shaitan and evil-doers.*
> *It seems our niqabi sisters are stronger in character than you give them credit*
> *for. . .*

MD:
> *We* BRITISH *Muslims have a clear choice: Do we want* ALL *Muslims to play the*
> *greatest role they can in British life? To join professions, get to the Boardrooms,*
> *Media Companies and in the highest Sporting fields? . . .*
>
> *A person can, of course, wear what they want in a democracy. There will always be*
> *fringe groups, weird people who dress up strangely and are tolerated (Hell's Angels,*
> *Satanists, Hare Krishnas, Hippies etc). Is that what we Muslims are? Weird people*
> *who dress in strange ways? I do not want us to be that group. I want us to be dy-*
> *namic, productive people, people who punch above our weight economically and*
> *socially. An example to Muslims and Non-Muslims in Europe. Niqab is without*
> *doubt a problem. It is a* MASSIVE *barrier to participating fully in British life. No*
> *Government Department will employ a woman who refuses to show her face.*
> *Is it asking for the earth to ask a person to make just a small sacrifice—a tiny*
> *sacrifice, one for which you won't go to hell, so that you are and are* SEEN *to be,*
> *a* FREE, BRITISH, CITIZEN.

At one point in the discussion, Hater of the Wall suggests that perhaps Muslim Democrat was not a Muslim at all and that he should give proof of his identity by showing his
religious knowledge:

HOTW:
> *This computer forum itself is a veil behind which we all communicate unable*
> *to see the identity of each other. Therefore I seek verification . . . You call yourself*
> *Muslim Democrat. Can you kindly look through my previous posts and reply to*
> *at least the most serious of the religious issues I raised . . . i.e. can we hear a few*
> *words from the 'Muslim' not just a 'democrat'?*

MD:
> *I* COULDN'T *care less what anyone thinks about me, whether people think I'm*
> *a Muslim or not. I'm just* ONE *person, Criticise my viewpoint not me. I'm the*
> *2% minority! My skin colour and my name means I'll never hide my Muslim*
> *identity.*
> *This Forum is indeed a veil. If it wasn't I'd probably be hunted down by fun-*
> *damentalist thugs and decapitated for being a hypocrite. What a sorry state of*
> *affairs! When a person can't even discuss an issue without being labelled a non-*
> *Muslim!*

Common in discussions concerning niqab is the conflict between those emphasizing an
individual's religious path or duty and those more concerned with the wider social impli-
cations of niqab wearing. Clearly Hater of the Wall is not interested easing relationships
or opening up communication channels to others. Infused with religious zeal, she sees
herself as following in the footsteps of the Prophet's wives and striving against potential

sin and temptation in Allah's name. Muslim Democrat's arguments, which are remarkably similar to Jack Straw's, though much less delicately phrased, are entirely antithetical to her uncompromising scripturally fortified reasoning. For her the niqab is a means of establishing 'focused interaction' with God rather than other humans. But Muslim Democrat is concerned by the wider social effects of niqab on others—its potential in a Western context to make Muslims look like members of some 'weird sect'; its implication that men cannot control their lust; its association with patriarchy; its role in impeding women's economic and political participation in society; and its segregating effects on the Muslim community as a whole. His arguments also reveal how, contrary to forcing women into niqab, Muslim men can be highly critical of it. Interestingly, when asked what he thought of Jack Straw's comments about niqab, the high-profile Swiss Islamic scholar and philosopher, Tariq Ramadan, replied, 'They are the right comments made by the wrong person at the wrong time.' In his books and speeches, Ramadan calls on Muslims in the West to engage in dialogue with others and to participate in mainstream politics as modern European Muslim citizens rather than withdrawing or becoming over-pre-occupied with issues of self-protection and identity.[14]

Attitudes to niqab do not, then, follow strict gender lines. The niqab has both male and female critics and supporters. On the whole, whatever position men take in niqab discussion forums, they are usually criticized by women who resent their interference. In a discussion thread entitled 'Niqab or No' on the Shia Web site, AhlulBayt,[15] one man posted a picture of a Kuwaiti woman in an 'over the head abaya', suggesting, 'Women should wear these.' Women's responses were highly derogatory. One woman commented, 'I don't think I want that woman to appear to me at night (play the ex factor music files)!' Another replied curtly, 'I hope the same extreme modesty that you apply to your wife you apply to yourself.' In this thread, the majority of women were more critical than defensive of the appropriateness of wearing niqab in a Western country.[16] Many pointed out that it attracted rather than detracted attention, encouraged staring, and in some cases, poking and prodding, which were entirely contrary to modesty and that the niqab made communication difficult. One woman also suggested that men were even more attracted to women in niqab since they were curious to know what was underneath[17] (a comment that appears in several discussion threads and would seem to be supported by some male interventions). In other niqab discussions on the same Web site,[18] some women put forward the argument that it is not up to women to protect men from sin but up to men to control themselves. One woman also asked, 'Can we truly compare 6th century Arabs in the Arabian Peninsula to 21st century people living in the West?' Words used to describe niqab were 'drastic' and 'extreme', although some defended it as highly recommended in Islam. Here again it was noticeable that it was a white convert who is most in favour of niqab, recommending it on religious grounds and as 'a test of bravery' and arguing that 'the biggest jihad is with your own self'.[19]

Taken as a whole, the niqab threads on this site reveal the concerns of women that the niqab attracts too much attention in a Western context, that it acts as a hindrance to communication, that it can incite lustful gazes, mockery and racist attacks and that it presents a scary and off-putting image to outsiders and sometimes even to the self. Some women expressed how niqab conjured up images of Darth Veda, ninjas and balaclavas. One woman described how she was experimenting with face veiling in preparation for a trip to Saudi Arabia when she caught a glimpse of herself in the mirror and was shocked: 'My first reaction was Holy Crap!—it really scared me, believe it or not. It was like there was nothing I could relate to … nothing external to let you know what this person is about, nothing you could recognise as common between yourself and this image before you, no identity presented apart from this all enveloping black.'[20]

Yet it is precisely this aspect of screening that makes the niqab appealing to some women who describe the pleasure and security they feel in being 'protected' and 'shut off from everything outside'. This desire to protect oneself from the environment is also linked to perceptions of the environment as being fraught with danger and immorality. As one niqab wearer from Stamford Hill put it to me in an interview: 'When you see all the filth there is around you in the streets, you just think, I don't want to have anything to do with any of that.' What she sees is a world of sexual laxity, female nakedness and moral decline exemplified in posters displaying naked flesh, young girls flaunting their sexuality in tight and revealing clothes and a culture of 'reveal all' reality TV. It is a vision stimulated not just by her immediate environment but also by an ideological heritage in which the strong and pious veiled Muslim woman is pitted against the weak appearance-obsessed Western woman whose nakedness represents decadence and moral decline.[21] For her the value of niqab is not so much its capacity to protect her from the male gaze as its role as a shutter against the perceived sinfulness of British, and by extension, 'Western' society.

The sense of physical closure attained by the face veil operates both outwards and inwards. It has the effect of turning people in on themselves, enabling them to concentrate more fully on the issues of self-discipline, self-restraint, self-mastery, devotion and prayer. One chatroom participant who calls herself 'Sister in Faith' describes this process as follows: 'I think that this is the main purpose of any form of hijab [including niqab], to be constantly aware of yourself, actions and deeds and to keep them in accordance with Allah's will. Hijab is just a TOOL that makes it happen … If wearing niqab makes you feel more at one with God, in peace and more mindful of your actions then I think you are setting yourself up as a pure example for mankind.'[22] Similarly, the author, Na'ima Robert, a black British niqab wearer who converted to Islam whilst studying in East London, and now edits a religious lifestyle magazine, entitled *Sisters* (founded by Robert in 2006), links the feeling of protection offered by niqab to the sense of closeness to Allah. Her argument is cyclical. When she wears niqab, she feels Allah is protecting her because she is doing what pleases him. She sees the niqab as a chance to 'test' her strength of faith, 'do something better' and keep her 'eyes fixed on Allah'. At the same time her desire to keep her face private is matched with a certain pleasure at the sense of 'mystery' attached to the anonymity and at the fact that friends would tell her, 'You're so extra!'[23] Her account is also interesting in terms of the geography and accumulative logic of covering. It was seeing so many covered women in Whitechapel that made her begin to 'feel exposed' and gave her the inspiration to 'step up a gear' and deepen her spiritual commitment by taking covering to a different level. It was, she felt, 'the least she could do' to express her gratitude and submission to Allah. Later, she describes feeling comfortable and confident wearing niqab in 'the mini bubble that is the East End', though less comfortable with the way she is stared at and insulted in some other areas of London. She tries to combat the feelings of stigma and isolation induced by niqab by 'working extra hard' to appear friendly and get people to relate to her through and in spite of the cloth. She sees niqab wearing as an act of principle 'akin to working by a code of ethics in an unethical business environment'[24] and makes numerous public appearances on YouTube and Islamic events in which only her eyes and hands are visible. Her public image invites both criticism and admiration from other Muslims.[25]

These themes of protection, anonymity, security, self-discipline and worship are graphically described by 'Kareema', a regular participant in numerous AhlulBayt niqab discussion threads who describes herself as a white Western 'revert'[26] living in Scandinavia. She talks of the benefits of wearing niqab when she feels shy or nervous and wants to 'keep religious feeling' when walking out amongst '*Kaffirs*' (unbelievers). In spite of attracting comments like, 'Phantom Plot', she finds that beneath the niqab she is able to maintain her privacy and make *duaa* [prayers] and recite *ayas* [verses] of the *Qur'an*, thereby making the act of

Figure 6.6   Writer and activist Na'ima Robert giving a speech at the Urban Muslim Woman's Event, Marriott Hotel, London, 2008.

walking an act of prayer. At the same time, because her 'curtains are closed', she feels to some extent insulated from the negative comments and looks she attracts. She remains, however, concerned that people in the street can still see her eyes and recognize that she was 'originally one of them'. Her desire to cut off all possible channels of interaction borders on the obsessional and attracts a certain amount of criticism and concern from other discussants. She wants to cover her eyes but is unable to do so because of poor vision and the problem of her glasses steaming up. She does, however, practice lowering her gaze to prevent people from catching her eye and to conceal her feelings of happiness, sadness and anxiety. At one point, she suggests that niqab is a 'more healthy choice' than taking medicine for panic attacks and feelings of nervousness. Having constructed the world of unbelievers as a hostile and threatening environment, she talks of not wanting to 'give them a chance to comment on anything of her body or see any of her personality'. She feels that the niqab is especially necessary in a Western country where men are encouraged into perverted thinking, and she seems disturbingly pre-occupied with the fact that it is impossible to know what is going on in men's minds when they see a woman. At the same time, she describes her trials as a 'blessing' rather than a burden. The niqab is for her the ultimate act of privacy. She mentions with admiration and pleasure the fact that when she went to speak to a new Sheikh in her local area, he did not look at her at all. Complete invisibility is her expressed ideal.

Clearly, for some women, niqab wearing is an introverted ascetic practice, part of the cultivation of a pious self similar to that described by Mahmood in the context of Islamic movements in Egypt,[27] whilst for others it takes on more assertive attention seeking political connotations. What also comes across is the sense of isolation that can be induced or enhanced by niqab and the importance of the Internet for providing an intimate and legitimate space for interaction. These exchanges are often trans-national. The AhlulBayt niqab debates, for example attract participants from Britain, the United States, Canada, Scandinavia, Germany, Saudi Arabia, Pakistan and Iran. Such contact with other niqabis through cyberspace seems particularly important to people like Kareema living in contexts where there are very few niqabis. These intimate online exchanges include discussion not only of social and theological points but also of a number of practical concerns: how do you eat in niqab? How do you drink in public spaces? How do you cope with breathing difficulties and over-heating? What styles are available? Where can you obtain them? And which are best suited for wearing with glasses?

Other frequent topics of debate are the domestic and factional tensions linked to niqab: parents who object; husbands who encourage or forbid its wearing; grandmothers who refuse to accept it. On the Qatar-based Web site, Islam.Online, one distraught convert explains to a cyber counsellor that she is desperate to wear niqab but that her mother has threatened suicide if she does, and her husband thinks it better that she does not wear it at all than wear it on a part-time basis.[28] She is rather sensibly advised by the counsellor to forgo niqab in the interests of sustaining good relations with her mother. Two young Bengali women I met, who had recently come to Britain following marriages to British Bengali men in Somers Town, told me they had planned to wear niqab in London but had found that their husbands favoured a more modern image and were not even in favour of hijab, never mind niqab. Their compromise position was to dress in modest Western clothes worn with headscarves, thereby retaining their modesty but at the same time looking modern in conformity to their husbands' wishes. Sophie Woodward's intimate ethnographic study of British women's relationships to their clothes reveals how individual women's wardrobes and styles of dressing are often intimately linked to the expectations and desires of significant others with whom they have relationships, reminding us that the modification of a woman's appearance in relation to the expectations and projections of others is by no means a distinctive Muslim phenomenon.[29]

Adopting niqab for many young women means going against the crowd and for some, this may be part of its appeal. Shia girls, for example sometimes find themselves accused by their families of following *Wahabi* Sunni traditions. Many niqabis, including Kareema, claim to experience more hostility from Muslims than from outsiders. At the same time, because it is difficult to wear, it also attracts high levels of admiration from some Muslim women who admire 'the courage' of those who are 'brave enough' to wear it. Some comment with regret that they themselves lack such courage, whilst for some teenage girls the niqab figures as an aspiration they hope one day to fulfil. Whilst some niqab wearers take pride in covering their faces in all public contexts where marriageable men are present, others place emphasis on the importance of context and the impact of different visual norms prevalent in particular spaces. Several express with regret that they experience more hassle from men in Muslim countries than they do in Western countries, which leads them to conclude that whilst face covering is a necessity in Pakistan, Saudi Arabia, Afghanistan and Iran where it saves a woman from lecherous looks and verbal comment, it is a bad idea in Western countries where it is more likely to attract an unnecessary degree of attention. But here too the specificities of the local context are important. One professional Muslim woman I interviewed in Somers Town wore niqab only when going to the mosque. Though raised in Britain to liberal parents, she had married into a conservative Bengali family where her mother-in-law was opposed to women attending the mosque for worship. Wearing a niqab in this context was a means of maintaining anonymity in a conservative male-dominated mosque environment and of escaping the censure of disapproving relatives. At the Gay Pride march held in London in 2008, two lesbian Muslim women chose to wear niqab as a protective device with which to conceal their identities from disapproving friends and relatives opposed to homosexuality. Here its main purpose was to act as a form of disguise or mask.

For those who wear niqab on a more regular basis, textual religious sources and rulings are frequently invoked and play an important part in their reasoning and motivation. Whilst some of these bear witness to the popularity of austere and purist interpretations of Islam, others bear witness to the circulation of more progressive scholarly opinions. One recent discussion thread on MPACUK focused on the issue of how niqabi women reconciled niqab wearing with the widely accepted Islamic view that it is forbidden for women to veil their faces whilst performing *Umrah* and *Hajj*.[30] One participant, writing under the name, Faith28, made a number of interesting interventions in which she discussed the importance of attaining a balance between the responsibility of the individual to the self and to society. Her argument was that in a Western context it is highly recommended that a woman should not wear niqab since it increases division in society. To substantiate her view she referred to rulings made by Shaykhs in England, South Africa, Iraq and Lebanon. Unlike Muslim Democrat in the earlier MPACUK discussion thread, she made use of scholarly religious interpretations to contest conservative religious arguments. In particular, she cited the Luton-based cleric, Imam Luqman Ali, whose response to a woman who was calling for solidarity around niqab in relation to the Jack Straw controversy was:

> *I prefer to support Muslims in fulfilling the more important 'responsibility' of living and communicating the value and virtues of Islam through cultural language and conduct that is (1) comprehensible and appreciable to society at large and (2) is appropriate to time and place and (3) follows the phraseology of the Islamic story as told and lived by the Prophet (s) himself by evolving incrementally with the assimilative capacities of its adherent audience.*
>
> *These root Qur'anic principles that are borne out by the seerah of the Prophet (s) are higher in the hierarchy of principles that Islam espouses than the at best debatable subsidiary branch ruling of niqab ... Yet today the niqab and the beard and the short trousers* [for men] *are treated as if they were higher principles while the actual higher principles are neglected ...*
>
> *I fundamentally disagree that the niqab is a worthy deed, especially here in the West. Even strict scholars who support the thesis of the niqab, like Sh. Nuh Keller, counsel against it in the West due to the negative attention that it is likely to elicit. The scholars are anything but united on the issue of the niqab in terms of jurisprudence despite their reactionary and political show of unity in the face of provocation.*

When Jack Straw expressed his unease with niqab and his concerns about its visual and social effects, he was in fact raising issues of considerable unease and concern amongst many Muslims in Britain and beyond. Yet such is the political sensitivity of community relations and the political insensitivity of the British media, that far from bringing this complex and multifaceted debate to the surface, Straw's comments had the effect of bringing about a collective cover-up in which Muslim opinion became homogenized in the dual interests of Muslim solidarity and media sensationalism. Yet beyond the mainstream media in the intimate but public world of Islamic cyberspace, the issue of the place and effects of niqab in Western societies was already and still remains a subject of impassioned debate in which participants move beyond merely attacking and defending niqab towards a broader exploration of its social, moral, spiritual, political, visual and material effects.

In this chapter, I have explored these dimensions through a series of niqab-related encounters and contexts of looking. The aim was to move discussion beyond the issue of the rights of the individual to wear it towards an understanding of the role of niqab as a specific material and visual form which elicits different responses according to the contexts in which it is seen and worn. What these examples show is the futility of attempts to read fixed meanings into niqab. It is a garment which, like any other, acquires different meanings in relation to the lives of those who engage with it, whether as wearers or observers. For some niqabis, it offers safety, protection and conformity and is a question of fitting in with the crowd and maintaining a certain level of insulation. For others, it may simply be a matter of obeying the dictates of conservative religious textual interpretations. For others, it plays a more political role as a flag for Islam and a declaration of separation and difference. Yet others experience it as a tool in the cultivation of a pious and self-disciplined body and mind, a form of religious ascetic practice. Yet others may be attracted to it partly for its sense of drama or as a convenient means of attaining anonymity—a form of disguise. None of these interpretations are mutually exclusive. They form part of a repertoire of meanings and concerns experienced and expressed by Muslims in Britain and elsewhere.

Yet, whatever meanings niqab wearers may attach to their dress, the fact remains that the most distinctive aspect of niqab is the way that it conceals parts of the face in a cultural context in which facial recognition and expression are considered important elements of communication. A prominent niqab wearer like the author, Na'ima Robert, may prove through her eloquent public speeches and performances that it is technically possible to communicate to a wider public from behind a black niqab, but by her own admission, this requires 'working extra hard to get people to relate to you'. Whilst for Robert the conspicuous effacement achieved by niqab poses a challenge which seems to spur her into taking on ever more public roles, for the majority of niqab wearers in Britain face veiling is far more likely to act as a barrier to participation in public life, not only because of the restrictive patriarchal ideologies associated with it and the way it challenges normative models of communication, but also because of its physical properties as a visual and material screen.

NOTES

1. Goffman (1963).
2. Goffman (1963: 35).
3. Following a recent conference paper in which I had shown some newspaper images of women in niqab, one anthropologist from Ireland said that his immediate association on seeing the images was with Irish terrorists.
4. Ameli and Merali (2006: 37).
5. Unfortunately, when I printed this posting off the Web in July 2006, I did not make a note of the Web address and am no longer able to trace the reference.
6. The *Wahhabiyya* is a puritanical Islamic reform movement originating in the eighteenth-century Arab Peninsula. It now functions as the 'state religion' of Saudi Arabia. It propagates puritan and literalist interpretations of early Islamic texts in the attempt to replicate as closely as possible the lives of the earliest Muslims. 'Innovations' are perceived as a threat to the purity of Islam. *Wahhabi* ideas are disseminated in Britain through books, pamphlets, sermons, teachings and Internet sites. Many of these books and pamphlets are available in English translation at a very cheap

price. They usually consist of highly didactic texts concerning what is permitted and not permitted for Muslims according to religious experts' interpretations of early Islamic scholarly texts. Rulings on women's behaviour and conduct in such books are highly conservative and restrictive. Strict covering is promoted and women who do not abide to rulings on modest behaviour are castigated and often threatened with the consequence of entering Hell fire. For examples of such literature purchased in London, see, 'Women Who Deserve to Go to Hell' (Karachi 2004); 'The Hijab—Why?' (New Delhi 2002); 'The Obligation of Veiling' (USA 2003); 'The Islamic Ruling Regarding Women's Dress according to the *Qur'an* and *Sunnah*' (Jeddah 1985) and 'Islamic Fataawa Regarding the Muslim Child' (Walthamstow 2007). For critical discussion of the spread of such literature see Denis MacEoin's report, 'The Hijacking of British Islam: How Extremist Literature Is Subverting Mosques in the UK' (London, Policy Exchange, 2007).

7. Lecture delivered at a Sisters' Event by Shaykh Haitham Al-Haddad at the Brady Centre, 6 May 2007, available on www.knowledgeaudio.co.uk, also on YouTube. The lecture was delivered seven months after the Labour Cabinet Minister, Jack Straw, had publically expressed his reservations about niqab, unleashing a major media controversy and debate (discussed later in this chapter). The lecture can in this sense be regarded as a consequence and response to that controversy, although many of the ideas expressed pre-date the controversy.

8. His claim that all Islamic scholars agree on this point is untrue. There are a number of religious scholars who do not recommend niqab wearing and some actively discourage its wearing in a Western context. There are also a number of books written by women to encourage other women to dress correctly. These usually recommend that dress should be modest and that the head and body should be covered but not the face. They also base their arguments on close readings of Islamic texts and accepted scholarly interpretations but are less inclined to threaten the reader with hell than to prick the reader's conscience and dispel her doubts and 'excuses' concerning hijab. For examples see *The Hijab: Dress for Every Muslimah, an Encouragement and Clarification*, by Shazia Nazlee (Suffolk 2001); *A Muslim Girl's Guide to Life's Big Changes*, by Rayhana Khan (London 2005); *The Muslim Woman's Handbook*, by Huda Khattab (London 1993).

9. Ahmed (2005).

10. See Rozario (2006) for a feminist discussion and analysis of the recent spread of burqa wearing in Bangladesh. She argues that whilst the adoption of the burqa may seem an appealing option for some urban middle-class Bengali women, it is likely to contribute towards 'the ongoing violation of women's rights in Bangladesh'.

11. Ahmed's article on the subject is evocatively entitled, 'Tower Hamlets: Insulation in Isolation' (2005).

12. For interesting discussion of the relationship between religion and the new media, see Meyer and Moors (2006), especially the article by Hirschkind on the circulation of religious cassettes in Egypt.

13. As pointed out in the introduction, Western colonialist attitudes to the veil tended to focus on the need to rescue Muslim women from their oppressed state—an idea that was taken up by

local nationalists and feminists and continues to inform much modernist thinking about the veil. This desire to uncover Muslim women was also infused with eroticism, as evident in the considerable legacy of Orientalized paintings and literature depicting sensuous and alluring veiled Eastern women in various states of languorous recline (see Lewis 1996).

14. This was one of the key themes of his contribution to a debate on multiculturalism at the IslamExpo, held at Olympia in Earl's Court, London, in July 2008. See also his book, *Western Muslims and the Future of Islam* (Oxford: Oxford University Press, 2004).

15. 'Full Veil: Niqaab or No Niqaab', AhlulBayt Discussion Forum (2003–2005), http://www.shiachat.com/forum/index.php?showtopic=14772 (accessed 9 February 2006).

16. This may partly reflect the fact that this is a Shia Web site and some Shia consider the niqab a Sunni practice. There are, however, some niqab wearing Shia women who participate in discussions on this site.

17. In his book, *The Islamist*, Ed Husain describes how when a group of young Muslim women in Tower Hamlets began wearing face veils, it caused quite a sensation amongst 'the brothers', who on the one hand were intimidated by their apparently superior piety and on the other hand began to fall in love with them, partly because they seemed 'the truest Muslims' but also because the young men found themselves racked with a 'craving to unclothe the excessively clothed' (Husain 2007: 68–69). In one online discussion about niqab in Britain, a young man who admires niqab and advises Muslim women to wear it expressed sympathy for non-Muslims who stare at niqabis, confessing that he could not help staring at them himself. Here again one senses a mixture of admiration, wonder and thinly disguised sexual excitement in the language he employs:

> But the niqab? I wonder if it will ever reach a normative stage in society as the hijab nearly has. It is still far too shocking, far too exotic, asks far too many questions and provokes an incredible amount of emotion. Take me, for example; I will almost certainly every time look up at a woman in niqab more than any other normal non-covered girl in the street. I just will … Now that's an above-and-beyond emotional response. Also, whenever I see a sister in niqab I find myself grinning like an idiot—you know, that warm and happy feeling that only an *Iman* [faith] boost can ever provide; that mysterious rush which shares obvious parallels to your first day at work in the big multinational and you see the bearded brother at the far end of the table. And yet, there is always that added fascination with the one who wears niqab. It's such a massive step in someone's *deen*, makes such a huge difference to their entire life outside the home as one's every single action and movement comes under scrutiny. What is it that makes a person hit that level? … And this is all from someone like me! So what then from ordinary non-Muslims?!? … I don't blame them a single bit [if they stare] … It requires great character to continue as normal with someone whose face you can't even see. *Subhanallah*, most Muslims can't even do that. I know I can't.' (online response to an article on niqab published in *The Observer* in 2005, http://islamiblog.blogspot.com/2005/11/im-big-fan-of-niqab-and-almost-as-big.html)

18. See discussion threads: 'Shia Lady Using Niqab', 'Going for the Niqaab', 'Niqaab', 'How It Feels to Be an Outsider', 'Niqaab in the UK', 'Niqaab—Shia Point of View', all listed on AhlulBayt Discussion Forum, Sisters Section, http://www.shiachat.com/forum/lofiversion/index.php/t57676.html

19. In her study of niqab wearers in the Netherlands, where face veiling is practiced only by a tiny minority of Muslim women, Annelies Moors has noted the prominence of converts in niqab (personal communication, 2008).

20. See thread, 'Niqaab in the UK', AhlulBayt Discussion Forum (2005–2006), http://www.shiachat.com/forum/lofiversion/index.php/t57676.html

21. See Pedwell (2007) for discussion of the evolution of this stereotype.

22. 'Shia Lady Using Niqab', AhlulBayt Discussion Forum (2004–2005).

23. Robert (2005: 189–194).

24. Robert (2005: 196–205).

25. In July 2008 I attended a charity gala dinner entitled, 'Urban Muslim Woman's Event', at the Marriott Hotel in Grosvenor Square, London. Whilst the all-female audience was colourfully and glamorously dressed, several of the speakers, including Na'ima Robert, were clad in black wearing face veils. Two black British Muslim women seated at my table took offence to this, and one kept asking of Robert, 'Why is she wearing niqab? Why is she wearing niqab? I find it really offensive.' What they found objectionable was the implication of superior piety implied by a speaker feeling she needed to wear niqab in front of an all-female audience. The women later calmed down when they realized that the speeches were being filmed for the Islam Channel, which led to the assumption that the niqab was to conceal the speaker's face from the television audience which would no doubt contain men.

26. This term is favoured by those converts to Islam who subscribe to the assertion that all humans are born Muslim by nature, making conversion a matter of reverting back to type.

27. Mahmood (2005).

28. See 'Mom Threatened Suicide If I Keep Wearing the Niqab', http://www.islamonlne.net/QuestionApplication/English/display.asp?hquestionID=81.

29. Woodward (2007).

30. The greater and lesser pilgrimages recommended in Islam.

Figure 7.3   Homepage of thehijabshop.com, 2007.
Courtesy of Wahid Rahman.

Figure 7.4   Colour co-ordination interactive display feature.
Courtesy of Wahid Rahman.

and protest to the uplifting sound of rousing music. Clearly, thehijabshop.com is not just about the promotion of hijab *as* fashion but also the promotion *of* hijab *through* fashion.

External links listed at the bottom of the site include The Nasheed Shop (which sells religious music, opened by Wahid in 2005), adverts for Islamic men's fashions, halal skin care products, Islamic home ware and The Muslim Baby Shop (opened by Wahid in May 2007). The relationship between these various enterprises is emphasized by features like the 'Design a Baby T-shirt' competition in which customers send in ideas for designs and win a free hijab if their design is chosen. This gives Wahid a free design source whilst simultaneously drawing attention to the existence of thehijabshop.com. It also emphasizes how the relationship between production, design, marketing and consumption can be transformed through Internet technology.

Like all advertisements, The Hijab Shop's ones promise an improved lifestyle through consumer products—in this case a lifestyle that is fashionably Islamic, obtainable through the consumption of products whose Muslim credentials are visibly explicit—headscarves marketed as 'hijabs'; baby clothes with slogans like 'salam', '100% Muslim' and 'Born in a state of fitra' inscribed across them; skin care products made from 'halal' ingredients; and inspirational Islamic music.

A look at one of The Hijab Shop newsletters gives a taste of the flavour of this religious and commercial blend. The use of Arabic phrases, *Assalaamu Alaikum* [Peace be upon you], *InshalAllah* [God willing], the reference to the customer's *Imaan* [strong faith] and the plea that Allah might reward those who strive in His cause (presumably through promoting and wearing appropriate dress) all establish the Islamic credentials of the advert and provide a legitimate and worthy frame for introducing the new summer collection of hijabs.

Thehijabshop.com is by no means the only British-based Web site marketing cheap and popular Muslim fashions online, but it has undoubtedly played a pioneering role in

Figure 7.5   T-shirts from The Muslim Baby Shop.com, on sale at IslamExpo, Olympia, London, 2008.

Figure 7.6   The Hijab Shop newsletter.
Courtesy of Wahid Rahman.

offering attractive, affordable, practical clothing specifically for Muslims, favouring contemporary styles and fabrics and promoting the image of the confident and fashionable
young Muslim woman who leads an active, modern, Western lifestyle whilst at the same
time adhering to Islamic ideals of covering. The success of the site is evident not only in
its popularity and fame amongst young British Muslims and the frequency with which it

is cited in hijab blogs and online discussion threads, but also in the fact that many other entrepreneurs have since developed Web sites and products which would appear to take direct inspiration from it.

THE MAN BEHIND THE WEB SITE

Wahid is aware that most of his customers assume that he must be a woman simply by dint of the fact that he is selling headscarves but, as he points out, one of the advantages of an online store is that there is no gender segregation. The store is very much a manifestation of his personal vision, although he admits seeking advice and assistance from his sisters and now employs a young Muslim woman in his warehouse space.

Discussing his motivations for creating the company, Wahid is clear that they were both religious and commercial. He wanted to create his own business and 'make money' but he was also keen to serve what he calls 'the Islamic community':

> I wanted to do something that was also a religious thing, which was about being actively involved in the whole Islamic environment and what was happening there since 9/11, something that was about making changes. So it was either me getting involved in an Islamic organization and maybe promoting their activities through advertising or something—I still do do that kind of thing—OR it was setting up a business that would enable me to work with Islamic organizations like the MAB and IFE, to communicate with them and give something back whilst making some money at the same time. So, for example, I contribute something back by giving away 10 per cent of the profit. That's rewarding for me—to give something back to the community, not just taking away.

Wahid settled on the option of an online clothing store partly because he already had skills and experience in that domain but also because he was aware, from his own background, of a gap in the market. The Web skills he had accumulated through his job as a designer of fashion pages for the Web sites of the Arcadia Group. This had given him experience not only of fashion and marketing but also of photography, Web design, layout and maintenance. His initial idea was to market fashionably styled jilbabs that could be worn by younger Muslim women. Here he was drawing on his background as a young East End Bengali Muslim familiar with the clothing frustrations of his peers:

> There was a real problem for youngsters brought up in this country. I could see it with my sisters and their friends. Many didn't wear jilbabs because most of the jilbabs in the shops were catering for the older generation which the younger generation didn't fancy, so didn't wear. At the same time there were some sisters designing their own jilbabs but these weren't so widely accessible. So I thought I'd try branching into that and make them available over the Web.

When Wahid referred to sisters stitching their own jilbabs, he was referring both to his own four sisters and to their cousins and friends—all young British Bengali women in search of more fashionable covered dress. Some had been casually taking orders from

Figure 7.7   Wahid Rahman at work, Brick Lane, London, 2005.

friends and relatives for jilbabs to wear to weddings and other occasions. But they were not used to producing garments in bulk and Wahid did not have the resources to approach a factory with a template and commission large orders. So although Wahid's intimate local knowledge made him aware of a demand for modern fashionable, practical jilbabs for younger-generation Muslims, he did not feel able at this stage to develop the product.[4] It was then that he began to think about the benefits of focusing on headscarves instead:

> After about a year of trying to sell jilbabs, I hit on the hijab idea. I realized that the hijab is easy. It's compact, easy to stock and you don't have to worry about sizes. One size fits all. It's just a square or a rectangle, and everybody needs it, and they'll buy far more hijabs than they will jilbabs.

So the hijab was very much a business choice made for practical reasons. What is more, Wahid was able to accumulate stock with ease from his immediate environment—the shops and street stalls of Whitechapel market, which were already importing large numbers of scarves from India, Bangladesh, China and Pakistan which they sold at bargain prices. At the same time, precisely because hijabs were so cheaply available in London's many street markets, Wahid targeted Muslims living farther afield, realizing that for his business to be successful he needed to sell hijabs in places where they were not so easily available or

Figure 7.8   Shopping for hijabs in Queens Market, Green Street, West Ham, London, 2007.
Photo: Arzu Unal.

so cheap. The Web was ideal for reaching out to a wider audience, as were various Islamic events and charity functions where Wahid and his sisters would set up a stall, selling Hijab Shop scarves at discount prices and garnering publicity for the brand and Web site. Soon links to thehijabshop.com were appearing on a variety of Islamic Web sites and orders began to flow in from different locations. Wahid also established links with other entrepreneurs, some of whom would contact him, suggesting that he stock their products; others of whom he approached by e-mail after learning about their products on the Internet. It was in this context that he contacted the Dutch designer, Cindy van den Bremen, with a proposal to sell Capsters on his Web site.

Making the hijab seem fashionable and contemporary was an important priority for Wahid, partly because he knew this would appeal to young consumers but also because it was a way of encouraging young people towards hijab.

> My main intention is to make the hijab appealing whilst still sticking to the boundary of covering the neck, hair and ear. If you make it appealing, people will wear it!

His reasoning rested on the knowledge that many second- and third-generation Bengali migrants and other Muslims born in Britain were sometimes put off hijab because they felt

it looked unfashionable. They did not want to be bound by the conservative cultural practices their parents had brought with them from rural villages in Bangladesh and elsewhere.
On the other hand, they were attracted to elements of Islam they perceived to be liberating
and wanted to be able to combine their understanding of Islam with their experience of
living in the West:

> This is a generation who have seen their mothers and people back home being subservi-
> ent to men, not speaking to their husbands, spending almost all the time in the kitchen
> cooking and so on. But they themselves have been brought up in the West. They see the
> freedoms Western women have and they look at their parents and think, No, that's not
> right. But they don't want to just copy Western ways in everything either. Then they
> look to Islam and they find it's all there—women's rights, husbands having to respect
> their wives etc. So they are keen to push the Islamic side of things, rather than the cul-
> tural side, otherwise they will be digging their own graves, so to speak. The Islamic side
> is more liberating.

In Wahid's triadic reasoning[5] the 'Islamic way of life' has more in common with the
'Western way of life' than the 'Bengali way of life' but it has stricter moral tenets in terms
of the interaction between men and women and rules about female covering. A woman
leading an Islamic lifestyle so defined can be active in the public sphere, work outside the
home, be educated, follow fashion and participate in all sorts of mainstream activities, including sports, as long as she remains modest. And this is where Cindy van den Bremen's
Capsters come in. Designed for sports, using trendy materials, Capsters captured the idea
of the active modern Muslim woman that Wahid was keen to promote and this is one of
the reasons he gives them visual prominence on the homepage of his Web site.

THE WOMAN BEHIND THE CAPSTER

If Wahid inadvertently benefits from the ambiguity of his identity on the Web, so too does
Cindy van den Bremen, designer of Capsters. Although she has never presented herself as
a Muslim, many of her customers and supporters around the globe assume that she must
be one and some begin their e-mails with greetings in Arabic and with praise for the work
she is doing for her 'sisters' and for the betterment of the *deen* (religion). Honest and direct,
Cindy always responds by thanking people for their comments and by clarifying that she
is not Muslim but that she is delighted that her Capsters are a help to Muslim women.
So how did this Dutch woman who does not subscribe to any formalized religion become
involved in designing a modern-day sports hijab?

Cindy van den Bremen's engagement with hijab is no less personal than Wahid's. At
the phenomenological level, she is sensitive to the fact that some people like to cover their
heads. Sometime after she had developed Capsters, her mother reminded her that as a child
she had always insisted on wearing something on her head and used to refuse to leave the
house without a headscarf. Cindy laughs at the memory but is open to the possibility that
this may have made her sensitive to the plight of headscarf wearers. More influential is her

Figure 7.9   Cindy van den Bremen as pictured on her Web site (left) and aged seven (right).
Photos: Cindy age 7: Guus de Bruijn; Adult: Ruben Olislagers

belief in the importance of being able to wear what one wants in life without interference from others. An unflinching belief in the rights of the individual to freedom of expression lies at the heart of her interest in hijab.

This involvement began when as a student she had a Turkish boyfriend whose mother and sisters sometimes covered their heads. This roused her curiosity. It was her first direct encounter with the hijab in Holland. It was the 1990s when media debates in the Netherlands were dominated by the idea that women in headscarves were to be pitied. It was generally assumed that they were forced into covering their heads and were in need of liberation. But Cindy became interested in what the hijab meant to the people who were actually wearing it. She noted for example that her sister-in-law wore a headscarf at home in the presence of her parents-in-law as a gesture of respect for her elders. Yet she did not wear it when she went outside to visit an acquaintance in hospital, perhaps because she felt uncomfortable wearing it in a Dutch environment. This made Cindy aware that head covering was not merely about religious rules and regulations but also about contexts, interactions and relationships. Cindy also became acutely aware of the stigma attached to hijab in Holland which made it difficult for Dutch Muslims to wear it.

Observing people's responses to her own multicultural relationship and to the hijab made her keen to address issues of social integration in the BA research she was doing at college. As a design student she was expected to come up with a final project and product on which her degree would be assessed. Cindy proposed to work on the hijab, trying to resolve what she called 'its image problem in Holland' by thinking about how it might be re-designed to become better integrated with the Western wardrobe. Yet when she proposed this idea, she found her tutors sceptical and dismissive.

> They just thought they can wear a shawl in whatever material they like, with a Donald Duck print on it or whatever and that's it! They actually said that! And I was shocked. I thought, take it away from its entire context and look at it as a consumer item that has to meet certain demands. That is what we do with a cup or any other object we discuss in class when we want to work with it in design terms.

Determined to convince her tutors of the feasibility of the project, she set about researching the hijab and educating them about the problems faced by hijab wearers in Holland. She also published a book of hijab styles with extracts of interviews and quotations from Dutch Muslim women. When she visited women's organizations in Amsterdam, Rotterdam and Eindhoven she heard tales of how hijab-wearing women in Holland were stared at and insulted, of how one woman had had her hijab tied to her train seat, another had had her hijab pulled off, and others spoke of being ignored or of people refusing to sit next to them on public transport. Cindy found her discussions with these women enlightening. Far from being backwards and conservative as implied in the Dutch media, many were well-educated, outspoken and motivated by a strong sense of individual choice, religious feeling, community spirit and moral conviction and purpose. Yet however much she tried to discuss these social issues around hijab at college, she found her tutors persistently reluctant to listen.

Then something happened in Cindy's favour. She came across a case in which a Dutch girl was prevented from wearing hijab in gym classes on the grounds that it was considered unsafe. This gave Cindy a legitimate angle for her project:

> I was so pleased because this was something I could really focus on! There was a problem and I could try to solve it because there was a safety issue and this meant you could talk about it in terms of design … When I read that they were suggesting that girls wear swimming caps for gym, I thought this is not about covering at all but about the way we cover. I felt it was my duty to step in. So from then on I started to focus on sports.

Ignoring her tutors' blindness to the potential of the project, Cindy set about designing a hijab that would be in harmony with the Western wardrobe and was suitable and safe for performing sports. It had to meet Muslim womens' criteria of modesty in terms of what it covered, but conform to safety standards and be of a suitable material for sports activities. It also needed a trendy sporting image.

Cindy designed six prototypes, four of which she went on to develop. Each was designed to capture the image and ethos of a particular sport such as aerobics, tennis, skating or golf.

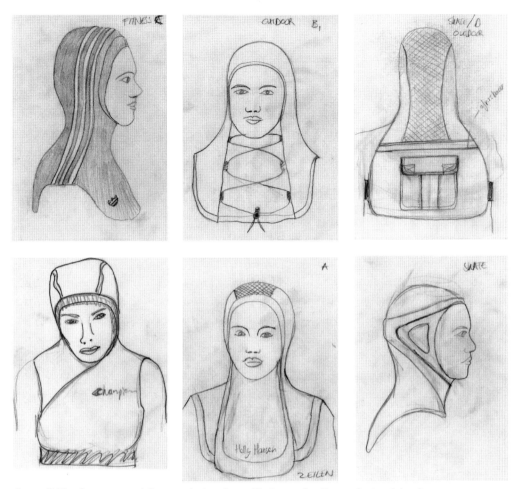

Figure 7.10   Prototypes of Capster designs from Cindy van den Bremen's sketch books.
Courtesy of Cindy van den Bremen.

She made sketches, matching particular colours and fabrics to each design using contemporary materials such as polyimide, polyester and elasthan, which gave the garments flexibility and stretch. She then returned to the Muslim women she had interviewed earlier to obtain wearer's knowledge and feedback. They gave her both encouragement and critical suggestions on which she based subsequent modifications. The large zipper she had incorporated in the 'outdoor model' was for example replaced by a Velcro fastening which women felt would be more comfortable. Cindy displayed her products at her graduation show and was awarded her degree without undue fuss. However, the next day she received a call from a journalist who wanted to write something about her designs. From that day onwards she became a prominent participant in debates about Muslims and integration in the Dutch media as well as receiving individual requests and orders for her designs from around the world. Alongside developing Capsters as a company, she has played an extremely active role in informing the Dutch public about hijab through publications, lectures, public debates and exhibitions. In this sense the Capster, like Cindy, has become a material ambassador for multiculturalism. It sits on display simultaneously at the Sharjah Museum of Islamic Civilization in the United Arab Emerates and at the Museum of Modern Art in New York.

In 2008 Cindy launched a new range of Capsters, expanding her repertoire to include 'casual' and 'exclusive' wear. The casual range includes a 'basic' model (slip-on black cotton hijab with Velcro fastening)—a response to requests from many Muslim women for something plain and black; a 'jeans' model, made from dark blue denim-look stretch cotton designed for a 'hipper' look; and an 'easy' model made from cool lightweight two-tone white and beige fabric, a response to requests from women in Singapore and Malaysia who wanted light, breathable head coverings. All are in keeping with the original ethos of Capsters, which provides practical modern solutions to covering which integrate with a Western wardrobe. On The Hijab Shop Web site these new designs are classified as 'easy-wear hijabs', ideal for 'active or busy Muslimas'.

Cindy has greatly valued her close contact with Muslims in Holland and elsewhere, but she also recognizes the discrepancy between her own liberal multicultural values and motivations and the hope of many of the Muslim women with whom she is engaged that she will convert to Islam. Just as her tutors had refused to see the broader social relevance of her project, so some Muslims are reluctant to accept that her interest in hijab is not based on a personal religious quest. Cindy did seek religious approval for her designs from an imam in Holland in order to make sure that they satisfied certain Islamic criteria of modesty, but she makes it clear that she has no intention of converting to Islam. For her, 'Capsters' was never a religious project. It was about addressing social issues, breaking down barriers and prejudice, encouraging diversity-based integration through design without forcing people to abandon their own terms of reference.

> The biggest compliment I got was from a woman in New York who was working and studying at University. She said, 'With your designs I show people I am willing to integrate with my own norms and values, my own set of beliefs' and that is actually what I had in mind when I made my designs.

But the Capster is also a piece of headwear which can be worn by anyone who wants to wear it, and for this reason on her own Web site, www.capsters.com, Cindy does not present it as a Muslim garment but as a practical piece of headwear which has its origins in the attempt to solve the problems faced by Muslim girls at school. When she receives e-mails saying, 'But you forgot about the Jewish market' or 'You forgot about the cancer patients', she replies that she did not forget about anyone, for Capsters are for anybody who wants to wear them. This includes her father who wears one when cycling on cold winter nights. This flexibility and openness is also captured in the recently launched 'lady' design, which is a gathered wrap which can be worn either over the head where it takes on the look of a hijab or simply draped on the shoulders where it functions as a wrap. In other words, whether or not it looks Muslim depends not on the garment's structure but how it is worn, by whom and in combination with what.

Cindy's non-sectarian approach to design was visible in her office in 2005 when the walls were decorated with three large Hindu calendar posters and she was working on producing a 'Hindu Inspiration Book'. Since this time, alongside developing and expanding Capsters, she has been working on ideas about how to 'adapt the sari into a more wearable form'. This design project was bound up with the re-generation of a poor run-down market area in South Rotterdam where cheap imported cloth from various Eastern countries is purchased mainly by people of Indian, Afghan and Moroccan origin but where those living outside the area rarely ventured. By buying cheap cloth in the local market, getting it stitched and embroidered by women through local community and mosque groups, then re-sold back in the market, Cindy's aim was to simultaneously improve trade for local merchants, encourage local women from migrant families to earn money and use their skills, and contribute to the improvement of the image and reputation of the market, making it more appealing to a broader range of consumers. Most of the designs use and re-work elements of Indian saris and Pashmina shawls into simple garments that are not directly associated with any particular religious or ethnic group but could be worn by anyone. They are garments grounded in an ethos of cultural diversity. In this sense Cindy's projects differ strongly from Wahid's more religious and sectarian approach to commerce. For him, the Capster is above all a sports hijab which carries with it modernist Muslim values and ideals. Cindy strongly believes in people's right to hold such values but she does not share them.

HEADSCARVES WITHOUT HEADS

Throughout the four years I have been following the progress of thehijabshop.com (2005–2009), Capsters has always featured on the homepage of the online store. Wahid considers them good for attracting attention partly because they are unusual designs which fit his

Figure 7.11   Capsters: outdoor, tennis and skate (left to right).
Photos: Peter Stigter. Courtesy of Cindy van den Bremen.

modernist ethos, but also because the professional photographs of models wearing them are eye-catching and appealing. The photos were commissioned by Cindy, using models of different ethnic backgrounds to convey a sense of the diversity of people who can wear the garment. This fits Wahid's desire to convey how Islam transcends narrow ethnic boundaries and has universal appeal. But in marketing Capsters as a 'revolutionary range of hijab' rather than as a religiously neutral form of headwear, Wahid also faces the problems and constraints of advertising in an Islamic milieu.

One of the challenges facing thehijabshop.com is how to advertise headscarves in such a way as to make them look attractive without at the same time drawing inappropriate attention to women's faces. The conservative solution to this problem is to advertise headscarves without heads. This technique is often found in Islamic shops which specialize in religious commodities from books, perfumes, tapes to dress and calligraphy. Here hijabs in sober colours can usually be found piled up in a corner at the back of the shop along with a few jilbabs and abayas displayed on hangers. It was also the solution favoured on most Islamic Web sites in 2004 when Wahid first started his business. Headscarves would be displayed either flat, folded, draped or photographed on models from behind, but Wahid felt such advertising would fail to evoke the fashionable and modernist image he was keen to convey and would not attract Muslim youth. Furthermore it went against his experience as a designer of fashion Web pages to show headscarves without heads. He therefore hit on the compromise solution of advertising his hijabs on a plastic mannequin whose pale skin and blue eyes also suggested a departure from traditional images of Muslim women. However, his choice was not entirely appreciated by all who visited the Web site. In 2005 he told me:

> One of the problems I have at the moment is that we have a plastic mannequin on the site. She is slightly pretty with make-up on and some sisters have taken objection to that, saying the hijab is not to beautify you but to keep you modest. My reply to that is that we want to make the hijab attractive so that more people will be encouraged to adopt it. So we don't want it to look black or dull. And that in the end is why most people won't wear it—because it looks so boring. If you make it appealing, then they might take the example of wearing. So I think the good outweighs the bad.

Such reasoning does not go down well with strictly orthodox Muslims, nor indeed with people (both Muslim and non-Muslim) who are opposed to the hijab altogether and who e-mail Wahid expressing their opposition to his entire enterprise. Whilst Wahid cannot do much about the latter, he remains sensitive to the concerns of the former whilst at the same time wanting to pursue his aim of enhancing the appeal of hijab for religious and commercial purposes. His decision to reproduce on his Web site images of live models wearing Capsters supplied by Cindy van den Bremen resulted in him having to devise a split advertising strategy:

> I use the sporting pictures because these attract more attention because they are modelled on real people. But then again there are groups who have complained. The sporting

SHOPPING

pictures were done in Holland using professional models who were non-Muslims and who had plucked eyebrows. So some have said to me, what are you doing? That's not what it's about. And obviously in religious terms you are not allowed to shave your hair, and it's quite obvious that these models have got plucked hair. So some Muslim media have rejected my advert showing the sporty hijab, and some have even rejected my advert showing normal hijabs on plastic models—they know they are going to get lots of complaints from others. So what they do is blur the face out. So now I say to them, I'll pay you this much for an advert with the face included, but I'll pay you a lower rate if you obscure the face because obviously the advert will get less attention. So now we have two sets of adverts!

Wahid laughs good-humouredly as he recounts all of this. He wants to encourage confidence and creativity and is happy to see that his own sisters have become adventurous in their hijabs over the last three years. At the same time he constantly has to ask where to draw the line between fashion, fun and religious propriety.

I did have a section on the Web site called 'Wild'. It had a cheetah-tiger sort of motif with dots, you know, drawn from wildlife. So I'd put it on the site as 'wild' as in 'wild-life'. But sisters took it to mean 'wild' as in the Western sense of the term, being wild! I just thought, OK, [he laughs some more], I'll go back to calling it wildlife!

At the other end of the spectrum, Wahid does not want to pander to those he calls the 'hard-line jihadist types'. Whilst he advertises his products in a large range of Islamic contexts, Web sites and events, there are some events he avoids for their aggressive or militant associations.

We try to be moderate and encourage people to be modest. We encourage them into hijab and then maybe once they are wearing it, they will find themselves attracted to hijab. It's more important to get people into the fold and then work on them maybe. Some people see our mannequins, think they look nice and realize that they too can look good in hijab … One woman e-mailed me, 'I never wore hijab before. But seeing your site makes me realize that actually you can look good with hijab without looking backward' … so when I read things like that, it encourages me, makes me feel that I'm on the right track!

A constant stream of Internet feedback from clients and others who surf on the site keeps Wahid alert as to how far he can push the boundaries and his sensitivity to both fashion trends and religious concerns seems to have paid off. By 2007, three years after launching The Hijab Shop, Wahid was no longer having to blur the faces in any of his headscarf adverts, and was getting away with displaying a wider and wider variety of ways of tying hijab on the mannequin, working on the basis that way-out styles would attract attention. In this he was influenced by his knowledge of the workings of the fashion industry.

I've been experimental on the site. I've had a few complaints but not too many. I mean, when you go to the cat walks in Western fashion, you don't expect people to actually wear what you see displayed, some of which is quite bizarre. So I'm using displays as a way of sparking comments and reaction, a kind of publicity but I've not gone too far.

Despite playing safe, Wahid has, over the three years since opening, gradually slackened his criteria of covering in line with what he thinks he can get away with without causing too much offence. He is still fastidious about keeping the neck of the mannequin covered but the length of the hijab has decreased in some images:

I don't always cover the chest but the main excuse I use is that we are selling the garment so we need to show as much of it as possible. If we do go too far down on the chest then

Figure 7.12   Hijabs, thehijabshop.com.
Courtesy of Wahid Rahman.

it will cut off some of the garment. That satisfies the crowd who complain that it has to cover the chest, but I still like to play quite safe. I don't expose the neck and ear. But I do get quite a lot of e-mails asking, how can I wear my hijab so that I can still show my earrings. I tend not to answer that one! They could dangle some hijab pins from the scarf I suppose!![6]

The success of The Hijab Shop has, he feels, sparked a number of other sites to follow his example. Blurred faces are getting less and less common and sites which rejected mannequins two years before are now using them. In this sense Wahid sees his shop as gradually pushing the boundaries of what can and can't be worn, encouraging a gentler interpretation of Islamic restrictions and blurring the boundaries between Western fashion and Islamic dress. A new range of jilbabs that he has been advertising since 2007 captures this two-way interplay between Western and Islamic trends.

JILBABI STREET FASHION

Jilbabs on the market in shops and street stalls of Whitechapel are mostly imported from the Middle East. They are usually made of synthetic material and are predominantly black, often displaying a little embroidery or beadwork on the sleeves, neckline and hemline. Although these were not generally worn by Muslims in rural Syhlet, they have become popular amongst married Bangladeshi women in the British context where many have been exposed to conservative interpretations of Islamic requirements of modesty and prefer to be cautious when venturing out in public. Many younger-generation Muslims are not attracted to such garments precisely because of their restrictive and conservative and traditionalist associations. It was, as we have seen, Wahid's awareness of this that lay at the heart of his online commercial venture.

It was therefore with considerable enthusiasm that Wahid heard a radio advertisement for a new modern, trendy, Western-styled jilbab that had been developed by two British Muslim entrepreneurs who were in search of retailers willing to stock their garments. It is this new range of jilbabs developed by Silk Route, and classified as 'sportswear', 'casual' and 'workplace', that now occupy a prominent place in thehijabshop.com Web site. These trendy new-look jilbabs differ from their Middle Eastern counterparts in several ways: they are made from materials such as cotton, canvas, airtex, jersey fabric and terricotton. Their cuts are simple and they incorporate design features which place them squarely within the category of urban street fashion: piping which mimics track suits, hoods taken from hoodies, metal zippers recalling combat gear, pockets for keeping mobiles and even slashes which play on the ripped effect popular in some street fashion. As such they also differ considerably Yasmin Arif's more exotic and feminine jilbabs designed for slightly older consumers.

Whilst the idea for the jilbabs came from two London Muslims, the designers were non-Muslim students from the London School of Fashion who had experience working for the popular fashion stall, H&M. Their brief was not so much to adapt a Muslim garment to Western criteria but to adapt Western fashions to suit Islamic criteria. They were provided

Figure 7.13   Silk Route sports jilbabs, as advertised on The Hijab Shop Web site.
Courtesy of Wahid Rahman.

with pictures taken from a variety of Western magazines which specialized in youth fashion
and told to adapt the garments in such a way as to cover arms and legs and de-emphasize
the body shape. Some of the jilbabs they came up with literally mimicked the effect of
wearing a two-piece skirt and blouse. These trendy urban styles are very clearly a new Western Islamic invention. In 2007 they were produced in bulk in Bangladesh and retailed at
£30–£35 a piece. The Silk Route Company has more recently shifted production to Egypt
in the interests of proximity and efficiency.

Wahid advertises the sports jilbabs with trainers and accessories such as footballs but,
he suggests, it is unlikely that women will perform sports in these garments. Like many
of the sports-inspired high street fashions on which they are based, they are more about
a sporty image than about sport. They are also, of course, about carrying the messages of
modesty and faith in a new contemporary form that enables the wearer to affiliate with
street style rather than take distance from it. It is precisely this aspect that is captured in
a short film advertising the product, made by the producers, The Silk Route Company,
in 2007, and supported by thehijabshop.com. The advert begins by evoking a scene of
Islamic fellowship with hands dipping into a collective meal of Eastern dishes. One hand
belongs to an attractive young woman dressed in a plain black jilbab and hijab who gets
up and embraces her mother before venturing out into the city of London. As she walks,
she leaves her imprint on the urban landscape in the form of printed messages. First, the
word 'modesty' appears on the graffiti-studded brick wall as she walks past, then, the words
'a new look' are printed on the bridge she crosses. Next, we see her strolling first through
a largely Bengali area of London, signalled by Muslim men with caps and white beards,
and emerging in a more upmarket commercial area. Here, she looks up and sees an advertisement which shows a model wearing one of Silk Route's trendy jilbabs with the words,
'a new look to modesty' inscribed. The girl sees her own image in the poster, and later
emerges transformed and smiling from the poster, dressed in a beige hooded jilbab and

off-white headscarf. She has been transformed from 'traditional' Muslim girl in black to trendy, modern, urban Muslim girl. She now walks with an added swing to her gait, as the advert draws to a close with the honeyed voice-over: 'Silk Route. The new look to modesty. Available from thehijabshop.com'.

The advert firmly fixed the new jilbabs as a form of trendy cutting-edge urban clothing. In 2007 it was available for viewing on Silk Route's own Web site. But Wahid did not include it on his own Web site owing to vehement objections from some quarters about the full body shots of the woman emerging from the poster. And this is where Wahid puts himself in a difficult position. On the one hand, he wants to promote jilbabs by making them trendy. On the other hand, many of the women most likely to be attracted to wearing jilbabs are likely to be fairly conservative in their views on modesty. For this reason, he cannot justify showing the faces of the models wearing jilbabs on his Web site. Whereas with hijabs and under-bonnets he can argue that it is necessary to show the face of the mannequin in order to demonstrate how the products look when worn, with jilbabs the face is not necessary for seeing how the garment looks. In 2007, Wahid told me:

> I must say I would rather show the faces of the models. It looks much nicer cos you get the whole package, the whole outfit, but I think people are reluctant still. It will change, but not yet. I think by next year I might be able to get away with showing the face!

On my last visit, Wahid's warehouse was stocked high with jilbabs, following a recent order of £40,000 worth of stock. One of his most popular styles was the slashed rip-effect black-and-grey jilbab, suggesting that there is indeed a new market for trendy Western jilbabs amongst British Muslim urban youth.

THE INTIMACY OF THE INTERNET

Cindy van den Bremen and Wahid Rahman undoubtedly have different objectives but their enterprises are intimately interconnected. Without Cindy's Capsters, Wahid's Hijab Shop would draw less attention, look less trendy, and have a more conventional feel. But the benefits are mutual. Without Wahid's Hijab Shop, Cindy's access to Muslim consumers would be more limited. Wahid is her most significant retailer and the popularity of his stall amongst Western Muslims gives her Capsters a high profile and a guaranteed audience. Furthermore, by being advertised in a Muslim milieu, their appeal to the Muslim consumer is inevitably enhanced. Meanwhile, the trendy modern jilbabs from Silk Route that Wahid advertises on the site no doubt add further appeal to the Capsters by reinforcing the legitimacy of Muslim urban youth wear.

Some might be tempted to see Wahid principally as a religious activist and Cindy as a social campaigner but the market fuses their projects and agendas. Though their philosophies and intentions differ, both participate in the wider project of promoting both diversity and integration by expanding the culturally sensitive options available in the market. Their aim is to deflate exaggerated claims to difference between Muslims and non-Muslims, whilst at the same time respecting the right to difference; in Cindy's case through education, communication and the development of safe, practical and trendy headwear which covers what many Muslims feel they need to cover; in Wahid's case by making garments with strong traditionalist associations more acceptable, fashionable and appealing to urban youth who wish to express their religious identity and uphold standards of modesty whilst participating in mainstream fashion. Both, through marketing products, are also concerned about changing societal attitudes—hence Cindy's participation in public debate through exhibitions and talks and Wahid's participation in Islamic charities and events. This interpenetration of objectives has been made possible by the Internet, which makes the activities of one man at his computer in East London and one woman at her computer in Eindhoven accessible to one another.[7]

At the same time the Internet makes these two individuals, both of whom are motivated by personal circumstances and local conditions, open to a wider unbounded public sphere. Both have been approached by public bodies who recognize the potential of finding material and sartorial solutions to social issues relating to Muslim participation in the public sphere. For example in 2003, Cindy was approached by the Justice Department of the Dutch government in relation to a case where a Muslim prison guard wanted to be able to wear the hijab at work. Her employer objected on safety grounds, arguing that there was a risk of strangulation but after conducting some research on the subject, realized that they did not have a right to refuse her request as uniform regulations for prison staff did not specify anything about headwear and footwear. This meant they would need to permit her to wear something, and they approached Cindy for possible designs. She developed something similar to her aerobics Capster which was tested for its conformity to fire, hearing and safety regulations. But before the Justice Department had taken any decision on the issue, Cindy's intervention was leaked to the press by a journalist with the result that she found herself on the front pages of the Dutch newspapers for several days, discussing heated issues relating to social, ethnic and religious integration and the neutrality of the Dutch state. At the same time, Cindy has been keen to participate in the international Muslim media when approached. For example in 2004, she participated in an online dialogue in the Qatar-based Web site, islamonline.net, where she responded to questions from Muslims around the world.[8] She has also been invited to participate in a fashion show in Saudi Arabia and her work has been exhibited in museums in Sharjah, New York and Rotterdam.

Wahid has also been approached by several outside bodies. In 2007, the Islamic Human Rights Commission, based in London, asked him to attend a meeting regarding the possible development of a hijab for use by Muslim women in the army. Similarly the director of Human Resources for the Edmonton branch of Ikea in North London came across thehijabshop.com when trying to find a suitable uniform option for South Asian and Muslim staff. They wanted him to design a whole outfit for Asian Muslims, but Wahid said he would focus just on hijab. He produced a two-piece stretchy slip-on navy blue bandana and headpiece combination with yellow piping and Ikea embroidered in yellow on the back. Press coverage of the Ikea model is posted on his Web site and has attracted the attention of Ikea HR staff in Australia and Canada to whom he has sent samples on request.

In this way, the garments marketed by Cindy and Wahid participate not only in the creation of new forms of Muslim visibility in the public sphere, but also the visual transformation of that public sphere. For example in the televised publicity for the Beijing Olympics, a tennis player wearing an aerobics Capster was seen on Dutch TV twice daily in the summer of 2008—thereby normalizing the idea of the active, modern hijab-wearing Muslim sports woman and including the Capster into the range of internationally accepted sportswear options for women. Cindy and her business partner are also developing co-operation with Women Win, an international women's fund which seeks to empower women through sports and has so far sponsored sports projects in Kenya, the Congo, Palestine, Malaysia, Morocco and the Netherlands. In the future Capsters will sponsor Women Win sports events and will supply Capsters at special rates to participants, thereby putting its philosophy into action and simultaneously spreading the brand name of Capsters internationally.

Whilst participating in the public re-coding of hijab, the work of Cindy and Wahid is simultaneously invested with highly personal meaning, not only for themselves as designers and retailers but also for consumers. Both find themselves recipients of e-mails from clients who share their intimate clothing dilemmas and identity concerns over the Internet. This chapter ends with a few extracts from Cindy van den Bremen's extensive mailbox, which gives a taste of the nature and geographic span of such correspondence:[9]

> *From the Netherlands:* I am very surprised to see this. Really it's great! I am a Muslim girl and I couldn't do any sport because of regulations of the school board. Really keep on doing this! Thank you!

> *From Los Angeles:* As a Muslim in America, every day seems to be an opportunity to share truths about Islam and abolish false stereotypes. Nevertheless the media has the power in their hands. My largest battle is my own family of Catholics … To share with you, wearing hijab is quite difficult for me brought up as I was. I wear it to Islamic events yet only on a few occasions do I wear it out in public. When I have, everyone notices me … I'd like not to stand out in a crowd as a Muslim, yet I do want people to know that I've made this decision and am so happy to finally uncover the truth … I am interested in the tennis and aerobics hijabs. Can you order hijabs in different colours?

> *From Canada:* There is a small group of ladies of whom I am a member. We are trying to print a poster on Muslim women to distribute around the city (Oakville, Ontario) in places like women's shelters, clubs and so forth. The poster is a form of *dawa* [drawing people to the faith] and good propaganda on the rights of women in Islam especially after September 11th … We need good photos of women in hijab (specially modern hijabs) … would it be possible to use at least one photo from your collection to promote Islam?

> *From school teacher in Connecticut:* I have a young Turkish Muslim woman in my class who wants to play basketball. Her loose headscarf presents a problem and she wants to

find something like the headscarves pictured in your article. Can you recommend where we can find some of the headscarves you have designed?

From South Africa: I live in a Western society in South Africa. It is a society where people do not understand Islam probably due to years of apartheid. I am fairly athletic by nature. I would find people staring at me while I was lifting weights in the gym, in a previously male territory … I am especially grateful to you designing these athletic scarves as it means a lot to me.

From Sydney, Australia: I think your idea is great as we girls in Australia have been looking for a solution to the problem of playing sports in a headscarf.

From Dusseldorf, Germany: First congratulations for your good idea designing headscarves for Muslim women. My sporting activities are exercises in the gym and horse riding and a traditional headscarf is really uncomfortable for that.

From Britain: I am a convert of seven years and have worn hijab ever since … What I found particularly attractive in your collection is how it integrates perfectly with the urban wear that is now so pervasive, thereby making it not only fashionable but also practical.

NOTES

1. Bunt (2003).
2. See Tarlo and Moors (2007) for a collection of articles on Islamic fashion around the world. See especially articles by Jones on Indonesia, Sandikci and Ger on Turkey and Abaza on Egypt. See also Navara-Yashin (2002) for discussion of the emergence of the Islamic fashion industry in Turkey.
3. The hijab pin has undergone rapid elaboration and diversification in recent years, now featuring as an elaborate piece of jewellery in its own right in many women's headscarf arrangements. For a taste of the range of hijab pins, broaches and chains available, see the Web site, PinzPinzPinz.com, first established in 2001. The site also features a hijab pin blog.
4. Wahid, like Yasmin Arif (chapter 6), was picking up on the unfashionable nature of many of the jilbabs locally available in Whitechapel, but in contrast to Yasmin, whose designs mostly have a strong Eastern flavour, he was in search of something more modern and Western that would be popular with a younger consumer.
5. Wahid's articulation of the problems faced by young British Muslims bears a striking resemblance to Gerd Bauman's articulation of 'the multicultural riddle' as a struggle between attempts to establish identity and rights on the basis of religion, ethnic identity and national identity (Bauman 1999). The way out of this triangle of apparently competing values is, according to Bauman, the promotion of internally plural praxis. Though he seeks to down-play the Bengali in favour of the Islamic, Wahid's Hijab Shop is in many ways an example of plural praxis. Unlike the interpretations of Islamic dress put forward by Hizb ut-Tahrir (chapter 5) and by Salafi

scholars (chapter 6) in which the aim is to eliminate all Western elements, Wahid's aim is to integrate Western and Muslim elements, demonstrating their compatibility.

6. Wahid is aware that most customers assume he must be a woman. He maintains this ambiguity by signing all messages on the Web site with the phrase, 'The Hijab Shop team'.

7. When Cindy and Wahid finally met for the first time in 2008, both were surprised to find the other quite different from what each had imagined the other to be like.

8. 'Designing Hijab for Integration', Live Dialogue Session, http://islamonline.net/livedialoque/english/browse.asp?hGuestID=UuMgyl (accessed 2 March 2005).

9. I am extremely grateful to Cindy van den Bremen for giving me access to the files of correspondence she has received from Muslims around the world, and to her own e-mailed responses to their comments. In the interests of maintaining the anonymity of clients, all names have been excluded.

8   ISLAMIC FASHION SCAPE

Is it possible to look both fashionable and Islamic? Ask that question to young British Muslim women today and many would almost certainly answer 'yes'. For some 'Islamic fashion' means wearing fashionable clothes 'Islamically', by which they mean in conformity with covering restrictions based on interpretations of Islamic texts. For others it means selecting from a new range of clothes designed and marketed specifically as 'Islamic fashion'. For many, it means a mixture of both. In an American Islamic fashion blog, launched in 2007 and 'dedicated to stylish Muslima', it is defined as follows: 'By Islamic fashion I mean clothing designed specifically with Muslim women in mind and other clothing that can be 'Islamized'.[1] Such a definition would have been unthinkable just one decade ago when most young Muslims living in Britain and other Muslim minority contexts in the West would have perceived the 'fashionable' and the 'Islamic' as being in tension, if not downright incompatible. Some British Muslim women did of course experiment with adapting Western fashion garments and wearing them in conjunction with hijab (see chapter 2), but they probably would have perceived themselves as fashionable Muslims rather than wearers of something called 'Islamic fashion'.[2] If such women wanted to wear explicitly 'Islamic' garments, then they would have been faced with two options: either purchasing jilbabs and abayas directly from or imported from the Middle East (available in mosque stores and Islamic shops usually run by men and specialized in the sale of religious items) or alternatively, stitching their own outfits. Neither of these options are likely to have been perceived as fashionable. The imported jilbabs looked distinctly foreign. They were usually black, made from thin fabrics ill-suited to the British climate and were often poorly stitched and stylistically incompatible with and impervious to the cycles of change intrinsic to the fashion system. The home-made option offered more potential for experimentation, but unless the person was particularly talented not only in stitching but also in design and innovation, she would have been unlikely to produce garments that would be perceived as fashionable. Such garments had yet to be imagined in the Western context. Furthermore young Muslims even one decade ago were generally less preoccupied both with the issue of covering and the idea of visual distinctiveness. Those women and girls who did wish to dress modestly and visibly express their identity and faith turned to the headscarf rather than to entire outfits which might be identified as Islamic.[3]

Today, however, a young woman who wishes to dress both fashionably and Islamically is confronted with a huge variety of sartorial possibilities in what might be described as a rapidly expanding Islamic fashion scape. This visual and material landscape is extensive and varied, combining both the local and the trans-national in particular ways. It does not exclude the mainstream fashions of the British high street but incorporates and re-works them. Young visibly Muslim girls know where and how to seek out garments which can be made compatible with Islamic constraints. They know which boutiques stock a good range of long-sleeved polo neck tops suitable for wearing under sleeveless dresses; which seasonal collections contain clothes good for layering and most in tune with Muslim tastes; which shops offer an interesting range of 'hijabable' scarves, headbands and shawls; and which 'ethnic markets' offer the latest and best-priced range of imported cloth, clothing, jewellery and accessories that might be incorporated into new Islamically aware outfits. Not only do they gain inspiration from what they see worn by other young Muslims in cosmopolitan cities and, in some cases, from travels abroad, but they can also glean ideas and advice from the rapidly expanding Muslim media, whether this be British Muslim lifestyle magazines such as *Emel* (launched in 2003) and *Sisters* (launched 2007), Muslim TV channels such as the Islam Channel which covers Muslim news and events in Britain and around the world, hijabi fashion blogs and discussion forums which offer advice on fashion matters and the increasing number of online boutiques displaying and marketing a new range of garments often classified specifically as Islamic fashion wear. They can also attend an increasing range of local Islamic events as well as high-profile international events, such as IslamExpo and GPU (Global Peace and Unity), both massive annual fairs held in London which attract thousands of Muslims from all over Britain and around the world to celebrate and trade in all things Islamic.[4] This includes a wide range of consumer goods, many of which are newly classified as Islamic, from halal marshmallows to hijab pins, Islamic financial products to children's stickers, chocolate Ramadan count-down calendars to talking Muslim dolls, Islamic literature, art and music to Palestinian soap and olive oil. Such events confirm London's place as an important node in the global distribution of Islamica as goods and ideas pour into the capital from around the world, and are in turn taken up and re-worked in other parts of Britain and Europe as well as in Muslim majority countries.

Such events are also an ideal place for consumers to scout out the latest Muslim fashion trends and for entrepreneurs, traders and designers to assess the marketplace, make contacts, pick up on new trends, launch new products and think about new ideas. At IslamExpo 2008, held at Olympia in Earl's Court, not only were there a number of stalls displaying and selling fashionable clothing and accessories explicitly marketed as Islamic, but there was also an Islamic fashion show staged thrice daily over the weekend in which the work of British Muslim designers was modelled in the secluded space of a women's only tent set up in the main exhibition hall. The huge queues of women jostling for admission at every session seemed to bear witness to the growing thirst and enthusiasm for what has become known as Islamic fashion.

The emergence of Islamic fashion designers and collections in the West can at one level be understood as part of a wider process whereby Muslim dress practices are undergoing new re-configurations in a global market. In Muslim majority countries like Egypt and Turkey, the adoption of Islamic dress in the 1970s and 1980s was at first a response to increased secularization imposed by the state whilst in countries like Indonesia and Mali, it became a means by which more strictly practising Muslims differentiated themselves from others they considered insufficiently Islamic. Whilst the turn to Islamic styles in such cases initially represented a self-conscious rejection and critique of fashion in favour of a purer and simpler understanding of Islamic authenticity, it did not take long before new markets emerged selling more elaborate forms of covered dress which soon became known as 'Islamic fashion'.[5] Elsewhere Annelies Moors and I have discussed the complex criss-crossing geographies of the global Islamic fashion scene as designers and entrepreneurs seek inspiration and new markets in different regional locations.[6] Hence whilst designers in Mali often turn to francophone Africa, Dakar and Abidjan for inspiration, designers in Egypt may look to India, Lebanon and Morocco as well as London, Paris and Milan. Meanwhile in South India and Yemen, black abayas imported from Saudi Arabia are considered an important component of the fashionable cosmopolitan Muslim wardrobe, even if the same garments may represent religious conservatism and restrictions elsewhere. In each case, what is apparent is a re-articulation of global and local trends which often involves a strong component of re-invention.

This final chapter traces the emergence of Islamic fashion design in Britain, examining the origins and ethos of particular brands and introducing some of the different ways the 'Islamic' is visualized and given material form. The chapter also considers the relationship between Islamic and mainstream fashions as well as examining the particularity of Islamic fashion in the global market. It suggests that whilst newly emerging 'Islamic fashions' catering to Muslims in the West draw on developments in Islamic fashion elsewhere around the world, they are borne out of a particular set of historical and trans-cultural circumstances and concerns which render them distinctive.

EXPERIENCES OF SARTORIAL ALIENATION

If there is one factor that the first generation of British Islamic fashion designers share in common it is an understanding of the clothing dilemmas of young Muslims living in the West who wish to dress in ways that are fashionable and modern on the one hand and faithful and modest on the other. It is a dilemma which most designers learned, not so much through savvy market research and economic foresight, as from their own highly personal experiences of being unable to find clothes which expressed both their feelings of identity and belonging to British (and Western) culture and their desire to express and uphold Islamic values and beliefs. Many, though by no means all, came from second-generation migrant backgrounds. Versed in ideas of individualism and freedom of expression and intimately familiar with British youth culture and fashions, these were individuals who felt uncomfortable at the idea of expressing their faith by plunging into imported Middle Eastern garments recognized as Islamic, either because they themselves could not identify with such clothes or because they found themselves perceived by others as alien and foreign if they wore them. At the same time, they were critical of the amounts of bodily exposure and the explicit sexual orientation of many high street fashions which they felt were incompatible with Islamic ideas of modesty and did not adequately cover arms, necks, legs and body shape. In short, they were in search of more modest contemporary forms of covered dress which could combine their sense of individuality and their interest in fashion and style with their Islamic belief and values. Such dress quite simply did not exist.

Figure 8.1a   Masoomah jilbabs on sale at the Global Peace and Unity Event, ExCel Centre, London, 2008.

Figure 8.1b   Sadia Nosheen, designer and founder of Masoomah.

In the case of some Islamic fashion companies, their birth can quite literally be traced not to awareness of emerging Islamic fashions around the world but to this experience of a lack of anything suitable to wear. The small Nottingham-based company, Masoomah, which specializes in tasteful contemporary jilbabs in muted colours and contemporary materials, did for example grow out of its founder Sadia Nosheen's frustration at the lack of options available to her when as a law student at Nottingham University, she became increasingly oriented towards studying and practising Islam and wanted to try to dress in conformity with her beliefs. The year was 1999:

> I was loving Islam and I wanted to cover. But there wasn't anything out there except the black Saudi jilbab. I was young and image was a massive issue for me. I wanted to be more Islamic but covering was the biggest put-off.

Similarly Sophia Kara, founder and designer of the more eccentric and experimental Leicester-based fashion company, Imaan, recalls having gone through a similar experience in the same year:

> To be honest when I wanted to cover I got the biggest shock of my life. I didn't know how to do it. I just couldn't find anything I wanted to wear. There was nothing suitable in the fashion shops but when I went to the local Islamic shop, it just really scared me. The clothes were all black and made from this awful frumpy material. They were imported from Saudi or Dubai or somewhere and were completely unsuited to our climate. I thought, this just isn't me! This is not my identity. I can't wear these. I bought one abaya because I really did want to cover. I was employed in jobs and pensions at the job centre but was on maternity leave at that time. I started fretting about the idea of being seen dressed like this, looking like my grandmother when I'd been into jeans and Doc Martins and used to wear ponytails and funky hairdos!

Like many other young Muslim women up and down the country, (including Wahid's sisters, chapter 7), both Sadia and Sophia tried to resolve the problem by making their own clothes, supplying their own demand as it were. Sadia, for example began making jilbabs using the same materials that she saw in fashion shops—denim, cord and cotton—and incorporating stylistic features such as hoods and pouches which signalled her awareness and sensitivity to contemporary fashion trends. These were clothes in which she felt confident and comfortable because they corresponded to who she was—a young British Muslim familiar with the grammar of fashion and Islam with strong attachments both to her British background and her faith. When she wore her clothes to college and events, she began receiving requests from other young Muslim women who had been experiencing the same sartorial alienation as herself, and it was this local demand which precipitated her into setting up her own Islamic fashion business from home.

The perception of a lack of suitable culturally relevant dress for Muslims living in the West was not restricted to the British Muslim experience. Zeena Altalib, the woman behind the American Islamic fashion company, Primo Moda (launched in 2004), was also stimulated into marketing Islamic fashion through her own frustration at the lack of styles available to women like herself:

> It all started with frustration, I was frustrated by the limited modest styles available. It took me so long to find just one shirt or skirt, I would have to spend hours shopping, running from store to store. Not only that, but every year the styles keep getting more revealing, tighter and skimpier.
>
> How can I find what I need? A constant consistent supply of trendy, fashionable modest clothing, and I am not talking about jilbabs or the traditional hijabs found in the Middle East. I was a professional woman who needed styles that could take me to meetings, conferences and conventions, fashions that would suit a woman who went to the office, who attended graduate school and lived her life in the mainstream, fashions that could take me from the board room to the mosque. I also wanted this for my friends, and all other women in my situation.

Until having children, Zeena Altalib had a high-paid job in the corporate sector and her lifestyle and social circles were no doubt very different from those of Sadia and Sophia in Nottingham and Leicester. One of her priorities was to develop not only modest professional wear but also Islamic swimwear and sportswear to cater to women like herself who wished to keep fit whilst remaining modest and covered. Unlike Sadia and Sophia, she does not design her own collections, but imports clothes from Turkey, Jordan, Syria and Saudi Arabia. Turkey, owing to its comparatively well-developed contemporary Islamic fashion scene, is her most important supplier and the source of the designer swimwear in which she trades.[7]

Neither was recognition of the inappropriateness of existing forms of Islamic dress for Muslims living in Western countries restricted to women. Anas Sillwood, founder of one of the earliest and most-established British and American Islamic fashion companies, Shukr, which specializes in both men's and women's dress, was also stimulated in part by his own experiences of sartorial alienation. Unlike Sadia, Sophia and Zeena who are all from Muslim backgrounds, Anas is of non-Muslim British and Greek Cypriot parentage. Raised

Figure 8.2 Islamic swimwear from Turkey as advertised on the Web site of Primo Moda. Courtesy of Zeena Altalib.

in the multicultural neighbourhood of Finsbury Park in North London, he converted to Islam at the age of twenty-one whilst studying at the London School of Economics. Travelling in the Middle East after his conversion, he was attracted and inspired by the beauty and dignity he saw in various local forms of men's dress but was aware that these were often poorly made and did not comply with what he saw as Western standards of production and finish. His initial idea was to produce high-quality versions of existing men's garments found in Asia and the Middle East. But he soon became aware of the limitations of merely transplanting such dress to a Western context:

> I was a bit of a fashion victim during my youth, following the latest fads of the youth culture of London where I grew up, a youth culture influenced by the inner-city culture of America. In this culture, clothing was partly a means of expressing one's alternative identity to mainstream society. After becoming Muslim and travelling to the Middle East to learn Arabic and study Islam, I became attracted to the traditional clothing I found Muslims wearing there, and adopted some of it even during my visits back home to England to visit my family. After wearing some of the outrageous clothing of my youth, I was used to receiving public stares, but the looks of shock I received this time round made me reflect about what image of Islam I was portraying to my family, friends and wider society. Many, or most, people in the UK and the West already had very unfavourable impressions about Islam, and it seemed like I was adding to an already generally widespread view, namely that Islam was a foreign religion totally unsuitable to the sentiments of Europeans and Americans. I stopped wearing traditional clothing in subsequent visits, and when SHUKR was launched wore instead some of the more culturally compatible styles we had designed, like the men's longer shirts and loose pants.

Anas had not only experienced unprecedented amounts of staring on public transport and in the streets when he wore a galabiyya but he had also found his young nephew asking why he was dressed as a woman and refusing to let him pick him up from school for fear of how his friends would react. Such experiences made him aware of the need for what he calls 'culturally relevant Islamic clothing' for Muslims living in the West. Through designing a range of loose-fitting men's clothes with a more Western flavour, he became

Figure 8.3   Anas Sillwood of Shukr and some of the clothes advertised on his Web site in 2008, including a bag with the Prophet's sandal motif.
Courtesy of Anas Sillwood.

increasingly aware that this was precisely what was 'was missing' for Western Muslims. His business began with a catalogue of men's wear in 2001. Within a year he had launched an online store, later expanding to incorporate women's wear. His business now employs a workforce of 100 tailors in Damascus with headquarters in Jordan where he employs a team of another 15 workers.

The pre-occupation with appearances and perceptions and concern about issues of integration, modernity and belonging emerged in the late 1980s and early 1990s and were part of a wider resurgence of interest in Islam amongst young Muslims both locally and globally. This coincided with and was to some extent nourished by the spread of the Internet in the late 1990s, which facilitated trans-national communications to an unprecedented degree, but it was also greatly exacerbated by the terrorist attacks of September 11, 2001, which marked the beginning of a period in which Muslims in the West found themselves under intense public scrutiny in politics and the media. The search for suitable clothing seemed to gain new urgency when it merged with the desire to counter the increasing barrage of negative images of Muslims and Islam. There were several elements to this. On the one hand, for many young people 9/11 initiated a period of self-discovery in which they sought to educate themselves about Islam and found themselves increasingly attracted to it in the process. On the other hand, the intense media scrutiny under which they found themselves increased people's feelings of self-consciousness in relation to their identity and appearances. Whilst many felt an increasing desire and need to identify themselves visibly as Muslim, partly out of solidarity with other Muslims around the world, but also as an expression of modesty, devotion and faith, some simultaneously felt motivated to design clothes which might better represent their interests and present a more positive public image. With their loyalty to Britain and 'the West' often called into question in politics and the media, the need for positive visual images and material forms which drew on their mixed heritage, rather than polarizing it, seemed ever more pressing. It was important both for their own self-confidence, comfort and sense of self-recognition as well as for conveying a positive public image which was explicitly Islamic without being threatening, traditional or foreign.

Sheeba Kichloo of Afaaf, for example recognizes 9/11 as the catalyst which drew her into finding out more about Islam and practising it more devoutly. This in turn inspired her to try to develop a collection through which she could convey her positive perceptions of Islam as a religion of beauty and peace, drawing her aesthetic inspiration from a wide repertoire of 'Eastern' and 'Islamic heritages'. Similarly, the writer and activist, Sarah Joseph, cites 9/11 as one of the triggers which prompted her into establishing Britain's first Muslim lifestyle magazine, *Emel*, through which she could offer positive, confidence-building images of Muslims like herself who were cosmopolitan in their outlook and creatively engaged in public life. Raised in the King's Road in a white British family with a father involved in fashion photography, she was keen to take distance from the hyper-sexualized images of women so pervasive in the mainstream media. For this reason the fashion pages of *Emel* display clothes without bodies inside them. The magazine covers both developments in

Islamic fashion design as well as the latest high street fashions, encouraging Muslims to select creatively from what they see around them rather than retreating to older, more archaic or ethnically coded forms of dress which often encourage conservative attitudes and ghettoization. As a convert Sarah Joseph is well-placed for conceptualizing de-exoticized forms of Islamic dress, though her childhood observations of the fashion industry have made her wary of fashion. She herself generally dresses rather plainly in inconspicuous modest clothes in muted colours. She claims to have very little interest in fashion, although she recognizes that readers of *Emel* are often very attracted to the fashion pages and take considerably more interest in their appearances.

The potential role of clothes in combating negative stereotypes of Muslims was also recognized by Anas Sillwood of Shukr. The clothes he markets are not about setting up a polarity between East and West, Muslim and non-Muslim, but about drawing on multiple aesthetic and design resources and inspirations. This involves both adapting old classic garments popular amongst Muslims in North Africa, South Asia and the Middle East and simultaneously taking what Anas and his design team perceive as the best of Western fashion trends as viewed from 'an Islamic perspective'. He feels one of Islam's strengths historically lies in the way it maintained its identity whilst adopting the best of local cultures rather than transplanting them, and it is this approach which he feels is in need of revival in dress and other aspects of life. In an interview for the British-based Muslim Web site, Deenport, he argued:

> Unfortunately, it seems that until now Muslims living in the West have not been entirely successful in understanding the local culture, feeling comfortable with it, and weeding out good from bad practices. We often see one of either two extremes: the completely West-washed Muslim whose inward and outward behaviour imitates non-Muslims; or the adamant ethnic Muslim who can barely speak English, let alone interact on a sophisticated cultural level with non-Muslim neighbours and acquaintances. Of course, what is needed is the traditional, moderate Islamic balance; maintaining one's Muslim identity whilst adopting the best practice and culture which the local land has to offer. An application of this traditional balanced approach will see the development of an authentic self-identity and culture, in which there is no tension between being both Muslim and Western.[8]

This desire to fuse and integrate different traditions rather than separate them out or opt for one or the other is shared by most of the people involved in Islamic fashion design. Sophia Kara of Imaan Collections expressed it as follows:

> Why can't we take advantage of both cultures, fuse them together, and create something different which is us after all? It's our identity. It's who we are and it can appeal to women from all walks of life. Modest dress doesn't have to be intimidating. Let's face it, we do judge a book by its cover and I can see why black can be intimidating and off-putting. I don't want to set up barriers; I want to break them down, help women integrate better, look nicer, more appealing and attractive. In Leicester we hold a women's only fashion

show every year and it's great because everyone is welcome, whatever their background, and they can all mix in, have a good time and exchange ideas.

Zeena Altalib of Primo Moda expressed a similar sentiment in a different context:

The fashions that I offer can help break down the barriers between Muslim women and Western society. For example, when I used to go to the local swimming pool with a 'make do' outfit, I felt that I was not approachable to others.[9] However, a surprising thing happened the first time I wore my Islamic swimming suit. Women came up to me at the pool and started conversations about the swimming suit and how great they thought it was. They were surprised that we can actually swim as well and that it is not forbidden in Islam. They also commented on how they liked the fact that it was colourful and not plain black.

Junayd Miah, one of the key figures behind the development of the British-based company Silk Route (designer of the trendy urban jilbabs) and the larger conglomerate, Islamic Design House, was also keen to convey that his company was not about weeding out the Western but using his cultural knowledge of Eastern and Western traditions to develop contemporary forms of Islamic dress with potential global appeal:

There was all this stuff coming in from Dubai, Syria, Asia etc but it was all full of cultural baggage, and we didn't fit into that at all. We're British. We have a sense of fashion and style. It's important to us. So we wanted to express that unique identity. And we were well placed for doing it because we were part of it. It was our own search for a means of expression for people like us and our younger sisters and cousins—the new generation who were turning to Islam.

Creativity and self-expression are so important in the West. Being British, we have the advantage in that respect and the responsibility to cater to the needs of people who want to lead an Islamic life-style and still maintain Western standards. It's about combining East and West and faith … It's there in the name we chose, Silk Route. It says it all. The Silk Route was an ancient trade route that joined the East and West together. And that is what we are doing—merging the cultures together in a very contemporary way.

REPRESENTING AND MATERIALIZING THE ISLAMIC

British and American Islamic fashion designers share a number of things in common: the desire to integrate faith with fashion; modernity with modesty; Islamic values with the standards of design and production associated with high-quality global fashion brands. Whilst some, like Arabiannites, have their own boutiques, most trade predominantly over the Web as well as through participation in fashion shows, exhibitions, trade fairs and Islamic events. The Internet gives them potential access to a global public and many have been successful at attracting Muslim customers not only in Britain, Europe, America and Canada but also in Singapore, South Africa and a variety of other Muslim minority and majority countries. The Internet is also highly valued by a number of women entrepreneurs for enabling them to work from home, keep flexible hours and combine business with raising children. From the point of view of consumers, shopping online not only provides access to fashions inaccessible nearer to home, but also offers the comfort of being able to buy them without having to make physical contact or risk bodily exposure.

To attract the maximum number of Muslim customers over the Web, the first Islamic fashion companies tended to frame their products both in terms of their Islamic credentials and in terms of their originality, specificity and particular appeal. One simple means of signalling the Islamic nature and feel of a collection is through the company's choice of name. Many British companies have opted for Arabic names through which they seek to communicate and convey the Islamic values and ethos of their collections.[10] The Shukr Web site, for example explains, '*Shukr* is an Arabic word found in the *Qur'an* which means gratitude or thanks. Allah Most High says in the *Qur'an*, "If you give thanks, I shall certainly increase you" (*Qur'an* 14:7) … The company SHUKR was named as a means of reminding ourselves and others of this important *Qur'anic* word and principle, in the hope that we might aspire to be among those whom Allah has increased because of their thanks and gratitude to Him.'[11] *Afaaf*, we are told, means 'purity in morals and modesty'. Similarly *Imaan* is the Arabic word for faithfulness and *Masoomah* the word for innocence. The latter Web site greets readers with the phrase, 'modesty at its best', whilst the Shukr Web site offers catchy modesty-related phrases such as the motto for 2007, 'Put Faith in Fashion' and the motto for the 2008 winter collection, 'Winter Essentials, We've got you covered!' Those companies which have not chosen classical Arabic names often make reference to the East by other means, as names such as Silk Route and Arabiannites testify. Most British company names have Islamic or Eastern resonance in contrast to some American online Islamic fashion companies such as Primo Moda and Artizara which have less obvious Islamic associations.[12]

The Islamic flavour of collections is also built through the use of Arabic names for particular garments. Words like *hijab*, *jilbab* and *abaya* have become part of a global dictionary of Islamic dress terms, though there is considerable ambiguity in how such terms are used in different contexts.[13] Whilst the pre-occupation with modesty and Islam is shared, how much these ideas are emphasized and how they are translated into visual and material form varies considerably from company to company, with some emphasizing the Oriental and exotic, some emphasizing the Western and professional, others arguing for a distinctive Islamic aesthetic and yet others presenting a playful Islamic take on mainstream fashion trends. A brief look at a selection of Islamic fashion Web sites and brands provides insight into some of the dominant themes emerging in the Islamic fashion scene in Britain and their links to Islamic fashion in other locations.

THE ETHICS OF AESTHETICS

Of all the Islamic fashion companies oriented towards Muslims living in the West, Shukr is the one most concerned with integrating Islamic principles and ethics into its production, design, finance, marketing and representation. At the same time it de-emphasizes the

Figure 8.4   Shukr homepage.
Courtesy of Anas Sillwood.

foreign, exotic and non-Western associations often attached to the idea of Islamic clothing. As a religiously oriented and religiously motivated British convert to Islam, its founder Anas Sillwood is concerned to convey that an Islamic way of life is suitable (and desirable) not only for people in Muslim majority countries but also for Westerners (whether born Muslim or not), and it is this ethos that informs the aesthetic, tone, organization and representation of his Web site and fashions which are targeted specifically towards Western Muslims.

The Shukr Web site is explicit about how Islamic ethics and aesthetics are integrated into the company and the clothes. The choice of displaying not only female but also male models without heads reflects recognition of the fact that both men and women are enjoined to practice modesty in the *Qur'an*.[14] The choice of muted colours, loose cuts, natural fibres and unfussy designs also conveys a subtle sense of dignity and modesty.

Asked what makes his clothing range Islamic, Anas replied:

> Perhaps we can say that, apart from the basic function of clothing which is to protect humans from the elements, both the *Qur'an* and the *Sunnah* identify two further

purposes: first and foremost to preserve human dignity by enjoining modesty in dress; and secondly to rejoice in the beauty and favour of God by wearing aesthetically pleasing clothing. According to a famous saying of the Prophet Muhammad, 'God is beautiful and He loves beauty.' So, taking this perspective, what is Islamic about our clothing is a) its modest appearance and b) its beauty.[15]

The relationship between the two relative concepts of beauty and modesty is, however, a delicate one, and Shukr has to some extent explored its permeable boundaries through trial and error. The company initially began by making very loose clothing but found customers complaining that the garments were too tent-like. When it produced more tailored garments, however, it had complaints that they were too tight. It now takes a middle-ground position, relying, according to Anas, on a mixture of 'feedback from customers, religious scholars, and our own sense of God-consciousness'. Similarly whilst colours are regarded as beautiful and therefore desirable, excessive brightness and ostentatiousness is avoided as the clothes are intended to be aesthetically pleasing without being attention-seeking as such. For this reason Anas Sillwood is reluctant to use the word 'attractive' to describe them.

The women's range includes skirts, trousers, dresses, coats and blouses that are Islamic more through the respect they pay to Islamic principles than to what are conventionally recognized as 'Islamic styles', though subtle references to the Islamic are incorporated into garments through design features such as embroidery and stitching. Interestingly, the men's collection contains more garments based on styles popular amongst Muslims in North Africa and the Middle East than the female collection, which retains closer affiliations with mainstream fashion.

In the accessories section the Web site also advertises a bag with an embroidered Islamic motif representing the Prophet Muhammad's sandal. This section contains a link to a substantial essay on the significance of the Prophet's sandals both to his earliest followers and to subsequent scholars. It is suggested that the sandals represent love and humility in relation to the Prophet's greatness and numerous 'evidences' are given from the works of different Imams on the theme, perhaps to ward off the possibility of potential objections from some quarters.

The Shukr Web site is packed with information, providing lucid, and at times, scholarly, explanations of different aspects of the company from its philosophy and ethics to the quality and characteristics of fibres. In this sense the clothes promoted become agents of a larger vision. Customers are informed:

> We aim to produce designs which identify ourselves as Muslims, but yet which are suitable to wear to school, college, work, as well as the mosque and Islamic events. We at SHUKR see this as a necessary stage in the development of our growing self-identity as Muslim Americans, Muslim Canadians and Muslim Europeans. Whilst habits of dress are only one aspect of this growing and developing collective self-identity, it is an important aspect, because how one looks on the outside often reflects alot about how one feels on the inside. SHUKR is proud to be able to serve the Muslims in this regard and

encourages all Muslims to take an active part in this quest for Islamic authenticity in the new environments which we have been destined to live in.

This idea of 'Islamic authenticity' is not just about appearances but also about maintaining ethical consistency. Shukr philosophy is, we are told, founded upon the Islamic concept of *Itqan*, ('perfection'), which translates into the idea of striving to produce the highest quality as well as maintaining high ethical standards. In a section entitled, 'Is Shukr expensive?', we are informed that Shukr is against sweatshop production, paying its workers above-average wages and guaranteeing worker rights concerning hours, overtime, sick leave and opportunities to pray at work. All of the full-time employees are Muslim. The company also follows Islamic principles on finance by avoiding the interest-based system and financing growth by re-investing profits.

Most of Shukr's business takes place over the Web and is oriented to the British and American markets, although Anas Sillwood and other members of the company also attend major international Islamic events and have some customers in Europe and beyond. In 2008, his clothes were exhibited both at London's Global Peace and Unity event and at IslamExpo, where they also featured in the highly popular fashion show.

THE POETICS OF SPIRITUALITY

A somewhat different way of translating Islamic principles into dress is by reference to the spiritual and ethereal. The Afaaf Web site, for example offers what might be described as a sensory and poetic Islamically inspired experience without making explicit references to Islam as such. A film draws potential customers into a dreamy world of soft-focus images in subtle shades of white and grey to the sound of trickling water and exotic birdsong. Textiles first emerge on the screen in soft focus, their patterns progressively traced by lacy white lines which creep across the screen, highlighting motifs of flowers, birds and concentric circles. Images appear in and out of focus in slow motion, taking on an inspirational quality and evoking a sense of beauty, tranquillity, mysticism and peace. The sound of water and the peaceful dream-like quality add to the other-worldly atmosphere of the site. Particular garments from the collection appear discretely in soft focus at one side of the screen as if they are just one more part of the creation story. The emphasis is on the beauty and sensuality of texture and sound. Though modelled on people, the bodies of models are almost invisible and their heads obscured. What the onlooker sees of the garments is their texture, detail and flow. With each new image a phrase emerges introducing the collection and conveying the ethos of the products and the company:

An expression of inner peace and outward harmony
A language of refinement, tranquillity, simplicity and style,
Textiles and patterns that are inspired from all around the world. Delicate hand embroidery and refined detail,
A rich fusion of Eastern, Arabic classics and contemporary Western cuts …
Afaaf—pure reflections—an expression of harmony.

Figure 8.5   Shukr clothes on sale at the Global Peace and Unity Event, ExCel Centre, London, 2008.

The film, which carries on repeating itself until switched off by viewers, has the hypnotic quality of walking round a garden of paradise. Once switched off, viewers are invited to explore different sections of the Web site: the women's collection, men's collection, jewellery and artefacts. The Web site operates as an advertisement rather than an online store. People wishing to make purchases from Afaaf are invited to make an appointment to visit the show room in Battersea in South London.[16]

Under 'Inspirations and Reflections', detail is given of the professional background of Sheba Kichloo, founder of the company. Her professional status is made clear by reference to her years of working for Harrods, her experience of management consultancy, her extensive travel and her involvement in charity work, all of which lend legitimacy to the exclusivity of her collection. This is combined with statements about the ethos of Afaaf as a company designed not only to promote the concept of modesty but to raise awareness of its beauty both ideologically and aesthetically. Frequent references are made to the 'deep spirituality' of beautiful things and to people's search for 'deeper meaning in life'. The delicate silks, wispy scarves, floating kurtas, gracious abayas, soft and luxurious Kashmir and Pashmina shawls seem to suggest some sort of timeless aesthetic, independent of more transient and superficial fashion trends. Many of the garments are modifications of popular Western and South Asian styles and feature embroidery and motifs which are recognizable as Kashmiri or Palestinian.

'What is true expression?' asks Sheba, 'Is it being trapped in the world of fashion, the exposure of flesh to …, the race of being in vogue?' or might it instead be about 'pure reflections, an expression of inner peace with outward harmony, a language of refinement, tranquillity and style?'

Figure 8.6   Clothes as advertised on the Afaaf Web site, 2007.
Courtesy of Sheba Kichloo.

At one level this presentation shares much in common with the marketing techniques of a whole range of companies offering peace, fulfilment and exclusivity to elite international clients whether through yoga, travel or various types of therapy. But the focus on the beauty of modesty is what makes it distinctively Islamic. The Web site includes a poem, written by Sheba, which is about light, purity, peace and the search for answers. It ends with the phrase,

> What is this beauty I ask?
> This is the light of simplicity.
> This is the beauty of modesty.

The quest for spirituality and peace mirrors Sheba's personal experience. Raised in London to parents of Kashmiri and Pakistani origin, she was born Muslim but it was only in her twenties that she went on what she calls a 'spiritual journey', something she also described as a 'crisis of recognition' post-9/11. She became inspired by what she learned about Islam and enthused with a desire to counter ignorance by projecting her perception of its positive qualities and values. She herself adopted hijab in 2002 as an expression of her personal transformation and her desire to align her 'outer appearance' with her 'inner self', and she went on to develop Afaaf in 2004 as part of her inspirational vision. She wrote the poem about modesty at a time when she was listening to a series of lectures about paradise. She was inspired by the descriptions of fountains and rivers of milk and honey, and found herself envisaging a beautiful girl in paradise who was fully covered and was like a column of light. It is this image of modesty illuminated in paradise that she wished to capture in the Web site.

Afaaf clothes differ from those of Shukr in several ways: they are exclusive and luxurious rather than catering to everyday wear; they draw heavily on South Asian, and to a lesser extent, Arabian traditions both in terms of styles and design features; they are more elaborate in terms of decorative elements and the choice of luxury materials; they are less bound in with cycles of mainstream fashion and they are produced by Muslim craftsmen scattered in different locations: India, Pakistan, Morocco, Egypt and Palestine. Furthermore, whilst Shukr products are framed first and foremost as Islamic, Afaaf products are framed in terms of beauty, modesty, spirituality and peace without making explicit reference to Islam.[17]

THE EXOTICISM OF THE EAST

One theme exploited in a number of fashion Web sites and collections is the association of the Islamic with the Arab world. The Arabiannites Web site, for example evokes ideas of the mystery and exoticism of the East in its heavy use of black, its Arabic-inspired calligraphy and its sketches and images of women peering mysteriously from behind semi-opaque hijabs. This mode of representation is a form of self-conscious self-Orientalism.[18] Visitors to the Web site are first presented with a black screen, on which the word *Arabiannites* emerge out of the darkness in a script which replicates stylistic features of Arabic lettering. A crescent moon appears illuminated above the words, and small stars twinkle in the night sky. The homepage of the Web site contains the headings, 'Arabian Beauty' and 'Behind the Veil', both of which might equally be titles of popular Orientalist novels. The clothes, which are classified into casual wear, evening wear, timeless black, loungewear and 'your own designs', are described as 'Arabian influenced products' based on 'Middle Eastern or Indo-continental traditions'. This Arabian feel is further emphasized by a background of geometric patterns reminiscent of Islamic tiles.

Unlike Shukr and Afaaf which in many ways represent a move away from explicitly Middle Eastern styles associated with Muslims, Arabiannites focuses on full-length long-sleeved gowns and outer robes such as abayas, jilbabs, kaftans and gelabiyyas which have immediate Islamic resonance and which highlight the foreign, Eastern and exotic connotations. A strong sense of drama is built into both the clothing and the Web site. Models' faces are not concealed on the Web site (though they are on billboards and posters) but are often partly obscured by cloth, emphasizing the sensuous and seductive potential of draped fabric and the allure of what cannot be fully seen. This rendition of modesty with Eastern promise is very different from the more purist de-sexualized interpretation of modesty found on the Shukr Web site, highlighting the fact that Arabiannites, whilst being more Eastern-oriented, is less explicitly religious in its frame and ethos. Yasmin Arif, the designer and founder of the company, is keen to encourage women who cover to explore the drama

Figure 8.7 Model posing on the Arabiannites Web site, 2008..
Courtesy of Yasmin Arif.

and pleasure of luscious sweeping fabrics. Whilst concerned to respect religious concerns of her customers regarding covering, her orientation is in many ways more aesthetic, reflecting the fact that she was inspired both by the experience of working on British ball gowns and her travels to Dubai where full-length covered dress is often glamorous, fashionable and at times ostentatious.[19] The glamour of Arabiannites clothes was highly visible in the fashion show at IslamExpo 2008, where shimmering embroidered robes in dramatic colours (reds, peacock blue, purples) were worn with high-heeled gold shoes and glittering hijabs, giving the impression that the models could quite literally have stepped out of a rendition of *A Thousand and One Nights.* Similarly the Arabiannites boutique conjures up the image of an exotic treasure trove, with its colourful displays of rich fabrics, embroideries, silk scarves, elaborate necklaces and hijab jewellery as well as the long black robes on display. It represents a reclaiming of the sensual pleasures of the exotic by people who have conventionally been exoticized.[20]

It would be wrong, however, to assume that Arabiannites garments are simply a replica of what is found in the Middle East. A closer look at the designs reveals an element of eccentricity and play often through small details, such as extravagant sleeves, extended hoods, ruffs and unexpected colours or embroidered features, all of which identify the clothes as designer fashion wear. Yasmin's aim is to 'get the feel of the East' but simultaneously remain 'in touch with Western designs'. These are clothes conceptualized in Britain by someone with a professional background in fashion design who also uses her knowledge of Eastern styles and fabrics and her contacts with producers in India and Dubai to create some sort of designer fusion wear. Her experimental impulse is to some extent constrained by the demands of some of her more conservative customers in East London who, as we have already seen, often favour a more austere interpretation of Islamic dress and sometimes request simpler styles in black. When customers point to some of the evening wear and worry that the colours are perhaps too bright to be considered modest, Yasmin reminds them that rich red or turquoise gowns can always be teamed up with darker abayas for outdoor use. She is keen to show Muslim women of South Asian origin that the sari is not the only option they have for formal occasions such as weddings, festivals and parties. Her evening wear suggests that covered dress can be stylish and elegant, enabling covered women to circulate at functions without having to worry in advance about whether or not the event is gender segregated.[21] The idea of modesty is built into these clothes, not through any restraint in the use of colours or luxurious fabrics, but through the fact that all of the garments cover the body from the neck to the feet without outlining the body shape.

In this sense the clothes differ from some of the clingy, black, glamorous jilbabs being imported from Dubai by companies such as the recently launched Lareine, which displayed its first collection at the GPU event in 2008. These jilbabs were tight and clingy with embroidered and beaded decorative features placed so as to emphasize the curves of the female body. They had the look of elegant evening dresses and their status as modest was not immediately obvious, something acknowledged by one observer from another company who commented, 'You'd need to wear another jilbab on top of one of those!' Other Eastern-

Figure 8.8 Interior of Arabiannites boutique, East London.

oriented interpretations of Islamic dress are offered by Islam Orient, an online company set up by a family of Chinese converts in East London who aim to bring a South East Asian flavour to Islamic fashion. More common are the many companies importing clothes directly from the Middle East targeting women from Asian and Arab backgrounds.

URBAN STREET STYLE

Moving explicitly away from the association of the Islamic with the exotic are various new forms of Islamic dress classified as urban street wear, such as Silk Route's trendy urban

Figure 8.9   Arabiannites abaya.
Courtesy of Yasmin Arif.

jilbabs (see chapter 7) which are about creating everyday forms of dress that are in tune with British Muslim youth culture. They share with Shukr the desire to create a culturally relevant dress for Western Muslims, but their interpretation of what that dress should be is more urban, edgy and assertive. It is less about translating Islamic philosophical principles into dress than about visibly asserting a confident, viable and trendy sub-cultural style for Muslim youth. Though very much rooted in their experience as British Muslim Londoners from South Asian backgrounds, the five entrepreneurs behind the company (three men and two women) have global ambitions for their products. In 2008 they founded the umbrella company, Islamic Design House, which brings together different individuals and enterprises involved in developing Islamically inspired and oriented forms of visual expression: Silk Route, Visual Dhikr (calligraphic art), *Sisters* (Islamic lifestyle magazine) and Aerosole Arabic (Islamic graffiti artist).

A Silk Route advert on the back cover of the *Emel* magazine, Summer 2008, shows a woman in a zip-up hooded jilbab. Her face is cut off and her body obscured by the inscription: 'to dress is to express my faith, to be heard is to be seen to be free to live my *deen*' [religion]. This is clothing with a message aimed directly at recently Islamicized Muslim youth around the world. Though modelled in many ways on British youth culture, the trendy urban image is marketable abroad. The company recently shifted its manufacturing from Bangladesh to Egypt and hopes to capture a global Islamic youth market. It currently

Figure 8.10   First collection of Lareine jilbabs on display at the Global Peace and Unity Event, London, 2008.

Figure 8.11   'Throw yo' hands' hoodie, as advertised on the Elenany Web site, May 2009.
Courtesy of Sarah Elenany.

employs designers in India, France and Britain and has attracted customers in Egypt and Nigeria with its trendy youth-oriented designs.

An alternative interpretation of Muslim youth dress is offered by the company Elenany, launched in 2009 by Sarah Elanany, a young British Muslim woman of Egyptian and Palestinian parentage who was born in the United States but raised in Mitcham near London. The company sells trendy but modest long-sleeved cotton tunic dresses, jackets and coats which are not recognizably Islamic in style but which are made from fabrics with graphics intended to capture the spirit of Islam. The graphics in Elenany's first collection are based on repeated hand motifs which recall gestures of prayer and protest. The graphics are bold and angular reminiscent of the Russian constructivist movement, though Sarah perceives the repetition and angularity as features of Islamic artistic traditions. It was a trip to Morocco that had reminded her of the importance of pattern in Islamic art and of the possibility of integrating Islamically oriented patterns and motifs into everyday clothing, but she was keen to find graphics that would be relevant to contemporary British Muslims. The design, 'Testify', consists of hands with one finger pointing upwards, recalling the Muslim obligation to testify to the oneness of God, but, as she points out on her Web site, 'the fact that it also looks like a number one to everyone else ain't a bad thing either!'. Another print, 'Throw yo' hands', shows raised fists and fingers. Sarah explained the design as follows:

Figure 8.12 *Dua* (prayer) pattern, Elenany.
Courtesy of Sarah Elenany.

> As a young Muslim person I go on protest marches and demonstrations quite a lot. The design speaks to the experience of many British Muslims. Demonstrations are the essence of Britishness in a way—that ability to stand up for what you believe in. I wanted to convey that in a bold way. I don't think we should have to apologize for being who we are, to mumble under our breath. The clothes are a kind of release. They're saying, it's OK, it's cool!

The dua pattern consisting of hands raised in prayer comes printed on different coloured backgrounds, one of which is bright red. This Sarah uses as the inside lining for jacket and coats, thereby retaining the more muted modesty-associated colours of black, white and grey for externals. Though oriented specifically to cater to what Sarah considers the 'needs' of young British Muslims, she is also keen to attract other customers and for this reason the model on her Web site does not wear a hijab. The reasoning is that non-Muslims would be put off clothes modelled on a hijabi whereas hijab-wearing Muslims are used to non-hijabis modelling most of the clothes they buy. Like the entrepreneurs of Silk Route, Elenany associates Britishness with a certain cool. In response to the suggestion that she should cater to foreign markets, she replied, 'I do feel like it's a very British brand and I'd like to keep it that way. That's cool. We can attract foreign buyers by exporting Britishness which is what a lot of people are after anyway.'

Recognition of the potential market for Islamic urban street wear is not restricted only to women's fashions. In 2006, Faisel, a young Muslim man of Gujarati origin, born and raised in Preston in the North of England, launched a range of cutting-edge men's Islamic dress, consisting of long *thobes* (long-sleeved long garments) designed as modern versions of the style of garment worn by the Prophet Mohammed, whose example Muslim men are enjoined to follow. Interestingly the company's name, Lawung, does not have any Arab or Islamic association, but apparently means 'old King' in ancient Chinese. At the same time the British credentials of the brand are actively asserted in photographic representations in the catalogue and Web site where a trendy young man with designer stubble poses in various urban and rural British settings. The word 'England' is also inscribed after the brand name in the catalogue, suggesting that what is on offer is a form of British Islamic men's wear, even if, like many so-called Western fashion garments, they are made in China. The garments represent a radical departure from more traditional Middle Eastern styles of thobe available in Britain in their use of contemporary materials and their incorporation of design features such as zips, ribbed collars, hoods, ribbed sleeves and combat-style pockets. At the Islam Expo and GPU events in 2008, they were displayed on futuristic mannequins and appeared to be attracting a considerable amount of interest and enthusiasm both from young and not-so-young men. Names such as 'Urban Streetz', 'Urban Navigator', 'Urban Military', 'Urban Executive', 'Urban Warrior' and 'Urban Extreme' testify to the assertive modernist intentions behind the clothes.

The young man behind Lawung has picked up on the fact that most young Muslim men in Britain are embarrassed to dress in long tunics or robes in their daily life, partly

Figure 8.13   Lawung men's thobes, IslamExpo, London, 2008.

because they feel such dress is foreign, outdated, and unfashionable and also because they are aware of how it is often perceived as an indicator of religious fanaticism or political extremism. As a result they might wear such dress for attending Friday prayers or possibly also for relaxing at home, but are unlikely to wear it in everyday working contexts. Faisel sees his explicitly trendy thobes as important for encouraging young Muslim men and boys 'to dress Islamically'. Taking a literalist interpretation of the Islamic principle that all Muslims should follow the *Sunnah* (the religious norms built on the example set by the Prophet), he considers the wearing of long robes and the sporting of a beard an Islamic obligation in the same way that many Muslim women perceive the wearing of headscarves obligatory. In this sense his collection is also part of the search for culturally relevant forms of Islamic dress for fashion conscious young Muslims living in the West. At the same time, like a number of other Islamic fashion designers and companies, he also has ambitions to expand into the Middle Eastern market. Lawung products were initially distributed through Islamic shops in towns with significant Muslim populations in the North of England and the Midlands (Blackburn, Dewsbury, Bradford, Bolton, Leicester, Coventry, Preston, Oldham). However, they are now available online and in various stores in London and, since IslamExpo 2008 where Faisel established contact with Wahid Rahman, they have been advertised on The Hijab Shop Web site. The company is currently developing connections with a major retail company in Saudi Arabia where it hopes to attract Saudi youth by offering a contemporary British take on Islamic men's dress. This raises interesting questions regarding the potential of the Middle Eastern market for Islamic fashions designed in Britain.

ISLAMIC THROUGH INSCRIPTION

At the popular end of the market for contemporary urban Islamic street wear is the designer T-shirt with Islam-oriented messages, declarations and slogans which assert their Islamic credentials directly through written messages and inscriptions. At IslamExpo and GPU 2008, large numbers of young volunteers and visitors sported T-shirts, some advertising Muslim charities and initiatives with punchy and often humorous religious slogans, others simply asserting religious and political views. These were worn by many in conjunction with the chequered scarf (*keffiyah*) worn as a scarf, headband or hijab.[22] There were also a number of stalls selling T-shirts, hoodies, baby clothes, bibs, armbands, headbands, baseball caps and other items of clothing and paraphernalia which bore declarations of Muslim identity, politics and belief. These varied from simple messages such as 'I love Islam' and '100% Muslim' to more assertive messages of political and religious allegiance, such as 'Allegiance to the Deen', 'Google Islam = Truth', 'Jihad vs G8 summit' and the *Shahada* (Muslim declaration of belief) written in Arabic[23]—many of them produced by the aptly named East London–based company, wearaloud.com.[24]

Clearly such events provided a space where young people felt proud to declare, celebrate and assert their Muslim identity in the same way that fans at a football match sport football paraphernalia or activists at a rally wear T-shirts in support of a particular cause, whether

Figure 8.14   Faisal Ibn Dawood Atcha (right), founder of Lawung, with his cousin, Global Peace and Unity Event, London, 2008.

it be animal rights or organic farming. Though visually asserting Muslim particularity and, in some cases, calling for Muslim-based political action, such dress should be seen less as proof of Muslim separatism and difference than as evidence of the ubiquity of the T-shirt as an iconic item of a global youth culture in which Muslims participate.

Whilst there are several companies selling Islamic T-shirts and related paraphernalia in Britain, there are many more in the United States where the T-shirts jostle for position alongside a whole range of other identity and belief-oriented T-shirts. On the 'Islam' page of the Cafepress.com Web site, 'related' products are listed as follows: 'agnosticism, Koran, anti-religious, Jew, Muslim, atheist, religious, bible, Jesus, Christian, religion, humor', reminding us that Islamic T-shirts sit alongside a wider range of American religious and anti-religious T-shirt fashions.[25] At the same time they do, of course, play a part in the development and assertion of a global Islamic youth culture which includes Muslim hip hop and graffiti art. The global pretensions of entrepreneurs marketing such clothes is often explicitly apparent in the names of companies. Obvious examples would be the US-based company, Islamicstatewear.com, and the Australian company, Ummahgear.com, both of which distribute T-shirts within and outside their own countries.

Figure 8.15,   Scenes from the Global Peace and Unity Event, London, 2008.

ISLAMIC AND OTHER FASHIONS

In a recent article in the journal, *Fashion Theory*, Heather Marie Akou describes the global emergence of Islamic fashion Web sites in different parts of the world from Kuwait to Canada, Saudi Arabia to Britain as 'a non-Western world fashion system' that is both 'distinct from Western fashion and often directly opposed to it'. She ends by asking, 'Just how well the Islamic world will be able to further build and maintain a system of dress distinct from the West remains to be seen. For now, these Web sites are opening up many possibilities.'[26]

Akou is certainly right to point out that the emergence of Islamic fashion is a global phenomenon despite local variations as to what counts as fashionable or Islamic.[27] But how correct is she in assuming the existence of a pan-Islamic fashion system independent of 'Western' fashions? One striking feature of the Islamic fashions that have emerged in the British context is the extent to which they build both on visual resources and skills from around the world and on the local dress practices and experiences of British Muslims. As we have already seen, many of the people involved in the Islamic fashion industry in Britain and the United States seek quite explicitly to integrate what they perceive as 'Western' and 'Islamic' elements rather than select one above the other. In fact there is considerable ambiguity and at times a deliberate blurring of the boundaries between Islamic and mainstream fashions both for a mixture of moral, social and commercial reasons.

Many of the promoters of Islamic fashion identify an element of outreach in their work, some claiming that it is a form of *dawah.* By making clothes more appealing, they seek to draw Muslims towards perceiving the benefits of covering whilst at the same time encouraging interest in the faith from non-Muslims. Some referred to their collections as 'educational' to the extent that they challenged negative stereotypes of Muslims and demonstrated the potential beauty of covering. Anas Sillwood, for example stressed that 'Muslims can educate people simply by their appearance', adding that Shukr took that 'responsibility' very seriously. This educational imperative does, of course, combine with commercial interests. In Afaaf advertisements, for example models are shown without heads. Contrary to what I had originally assumed, this mode of representation was chosen, not in order to comply with restrictions on representations of the body and face favoured in conservative Muslim circles, but in order to avoid discouraging Muslims who do not cover and non-Muslims from taking an interest in the clothes. The reasoning was that if the faces of models were visible, it would have been necessary to put them in headscarves since the collection was about modesty, but if they had worn headscarves this would have implied that the clothes were first and foremost religious dress for hijabis only. The decision to remove heads was in this case motivated by a desire to reach out to the broadest range of customers possible. It was a similar desire that had motivated Sarah Elenany to model her collection on a woman without hijab.[28]

This blurring of boundaries between Islamic and other fashions is particularly apparent on the Web site of the Manchester-based company, LOSVE (founded in 2008). What is distinctive about the Web pages of this online store is that there are not any references to religion at all. Instead, the company advertises long-sleeved tops, long skirts and scarves in trendy patterns with the slogan, 'Long is beautiful'. Even the scarves on this Web site are displayed around the necks of models rather than being worn as hijabs. Whilst Muslim customers find the site through Muslim networks and hijab blogs where the clothes are recommended, other customers come across them by typing the words, 'long skirt' into the search engines of their computers. LOSVE models its clothes on high street fashions but produces longer versions of them with the idea that women who want to cover can purchase the latest fashion fabrics and styles without having to worry about the issue of how they

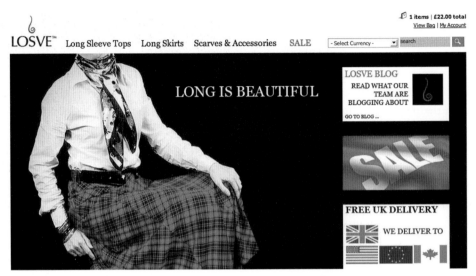

Figure 8.16   Advertisement for Losve clothes, 2008.
Courtesy of Abdul R. Hummaida.

are going to alter or layer them. Their 2008 winter collection had for example picked up on the high street fashion for tartan by producing a large range of full-length tartan skirts. According to Abdul Hummaidah, manager of the company, 40 per cent of his customers are non-Muslim.

In a similar vein Shukr has for some time been contemplating developing a second collection that would be marketed as modest rather than Islamic. This, Anis feels, would not only broaden the commercial outreach of the company but also help to encourage the practice of modesty in the mainstream and therefore have wider positive social effects. The modest range would be able to draw on the existing Islamic range since many of the clothes marketed are not conspicuously Islamic in style. The company already has a number of non-Muslim customers, some of them religiously conservative Christians and Jews who share similar concerns with modesty, and others who are simply women who like loose clothes and are attracted to the Shukr aesthetic. Similarly Sophia Kara of the Leicester-based company, Imaan, has found a number of non-Muslim women taking an interest in her collection, some of whom have become regular clients. As a result, when she re-designed her Web site in December 2008, she removed all references to Islam and reframed the clothes as 'contemporary modest designer wear' and used phrases such as 'faith friendly couture' to encourage the widest possible customer base.

The idea of inter-faith modest fashions is also explored by Sarah Ansari, one of the founders of the American company, Artizara (established in 2004), who states on the homepage of her Web site, 'We wanted to reach out not just to Muslims but women of all faiths who have an interest in modest dress and world style. We wanted to go out there and say Islam is Beautiful, and dressing modestly is cool.' In her fashion blog she includes an

Figure 8.17   Imaan Collections publicity, 2009.
Courtesy of Sophia Kara.

article by a Mennonite woman who expresses sympathy and empathy with Muslim women in hijab. Here again, what is aspired to is 'a symphony of East and West' rather than a self-conscious rejection of Western fashions. Such a symphony is, of course, made all the more possible owing to the fact that contemporary 'Western fashions' frequently draw on Eastern stylistic elements.[29]

The proximity of Islamic fashion to other fashions is further clarified by designers' responses to questions about the extent to which they followed or were inspired by mainstream fashions. Most responded that they keep abreast with fashion cycles, observing which colours and styles were predicted for upcoming seasons and following developments in fashion through magazines, forecasts, high street observations and blogs. All were also clear that they did not simply replicate these fashions but tried to incorporate some elements of them either through colour, design or cut. Some of the smaller companies which get small numbers of garments made up in different locations around the world find it logistically impossible to keep up with the colour predictions for particular seasons. Others do, however, follow contemporary high street fashions quite closely. Sadia Nosheen of the Nottingham-based company, Masoomah, has a 'basic range' which she gets made locally from roll ends of fabric which she obtains directly from wholesalers in the Midlands. This enables her to use not just similar fabrics to those found in local high street shops in a particular season, but actually the same ones. Selecting what she calls the 'murkier' colours from the range available, she makes up small quantities of jilbabs from each roll. This enables her to offer a rapid turnover of different coloured and textured jilbabs which are in tune with what is available in the shops.

Sophia Kara of Imaan Collections is also a keen observer and adapter of mainstream fashions. She follows fashion predictions closely and claims to use these as an 'inspiration' rather than a constraint. She argues that having an awareness of what seasonal colours are going to be 'in' is very important since her clients will be buying the latest accessories available in the market. Because she is aware of seasonal colour preferences, she is able to offer clothes which will match or blend with their bags, shoes and jewellery. As a fan of

1920s style, she encourages the wearing of long necklaces and enjoys incorporating fancy buttons and feathers into her outfits. Her clothes are distinctive for their asymmetry and quirkiness—a fact which allies them to the more eccentric side of British fashion.

The extent to which the larger online companies follow and replicate mainstream fashions varies considerably. Tabassum Siddique, the head designer at Shukr, argues that whilst she looks to 'Western trends in clothing, design and thought' at the beginning of each seasonal cycle, she does not feel too bound by them. She relates her work to that of an interpreter, translating 'Western styles into Islamic Styles'. By contrast, Zeena Altalib of Primo Moda follows Western fashion predictions extremely closely, attending forecast shows in New York and making sure that her collections correspond to the latest American tastes. Many of the clothes she sells are highly tailored by comparison to British equivalents and are less obviously Islamic in style, reflecting both her desire to capture the tastes of professional middle-class American women and the fact that American Muslims are on the whole less visually distinct than their British counterparts. Similarly the American company Arti Zara offers far more fitted body-hugging outfits than commonly marketed on British Islamic fashion Web sites. Many of the garments offered would not be out of place in mainstream fashion outlets.

As far as business is concerned, with the exception of Shukr and Silk Route, there does not seem to have been much attempt to incorporate Islamic financial principles into the economic organization of companies. And whilst the managers of Silk Route seek to avoid interest-based finance, they nonetheless speak the language of capitalist business enterprise and the culture of accelerated mass consumption. 'We've studied all the business models out there', Junayd Miah told me. 'We love the Zara model, where you can get a design out within just two weeks. Women love shopping and we want to give people options, lots of variety.' A number of entrepreneurs further expressed the fact that they wanted their clothes to match the professional standards of reputable Western fashion companies, whether in terms of production, design or labelling.

What all of these examples seem to suggest is a relationship of proximity between newly emerging Islamic fashions and mainstream fashions in the West. And like all close relationships, it is not without certain tensions. In many ways the Islamic fashion industry is predicated on the idea that mainstream fashions are 'un-Islamic' or at least incompatible with Islamic ideals of modesty, an idea which may sometimes be exaggerated. What Islamic fashion designers and manufacturers seek to offer, then, is something alternative which resonates with the needs and desires of Muslim women who cover. A sense of the 'Islamic' is therefore built into many clothing collections whether through the cut, colour, fabrics, graphics, styles or provenance of the garments. More essential still, however, is the emphasis on modesty which defines the ethos and parameters of Islamic fashion whilst at the same time attracting some non-Muslim customers.

How to define and interpret modesty remains, however, a difficult challenge and many of those involved in the industry speak of tensions over this issue. Some, like Shukr, have been confronted by the problem that, although customers want to cover for reasons of modesty, they are often also attracted to more fitted clothes and sometimes make requests for tighter versions of what is on offer. As a result those who deal with customers face to face often end up having discussions about modesty with their customers. Sadia Nosheen of Massomah, for example refuses to take in garments in response to customer requests. 'I just say, no', she told me, 'then I talk to young girls, and ask them why they want to wear the jilbab, and if they know why they are wearing it, then they need to keep that purpose in mind. Otherwise they can just go to any shop and buy whatever they want.' Similarly Sophia Kara of Imaan refuses to make her designs more fitted, as this is not what her collection is about. At the same time she recounted how she sometimes has to 'keep a check' on herself as she too can 'get too carried away'.

The issue of modesty is also a cause of considerable tension when it comes to the issue of representation in posters, advertisements, fashion shows and Web sites (see chapter 7). Many, as we have seen, choose not to display faces on posters or Web pages for a diversity of reasons and, in this way, they take distance from mainstream fashion advertisements, although some mainstream online stores also choose this mode of representation. Finding fashion photographers willing to go along with the headless model concept in photo shoots has also proved difficult for some. All companies face the problem that they want their products to look attractive but want to avoid sexually provocative advertisements. At the same time, they recognize that sex sells and that even modest hijabi women may find themselves more attracted to clothes which are modelled seductively. Here too different companies set different standards regarding what may or may not be considered a provocative or seductive pose.

Participation in Islamic fashion shows is generally less controversial as these tend to be gender-segregated events in the British context. But invitations to participate in mixed shows or in shows that are not framed as Islamic are sometimes rejected, particularly if the other clothes being marketed are entirely at odds with the idea and ethos of modesty. On the other hand, within the protected space of an all-female environment, concerns about the sexualization of the female body are often considered irrelevant as the alluring postures of models and the ample use of make-up and high heels suggest. This conforms to the idea that whilst women are supposed to hide their beauty and sexuality from male strangers, they are encouraged to express it in relation to their husbands. Here again, Shukr is perhaps distinctive in down-playing sexuality in the presentation of its clothes even within a female environment.

The liberty of Islamic fashion designers to experiment with colours, fabrics and styles is also to some extent regulated by the expectations and desires of their customers. Online traders keep close tabs on customer responses and display positive feedback on their Web sites. In Britain, however, austere interpretations of Islamic requirements of modesty are not uncommon, leading a number of married women to feel they should be wearing black even if this is not a *Qur'anic* requirement. Hence, Yasmin Arif of Arabiannites found herself producing more black garments than originally intended in order to satisfy conservative local tastes. Similarly, Sadia Nosheen of Masoomah finds that most of her clients are attracted to muted colours, which limits her capacity to experiment. By contrast, Sophia

Kara of Imaan, irritated at the way some women in Leicester 'ruined the look' of colourful evening gowns by wearing black niqabs, decided to offer coloured niqabs to match outfits for those women who wish to cover their faces at public functions. She is keen to bring a sense of fun into Islamic dress and to combat the austerity and negative connotations of head-to-toe black outfits. A bright pink silk Imaan gown with matching pink niqab was, for example modelled in a fashion show in Leicester and was later purchased online by a Canadian Muslim who had seen coverage of the show via the Internet.

Finally, like all segments of the fashion industry, Islamic fashion designers and entrepreneurs have to cope with competition both from mainstream retail outlets and from others involved in the Islamic fashion industry. Whilst the first wave of individuals entering the field was, as we have seen, motivated by a mixture of personal, political, ethical, aesthetic and commercial interests, they now face competition from others who recognize the commercial potential of Islamic fashion but who are less concerned with issues of Islamic ethics and values. Shukr for example has found it necessary to place a warning to customers on its Web site about cheap imitations available on the market and how these represent Muslims doing harm to other Muslims. A number of other companies have found their designs and marketing techniques replicated by others. One entrepreneur at IslamExpo 2008 who was selling a wide variety of Islamic headwear and accessories from hijabs and niqabs to sleeve extensions and bonnets from Egypt, Africa and the Middle East confessed that until he came to Britain from East Africa some eight years back, he had never even heard of an Islamic shop. He now runs an online store called muslimbase.com and gives demonstrations on YouTube about how to tie the hijab, not because he feels hijab wearing is obligatory, but to give publicity to his Web site and products. His stated ambition is 'to become the Tescos of the Islamic world!'

A brief look at the emergence of Islamic fashion companies in Britain and the United States suggests that, far from being independent of mainstream fashion, they are very much entangled with it, playing simultaneously on notions of similarity and difference. Most pioneering Islamic fashion designers and entrepreneurs were self-confessed lovers of fashion and it was their desire to reconcile their love of fashion with their desire to express their faith that motivated them into the industry. At the same time, they draw on transnational Muslim networks and a wide variety of visual, material and ideological resources from around the world in their understanding of what might be considered 'Islamic' and fashionable.

The close relationship between Islamic fashion and other fashions is evident not just in the actions of producers, but also in the behaviour of consumers. Women and men who wish to visibly express their Muslim identity and faith through fashion do not rely exclusively on Islamic shops and online stores for their purchases, but select from a wide variety of outlets, including mainstream fashion boutiques, online stores and street markets. What is emerging here is not so much a 'non-Western world fashion system' as a global Islamic fashion scape in which designers, entrepreneurs, consumers, Internet users and media commentators are expanding the range of sartorial possibilities open to them, not only by devel-

Figure 8.18 Purple-print set as posted on the Hijab Style blogspot.
Courtesy of Jana Kossaibati.

oping distinctive Islamic styles inspired by different types of regional dress but also selecting, altering and re-combining elements of mainstream fashion to create new Islamically sensitive outfits. Nothing epitomizes the wide-ranging and eclectic nature of this Islamic fashion scape more clearly than the recent emergence and spread of Hijabi Fashion blogs in Britain and the United States.[30] Here young Muslim women blog about fashion and appearances; discuss and advertise international fashion events whether in Britain, Canada, the United States, Turkey, Egypt, Dubai, Indonesia, Oman or Europe; offer links to Islamic fashion outlets; write reviews of glossy magazines and TV programmes related to fashion; and give advice about how to tie the hijab in different styles. One key feature of these blogs is the creation of fashionable ensembles in the form of clothing collages or 'sets' which include accessories such as shoes, bags, jewellery and lipstick. The outfits created on the Hijab Style blog, established and run by the British medical student Jana Kossaibati, are culled mostly from popular high street brands such as Topshop, Debenhams, Principles and H&M, combined with occasional items from a global selection of Islamic online stores. For increasing numbers of young Muslim women living in the West, such images represent the birth of a modern Western Islamic fashion in which distinctions of ethnicity have become irrelevant.

NOTES

1. Islamic Fashion Blog, http://caribmuslimah.word press.com/aboutthisblog (accessed 10 December 2008).

2. The term 'fashionable Muslim' might be applied to anyone from a Muslim background who dresses fashionably, regardless of whether or not her clothes have religious connotations. By contrast to say someone is wearing 'Islamic fashion' suggests that her dress is a fashionable form of dress associated with Islam.

3. This process is well-described by Clare Dwyer who conducted research in two schools with significant British Asian Muslim populations in the early to mid 1990s. She describes how some Muslim pupils were differentiating themselves from others by adopting headscarves on a full- or part-time basis which they wore with skirts or trousers. This was also a way of avoiding more Asian styles of dress and asserting a certain degree of autonomy in relation to their parents (Dwyer 1999).

4. In 2008 I attended IslamExpo, which was held in Olympia in Earl's Court, and GPU, which was held at the vast ExCel exhibition centre in East London. The latter event claims to attract approximately 60,000 visitors over two days and makes claims for being the largest international event in Europe.

5. See Jones (2007) for Indonesia and Abaza (2007) for Egypt.

6. Moors and Tarlo (2007).

7. Companies which specialized in the production of Islamic fashion emerged in Turkey as early as the 1980s, catering to a new generation of religiously motivated young women who wished to cover. In a political and historical context where the religious and the secular are perceived in oppositional terms, the emergence of 'Islamic' businesses offering a new range of Islamically coded goods played a significant role in popularizing the 'Islamist movement' (Navaro-Yashin 2002). For further details of the emergence of Islamic fashion in Turkey, see Sandikci and Ger (2005, 2007).

8. Extract from Anas Sillwood's responses to an online interview with Omar Tufail and Hisham al-Zoubeir for Deenport, a popular Muslim Web site based in Britain (access to interview courtesy of Sillwood, July 2007).

9. In Britain, as in the United States, a number of Muslim women swim in 'make do' outfits (such as leggings or shalwars with T-shirts or tops) and are reluctant to wear swimming costumes even if pools offer women's only sessions. In this context Islamic swimwear which is designed especially for water sports provides a practical alternative.

10. For further discussion of Web site names, see Akou (2007).

11. http://www.shukr.co.uk/Merchant.mvc?Screen=shukr (accessed 5 July 2007).

12. Whilst Arabic names and Islamic frames attract attention from religiously oriented Muslims, signalling that a particular Web site might interest them, they can also put off those less religiously inclined. For this reason, some companies have recently toned down their overtly Islamic image in an attempt to broaden their customer base.

13. See Moors and Tarlo (2007).

14. In the *Qur'an* believing men are enjoined to lower their gaze in the presence of women and to keep their *awra* (those parts of the body that are considered sexually charged) loosely covered (*Qur'an* 24, 30). In the *Hadiths* further references are made to the importance of dignity and modesty in men's dress. Some men consider that in order to follow the example set by the Prophet Mohammed, it is advisable to wear long garments. These should not be ostentatious. Men are also prohibited from wearing gold jewellery and silk.

15. Extract from the author's online interview with Anas Sillwood, July 2007.

16. When I interviewed Sheba Kichloo in 2007, she was in the process of moving to Dubai where her husband had been posted and had ambitions to expand her business there.

17. This visualization of Islamic spirituality and peace in terms of an aesthetics of lightness is not dissimilar to that expressed by the textile artist, Rezia Wahid (see chapter 2).

18. For a wide-ranging discussion of the circulation of Orientalist logics in the fashion industry, including self-Orientalizing strategies, see Niessen, Leshkowich and Jones (2003).

19. Interestingly, Yasmin Arif is the only female Islamic fashion designer I have met whose business did not develop as an extension of the personal dilemma of how to dress Islamically and fashionably. Unlike the others, she was not a hijab wearer before entering the field of Islamic fashion but became one in the process.

20. At one level, this represents a reversal of the Orientalist order and, as such, presents a challenge to imperialist discourses and stereotypes. At the same time, it reproduces the association of the Asian with the feminine and exotic and, to this extent, may serve to further re-entrench stereotypes (see Jones and Leshkowich 2003).

21. Saris, owing to the flesh they reveal around the neck and stomach, are not considered sufficiently modest by many hijab-wearing women. As a result, at mixed functions, a number of women cover their glamorous saris with jilbabs or abayas. By offering glamorous long gowns with matching abayas in rich fabrics, Yasmin Arif feels she is giving women the possibility of being simultaneously feminine, covered and glamorous rather than considering their femininity as something shameful and in need of hiding.

22. A form of Arab headwear, the *keffiyah*, became a powerful symbol of Palestinian nationalism in the late 1930s and was adopted in the 1960s by the Palestinian leader, Yasser Arafat, who wore it for the rest of his life. At the same time, it has been taken up in America, Britain and Europe by a variety of left-wing activists and sympathizers, whether in the struggle against the Vietnam War in the 1960s or in sympathy with the Palestinian cause in later years. In recent years it has been worn as a form of face covering by armed Muslim militants seeking to disguise their identity whether in Afghanistan or Iraq. Though originally worn only by men, it has become popular amongst Muslim teenagers of both sexes as a sign of Muslim solidarity over Palestine and of Muslim identity more generally. The *keffiyah* available today are mostly imported from China and have become incorporated into youth fashions. They come in an increasing variety of colours and patterns and many young people who wear them are largely oblivious of the garment's history and associations. A short film entitled *Keffiyah Infiltrates Our Nation's Youth* provides an amusing skit of American anxieties about the popularity of the *Keffiyah* (http://www.kabobfest.com/search?q=kaffiyah).

23. The *Shahada* written in Arabic script on a black background features on the Hamas flag. Armbands and headbands bearing this message have been worn by a number of self-declared jihadists, including suicide bombers, and are associated with aggressive militaristic assertions of Islam.

24. In 2007 the homepage of wearaloud.com used to show the company's name sprayed graffiti-style onto a wall. It also used to advertise a VIP lounge offering what it called 'exclusive and forbidden items' but these were no longer advertised when I last consulted the site (11 December 2008), http://www.wearaloud.com/shop/componenth.

25. Anyone assuming that such T-shirts express more moderate and tolerant views should check out the explicit anti-Islamic slogans available through Cafepress.com (http://www.cafepress.com/antireligion/1196929), or the Web site Boffensive.com (http://www.boffensiv.com/offensive-tshirts/religion.htm).

26. Akou (2007).

27. For discussion of how local circumstances and ideas shape variations in Islamic fashion in Turkey, Indonesia, Iran, India, Mali, Yemen, Egypt, Britain and the United States, see *Fashion Theory*, 2007, vol 11, 2/3.

28. Elenany invites online viewers to propose themselves as models for her collection online. Her aim is to avoid reproducing the stereotypical image of the model as vacant and emaciated and to choose instead 'real women with character'. Presumably, there are also added financial benefits to using customers as models.

29. For further discussion of this process, see Niessen, Leshkowich and Jones (2003), who explore how East/West relations and hierarchies are played out in a fashion system which, they argue, is thoroughly globalized on the one hand, but remains largely defined by the West on the other.

30. See Islamic Fashion Blog, http://caribmuslimah.wordpress.com, Hijabi Fashionista, http://hijabifashionista.blogspot.com, and Hijab Style, http://hijabstyle.blogsopt.com.

AFTERWORD

Walking down Green Street in October 2009, I find myself entering the newly opened boutique of Islamic Impressions. Up to now I had only ever encountered this company through its online store and at Islamic events. Checking up on the latest Web sites from my computer at home, I come across yet another hijabi fashion blog and yet another online company advertising new hijab accessories. Surfing the online fashion stores represented in this book, I view their latest collections and techniques of display with interest. Reading the newspapers I note how different media controversies have inflated and deflated over time. Meeting up with women whose experiences and images I have recorded, I am aware that their lives, like mine, are moving on. Babies have been born, marriages contracted and the issue of covering has taken on more or less importance in different individual lives as fashions, debates and priorities have changed over time. For a researcher and ethnographer, the temptation is to keep going back to the text, to update it one last time, adding yet another image or episode in the biography of an individual or company. But such an exercise would of course be futile, resulting merely in an endless work in progress which would never see the light of day. So instead I would like to end this book with a simple reminder that what is presented here is, above all, documentation of a moment of transformation. It is a moment characterized not by static introspection but by experimentation and rapid change. If there is one conclusion to be drawn from this documentation of visibly Muslim appearances in the first decade of the twenty-first century, it is that none of the people and fashions represented here will look quite the same in ten years time.

BIBLIOGRAPHY

Abaza, M. (2007), 'Shifting Landscapes of Fashion in Contemporary Egypt', *Fashion Theory*, 11, 2/3: 281–298.

Abbas, T. (ed.) (2005), *Muslim Britain: Communities under Pressure,* London: Zed Books.

Abu-Lughod, L. (1990), 'The Romance of Resistance: Tracing Transformations of Power through Bedouin Women', *American Ethnologist*, 17: 1.

Abu-Lughod, L. (2002), 'Do Muslim Women Really Need Saving? Anthropological Reflections on Cultural Relativism and Its Others', *American Anthropologist*, 104/3: 783–790.

Ahmad, F. (2003), 'Still 'In Progress?'—Methodological Dilemmas, Tensions and Contradictions in Theorizing South Asian Muslim Women', in N. Puwar and P. Gaghuram (eds), *South Asian Women of the Diaspora*, Oxford: Berg.

Ahmed, A. (1992), *Post Modernism and Islam: Predicament and Promise,* London: Routledge.

Ahmed, L. (1992), *Women and Gender in Islam: Historical Roots of a Modern Debate,* New Haven, CT: Yale University Press.

Ahmed, N. (2005), 'Tower Hamlets: Insulation in Isolation', in T. Abbas (ed.), *Muslim Britain: Communities under Pressure,* London: Zed Books.

Akhtar, P. (2005), '(Re)turn to Religion and Radical Islam', in T. Abbas (ed.), *Muslim Britain: Communities under Pressure,* London: Zed Books.

Akou, H.M. (2007), 'Building a New "World Fashion": Islamic Dress in the Twenty-first Century', *Fashion Theory*, 11/4: 403–421.

Alexander, C. (2000), *The Asian Gang: Ethnicity, Identity, Masculinity,* Oxford: Berg.

Ameli, S. and Merali, A. (2004), *British Muslims' Expectations of the Government: Dual Citizenship: British, Islamic or Both? Obligation, Recognition, Respect and Belonging,* London: Islamic Human Rights Commission.

Ameli, S. and Merali, A. (2006), *British Muslims' Expectations of the Government: Hijab, Meaning, Identity, Othering and Politics: British Muslim Women,* London: Islamic Human Rights Commission.

Ansari, H. (2004), *'The Infidel Within': Muslims in Britain since 1800,* London: Hurst.

Appadurai, A. (1998), *Modernity at Large: Cultural Dimensions of Globalisation,* Minneapolis: University of Minnesota Press.

Badr, H. (2004), 'Islamic Identity Re-covered: Muslim Women after September 11th', *Culture and Religion*, 5/3: 321–338.

Balasescu, A. (2003), 'Tehran Chic: Islamic Headscarves, Fashion Designers and New Geographies of Modernity', *Fashion Theory*, 7/1: 39–59.

Balasescu, A. and Niessen, S. (2007), 'Haute Couture in Tehran: Two Faces of an Emerging Fashion Scene', *Fashion Theory*, 11, 2/3: 299–318.

Bari, M.A. (2004), *Race, Religion and Muslim Identity in Britain,* Swansea: Renaissance Press.

Bauman, G. (1999), *The Multicultural Riddle,* London: Routledge.

Begum, H. and Eade, J. (2005), 'All Quiet on the Eastern Front? Bangladeshi Reactions in Tower Hamlets', in T. Abbas (ed.), *Muslim Britain: Communities under Pressure,* London: Zed Books.

Bhachu, P. (2004), *Dangerous Designs: Asian Women Fashion the Diaspora Economies,* London: Routledge.

Blank, D. (1999), 'A Veil Controversy: The Construction of the "Tchador Affair" in the French Press', *Interventions: International Journal of Post colonial Studies*, 1/4: 536–554.

Brenner, S. (1996), 'Reconstructing Self and Society: Javanese Muslim Women and "the Veil"', *American Ethnologist*, 23/4: 673–697.

Bryon, A. and Niessen, S. (2002), *Consuming Fashion: Adorning the Transcultural Body,* Oxford: Berg.

Bullock, K. (2003), *Rethinking Muslim Women and the Veil,* Herndon: International Institute of Islamic Thought.

Bunt, G. (2003), *Islam in the Digital Age,* London: Pluto Press.

Clarke, A. and Miller, D. (2002), 'Fashion and Anxiety', *Fashion Theory*, 6/2: 191–214.

Cwerner, S. B. (2001), 'Clothes at Rest: Elements for the Sociology of the Wardrobe', *Fashion Theory*, 5/1: 79–92.

D'Alisera, J. (2001), "'I Love Islam": Popular Religious Commodities, Sits of Inscription and Transnational Sierra Leonean Identity', *Journal of Material Culture*, 6/1: 91–110.

Donnell, A. (1999), 'Dressing with a Difference: Cultural Representations, Minority Rights and Ethnic Chic', *Interventions: International Journal of Post colonial Studies*, 1/4: 489–499.

Donnell, A. (ed.) (1999), 'The Veil', Special Issue, *Interventions: International Journal of Post colonial Studies*, 1/4.

Dwyer, C. (1999), 'Veiled Meanings: Young British Muslim Women and the Negotiation of Differences', *Gender, Place and Culture*, 6/1: 5–26.

Franks, M. (2000), 'Crossing the Borders of Whiteness? White Muslim Women Who Wear the Hijab in Britain Today', *Ethnic and Racial Studies*, 23/5: 917–929.

Gardner, K. (2002), *Age, Narration and Migration: The Life Course and Life Histories of Bengali Elders in London*, Oxford: Berg.

Gell, A. (1998), *Art and Agency*, Oxford: Clarendon.

Goffman, E. (1959), *The Presentation of Self in Everyday Life*, Edinburgh: University of Edinburgh Social Sciences Research Centre.

Goffman, E. (1963), *Behaviour in Public Spaces,* Glencoe: The Free Press.

Goffman, E. (1968 [1963]), *Stigma, Notes on the Management of a Spoiled Identity*, Harmondsworth: Penguin [New York: Free Press].

Göle, N. (1996), *The Forbidden Modern: Civilization and Veiling*, Ann Arbor: University of Michigan Press.

Göle, N. (1997), 'The Gendered Nature of the Public Sphere', *Public Culture*, 10/1: 61–81.

Göle, N. (2002), 'Islam in Public: New Visibilities and New Imaginaries', *Public Culture*, 14/1: 173–190.

Göle, N. (2003, September 22), 'The Voluntary Adoption of Islamic Stigma Symbols—Part 111: Individual, Family, Community, and State', *Social Research*.

Graham-Brown, S. (1988), *Images of Women: The Portrayal of Women in Photography of the Middle East 1860–1950*, New York: Columbia University Press.

Greenblatt, S. (1991), 'Resonance and Wonder', in Ivan Karp and Steven Levine (eds), *Exhibiting Cultures*, Washington, DC: Smithsonian Institution Press.

Guindi, F. El. (1999), *Veil: Modesty, Privacy and Resistance,* Oxford: Berg.

Hall, S. (1990), 'Cultural Identity and Diaspora', in J. Rutherford (ed.), *Identity: Community Culture Difference*, London: Paul and Co. Publishing Consortium.

Hebdige, D. (1987), *Subculture: The Meaning of Style*, London: Routledge.

Herrera, L. and Moors, A. (2003), 'Banning Face Veiling: The Boundaries of Liberal Education', *ISIM Newsletter*, 13: 16–17.

Hirschkind, C. (2006), 'Cassette Ethics: Public Piety and Popular Media in Egypt', in B. Meyer and A. Moors (eds), *Religion, Media and the Public Sphere*, Bloomington: University of Indiana Press.

Hizb ut-Tahrir. (2001), 'Dangerous Concepts to Attack Islam and Consolidate the Western Culture,' London: Al-Khilafah Publications.

Hizb ut-Tahrir. (2002), 'The Inevitability of the Clash of Civilizations,' London: Al-Khilafah Publications.

Hizb ut-Tahrir. (2003), 'The Western Beauty Myth,' London: Khilafah Publications.

Hizb ut-Tahrir. (2003), 'The Attack on the Veil', *Khilafah Magazine*, 16/7.

Hizb ut-Tahrir. (2002), *The Inevitability of the Clash of Civilizations,* London: Al-Khilafah Publications

Jones, C. and Leshkowich, A.M. (2003), 'Introduction: The Globalization of Asian Dress: Re-Orienting Fashion or Re-Orienting Asia?', in S. Niessen, A.M. Leshkowich and C. Jones (eds), *Re-orienting Fashion: The Globalization of Asian Dress*, Oxford: Berg.

Jones, C. (2007), 'Fashion and Faith in Urban Indonesia', *Fashion Theory*, 11, 2/3: 211–232.

Judge, H. (2004), 'The Muslim Headscarf in French Schools', *American Journal of Education,* 111 (November): 1–24.

Lewis, R. (1996), *Gendering Orientalism: Race, Femininity and Representation*, London: Routledge.

Lewis, R. (2007), 'Veils and Sales: Muslims and the Spaces of Postcolonial Fashion Retail', *Fashion Theory*, 11/4: 423–444.

Mahmood, S. (2005), *Politics of Piety: The Islamic Revival and the Feminist Subject*, Princeton, NJ: Princeton University Press.

Marco, O. (2007), 'An Ethnographic Approach to Hijabization Process: Some Mindful Bodies', Master's thesis, Brunel.

Mernissi, F. (1987), *Beyond the Veil: Male-Female Dynamics in Modern Muslim Society*, Bloomington: University of Indiana Press.

Mernissi, F. (1991 [1987]), *The Veil and the Male Elite*, Reading, MA: Addison Wesley.

Meyer, B. and Moors, A. (eds) (2006), *Religion, Media and the Public Sphere*, Bloomington: University of Indiana Press.

Misra, V. (1996), 'The Diasporic Imaginary: Theorising the Indian Diaspora', *Textual Practice*, 10/3: 421–447.

Modood, T. (1992), 'British Asian Muslims and the Rushdie Affair', in J. Donald and A. Rattansi (eds), *'Race', Culture & Difference*, London: Sage in association with the Open University.

Modood, T. (2007), *Multiculturalism*, Cambridge: Polity.

Mookherjee, M. (2005), 'Affective Citizenship: Feminism, Postcolonialism and the Politics of Recognition', *Critical Review of International Social and Political Philosophy*, 8/1: 31–50.

Moors, A. (2007), 'Fashionable Muslims: Notions of Self, Religion and Society in San'a', *Fashion Theory*, 11, 2/3: 319–346.

Moors, A. and Tarlo, E. (2007), 'Introduction', Special Issue, *Muslim Fashions, Fashion Theory*, 11, 2/3: 133–141.

Naghibi, N. (1999), 'Bad Feminist or Bad Hejabi? Moving outside the Hijab Debate', *Interventions: International Journal of Post colonial Studies*, 1/4: 555–571.

Navara-Yashin, Y. (2002), 'The Market for Identities: Secularism, Islamism and Commodities', in D. Kandiyoti and A. Saktamber (eds), *The Fragments of Culture: The Everyday of Modern Turkey*, London: I. B. Taurus.

Niessen, S., Leshkowich, A. M. and Jones, C. (eds), (2003), *Re-orienting Fashion: The Globalization of Asian Dress*, Oxford: Berg.

Nieuwkerk, K. v. (2004), '"Veils and Wooden Clogs Don't Go Together"', *Ethnos*, 69/2: 229–246.

Peach, C. (2005), 'Muslims in the UK', in T. Abbas (ed.), *Muslim Britain: Communities under Pressure*, London: Zed Books.

Pedwell, C. (2007), 'Tracing "the Anorexic" and "the Veiled Woman": Towards a Relational Approach', Gender Institute, *LSE New Working Paper Series*, Issue 20, 2–48.

Polhemus, T. (1994), *Street Style*, London: Thames and Hudson.

Poulter, S. (1998), *Ethnicity, Law and Human Rights*, Oxford: Clarendon.

Puwar, N. and Gaghuram, P. (eds) (2003), *South Asian Women of the Diaspora*, Oxford: Berg.

Ramadan, T. (2004), *Western Muslims and the Future of Islam*, Oxford: Oxford University Press.

Rozario, S. (2006), 'The New Burqa in Bangladesh: Empowerment or Violation of Women's Rights?', *Women's Studies International Forum*, 29: 368–380.

Said, E. (1978), *Orientalism*, London: Routledge and Kegan Paul.

Sandikci, O. and Ger, G. (2005), 'Aesthetics, Ethics and Politics of the Turkish Headscarf', in S. Kuechler and D. Miller (eds), *Clothing as Material Culture*, Oxford: Berg.

Sandikci, O. and Ger, G. (2007), 'Constructing and Representing the Islamic Consumer in Turkey', *Fashion Theory*, 11, 2/3, 189–210.

Scott, J. Wallach (2007), *The Politics of the Veil*, Princeton, NJ: Princeton University Press.

Shirazi, F. (2001), *The Veil Unveiled: The Hijab in Modern Culture*, Gainesville: University Press of Florida.

Starret, G. (1995), 'The Political Economy of Religious Commodities in Cairo', *American Anthropologist*, 97(1): 51–68.

Taji-Farouki, S. (1996), *A Fundamental Quest: Hizb ut-Tahrir and the Search for the Islamic Caliphate*, London: Grey Seal.

Tarlo, E. (1996), *Clothing Matters: Dress and Identity in India*, London: Hurst.

Tarlo, E. (2004), 'Weaving Air: The Textile Journey of Rezia Wahid', *Moving Worlds*, 4/2: 90–99.

Tarlo, E. (2005), 'Reconsidering Stereotypes: Anthropological Reflections on the Jilbab Controversy', *Anthropology Today*, 21/6: 13–17.

Tarlo, E. (2007a), 'Marjane Satrapi's *Persepolis*: A Sartorial Review', *Fashion Theory*, 11, 2/3: 347–356.

Tarlo, E. (2007b), 'Hijab in London: Metamorphosis, Resonance and Effects', *Journal of Material Culture*, 12/2: 131–156.

Tarlo, E. and Moors, A. (eds) (2007), Special Issue, *Muslim Fashions, Fashion Theory*, 11, 2/3.

Tawadros, D. G. (2003), *Veil: Veiling, Representation and Contemporary Art*, London: inIVA.

Turbin, C. (2003), 'Refashioning the Concept of Public/Private: Lessons from Dress Studies', *Journal of Women's History*, 15/1: 43–51.

Werbner, P. (2001), 'The Limits of Cultural Hybridity: On Ritual Monsters, Poetic Licence and Contested Postcolonial Purifications', *Journal of the Royal Anthropological Institute*, 7: 133–152.

Werbner, P. (2007), 'Veiled Interventions in Pure Space: Honour, Shame and Embodied Struggles among Muslims in Britain and France', *Theory, Culture & Society*, 24/2: 161–186.

Winter, B. (2001), 'Fundamental Misunderstandings: Issues in Feminist Approaches to Islamism', *Journal of Women's History*, 13/1: 9–41.

Woodward, S. (2007), *Why Women Wear What They Wear,* Oxford: Berg.

REPORTS

Muslims in Britain, by Humayun Ansari, Minority Rights International, 2002.

The Search for Common Ground: Muslims, Non-Muslims and the UK Media, Greater London Authority, 2007.

Living Apart Together: British Muslims and the Paradox of Multiculturalism, London, Policy Exchange, 2007.

Islamaphobia: A Challenge for Us All, London, Runnymede Trust, 1997.

The Hijacking of British Islam: How Extremist Literature Is Subverting Mosques in the UK, by Denis MacEoin, London, Policy Exchange, 2007.

Images of Islam in the UK: The Representation of British Muslims in the British National Print News Media 2000–2008, by Kerry Moore, Paul Mason and Justin Lewis, Cardiff School of Journalism, Media and Cultural Studies, 2008.

MAGAZINES

Emel
Khilafah Magazine
Q News
Muslimwise
Sisters

NOVELS AND AUTOBIOGRAPHIES

Ali, Monica, *Brick Lane*, London: Doubleday, 2003.

Husain, Ed, *The Islamist*, London: Penguin, 2007.

McEwan, Ian, *Saturday*, London: Jonathan Cape, 2005.

Robert, Na'ima B., *From My Sisters' Lips*, London: Bantam Books, 2005.

Satrapi, Marjane, *Persepolis*, vols 1, 2, London: Jonathan Cape, 2003.

ISLAMIC BOOKS AND PAMPHLETS ON DRESS AND RELATED MATTERS

Islam: The Choice of Thinking Women, by Ismail Adam Patel, London: Ta-Ha Publishers, 1997.

Purdah and the Status of Women in Islam, by Sayyid Abul A'la Maududi, New Delhi: Markazi Maktba Islami, 2000 [1996?].

The Obligation of Veiling and Women, by Abdul-Azeez bin Abdilaah bin Baaz, Muhammad bin Saalih Al-'Uthaimeen, Zayd bin Haadee Al-Madkhalee, USA: Al-Ibaanah Books, 2003.

The Islamic Ruling Regarding Women's Dress according to the Qur'an and Sunnah, Jeddah: Abdul Qasim Bookstore, 1991 [1985].

The Hijab—Why?, by Muhammad Ismail, New Delhi: Islamic Book Service, 2002.

The Hijab: Dress for Every Muslimah, by Shazia Nazlee, Ipswich: Jam'iat 'Ihyaa' Minhaaj al-Sunnah, 2001.

The Muslim Woman's Handbook, by Huda Khattab, London: Ta-Ha Publishers, 2006 [1993].

The Muslim Woman's and Muslim Men's Dress, by Jamal Badawi, London: Ta-Ha Publishers, 2006 [1980].

Niqab: A Seal on the Debate, by Kamillah Khan, Kuala Lumpur: Dar Al Wahi Publication, 2008.

The Return of Hijab, Parts 1, 2, by Muhammed Ibn Ahmd Ibn Ismail, London: Al-firdous, 2001.

Women Who Deserve to Go to Hell, by Mansoor Abdul Hakim, Karachi: Darul Ishaat, 2004.

Women in Shariah, by Abdur Rahman I. Doi, London: Ta-Ha Publishers, 1996 [1989].

ISLAMIC BOOKS FOR OR ABOUT CHILDREN

A Muslim Girl's Guide to Life's Big Changes, by Rayhana Khan, London: Ta-Ha Publishers, 2005.

I Can Wear Hijab Anywhere!, by Yasmin Ibrahim, Leicester: Islamic Foundation, 2004.

Islamic Fataawa Regarding the Muslim Child, compiled by Yahya Ibn Sa'eed Aale Shalwaan, Walthamstow: Invitation to Islam, 2007.

What Do We Say? (A Guide to Islamic Manners), by Noorah Kathryn Abdullah, Leicester: Islamic Foundation, 1996.

CLOTHING WEB SITES CONSULTED

www.aabuk.com/

www.afaaf.com

www.arabiannites.co.uk

www.artizara.com/

www.capsters.com/

www.imaancollections.com/

www.islamicdesignhouse.com/

www.islamicimpressions.co.uk

www.islamicstatewear.com

www.islamorient.com

www.lawungdirect.com

www.losve.com

www.masoomah.co.uk

www.muslimbase.com/

www.pinzpinzpinz.co.uk

www.primomoda.com/

www.shukr.co.uk

www.thehijabshop.com/

www.ummahgear.com

www.wearalound.com

HIJAB BLOGS CONSULTED

www.caribmuslimah.wordpress.com
www.hijabhigh.com
www.hijabstyle.blogspot.com
www.thehijablog.wordpress.com

OTHER ISLAMIC WEB SITES CONSULTED

www.1924.org
www.deenport.com
www.hizb-ut-tahrir.org
www.islamOnline.net
www.mpacuk.org
www.muhajabah.com
www.prohijab.net
www.shiahchat.com
www.sunniforum.com
www.thecitycircle.com

OTHER SOURCES CITED

'Modern Chronology of the Keffiyah Kraze', http://kabobfest.blogspot.com/search?q=kaffiya
Wharnsby, Dawud, 'The Veil', 2004, Enter into Peace, http://www.wharnsby.com/Lyrics/archives/
   000190.html

INDEX

Italic numbers denote references to illustrations.

pressure to wear, 141–3
pride in, 136, 138, 143, 147–9
as protection, 151–4
protection from, 151–4, 156
scholarly views on, 141, 155
in schools, 142, 145
self-sacrifice in wearing, 136, 147, 151–2, 156
styles of wearing, 134, 138
visual perceptions of, 131–5, 142–3, 151, 154, 158n17
Nosheen, Sadia, 193–5, 222–4
Nottingham, 92, 98, 194, 195

Oihana, Marco, 100n2

Pakistan, 6, 28–9, 35, 140, 170
Pakistani, 35, 38, 105
Pierre, 47–8, 52
PinzPinzPinz, 186n3
Poetic Pilgrimage, 14, 73, 81–92, 93, 98
police uniforms, 45, 68–9n2
Primo Moda, 194–5, 199, 201, 222
Prophet Mohammed, 7, 10, 215, 227n14

Qaradawi, Sheikh Yusuf, 43–4
Qur'an, 7–9, 40–1, 56, 59, 62, 74, 105, 109, 115, 117, 118, 152, 200, 201–2, 224, 227n14

Race Relations Act, 68n1
racism, 5, 10, 28, 58, 62, 68n1, 82, 91, 135
Rahman, Wahid, 161–5, 167–72, 177, 181–5, 186n5, 186n6
Ramadan, Tariq, 69n12, 100n6, 121, 150, 158n14
Rastafarian, 82–3, 85, 92, 98
Robert, Na'ima, 151–2, 156

saris, 20, 22–3, 29, 35, 40, 45, 88, 95, 163, 177, 210
    opposition to, 21, 114, 228n21
Saudi Arabia, 134, 138, 156n6, 184
schools, 21, 29, 36, 50, 103
    uniforms 10, 12, 14, 29, 36
    see also jilbab, controversy
segregation, 50–2, 64, 125
September 11, 10–11, 24, 31, 51, 58–9, 69n9, 106, 135, 169, 196–8, 206
shalwar kamiz, 29, 35, 40, 45, 71–2, 95–6, 97, 105, 114–15, 122, 163

Shireen, 92, 98–9
Shukr, 195–9, 200, 201–4, 208, 211, 220–4
Sikh turban, 4, 45, 68n1, *see also* turban
Silk Route, 181–3, 200–1, 211, 215, 223
Sillwood, Anas, 195, 197, 201–3, 220, *see also* Shukr
Sisters (magazine), 151, 190, 211
Soumaiyah, 92, 98
sportswear
    hijab, *see* Capsters
    jilbab, 181–2
    swimwear, 195, 199, 227n9
stereotypes
    of Muslims, 17, 27, 31, 33, 52, 57, 86, 103
    resistance to, 74, 81, 89, 90, 95, 185–6, 198
    of the West, 109–10, 113–14, 117–19, 122–7, 128n12
Straw, Jack, 10, 144, 150, 155
Sunnah, 7

T-shirts, 5, 27, 58–9, 89, 167–8, 217–19, 228n25
thobe, 7, 10, 47, 215–17
turban, 62, *see also* Sikh turban
Turkey, 3, 8, 16n14, 80, 100n4, 161, 181

ummah, 54, 113, 114–17, 118, 121, 161
ummahgear.com, 219
university students, 76–7, 84, 92–8, 112–3, 117, 128n14, 174, 176, 194, 196, *see also* FOSIS; Islamic Society (ISoc)

van den Bremen, Cindy, 161–2, 164–5, 171–8, 183–6
Veil, 2, 3, 4, 15n3, 42, 56, 63, 65, 137, 207, *see also* niqab
Virgin Mary, 54, 56, 90

Wahhabi, 141, 156n6
Wahid, Rezia, 13, 18–27, 34, 38, 40–2, 56, 62, 227n17
wearaloud.com, 218, 228n24
Wharnsby, Dawud, 56, 65
Whitechapel, 134, 138–43, 151–2, 163–4, 181
Wolf, Naomi, 114, 118
Wolstonecraft, Mary, 118
Woodward, Sophie, 154

Zarina, 72, 76–81, 82, 85